THINKLERS!™

A Collection of Brain Ticklers

Kevin Brougher

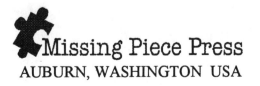
Missing Piece Press

AUBURN, WASHINGTON USA

THINKLERS!™
A Collection of Brain Ticklers

Printed in the United States of America
ISBN# 0-9703729-1-4
Library of Congress Control Number: 00-092033

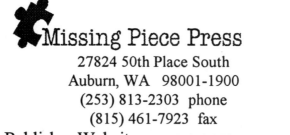

Missing Piece Press
27824 50th Place South
Auburn, WA 98001-1900
(253) 813-2303 phone
(815) 461-7923 fax
Publisher Website: www.MissingPiecePress.com

***Note to teachers and business presenters: Permission is granted for copying pages for use on an OVERHEAD PROJECTION system.   If you would like to copy pages to hand out to your students or staff, *please* write or call for permission. Thank you.

CONTENTS

INTRODUCTION

I probably struggled more with this introduction than any other part of the book. Mainly because I didn't know how technical I should get in describing the thinking that goes on when you are solving some of the riddles and puzzles in this book. I've decided to keep it short and let you get into the book and start having fun as soon as possible. Who reads these introductions anyway? But, for those of you who do...

The activities in this book are based on two main concepts.

1. <u>Cultural Literacy</u> - A concept made popular by E.D. Hirsch, Jr. The idea is that there are certain concepts, people, sayings etc. that are unique to our culture that everyone should know. For example, most people have heard the saying, "a bird in the hand is worth two in the bush", and they know that George Washington was our country's first president. There are not many jobs that REQUIRE you to know this but, because we live in America we should at least be aware of our unique cultural history.

2. <u>Thinking</u> - This is a broad term that encompasses such concepts as: cognition, metacognition, divergent (or lateral) thinking, convergent thinking, problem solving, creativity, remote associations, logic, synthesis, analysis, evaluation and on and on and on. (There are literally hundreds of books on this subject and new research is coming out everyday!)

The TWOsomes, THREEsomes, FOURsomes rely heavily on cultural literacy and knowledge. The Position Puzzles use a blend of culteral words and sayings with creative and divergent thinking. The Rhyme Time, Commonyms, and Ask Me More are especially good for practicing and developing some of the many types of thinking and creativity.

This book was written and compiled out of the strong belief that THINKING is FUN. Needless to say, I also believe that thinking and creativity are skills that can and should be developed.

This book is no way a panacea to good thinking but, it IS a tremendous **RESOURCE** of some activities that require thought, contemplation and pondering in a FUN way. Although written with students in mind, it can be a great book to share with adults in the work place, parties, or meetings. Families could challenge each other on the way to a camping trip. Teachers should enjoy sharing the challenges with their students on a day to day basis or by using the activities in a mini-unit on thinking. However and whenever it is used, I am confident that you, and the people you share it with, will get a tickle out thinking so hard. Enjoy the book.

The Author

POSITION PUZZLES

These types of puzzles have enticed minds for years. You might have come across them as "Wacky Wordies", "Word Rebuses", "Punzzles", or some other name.   I have called them POSITION PUZZLES because, for the most part, figuring them out requires that you look at the position of the words. The puzzles are words, letters, numbers, lines, and symbols that represent familiar words, items, places, sayings, movies, etc.   For instance:

$$\frac{\text{WEAR}}{\text{LONG}}$$

is the POSITION PUZZLE for "Long Underwear"!   Some will come easy. Some will be extremely challenging.   Enjoy and learn from this collection of over 1600 POSITION PUZZLES!

Note: For each of the following pages, the boxes are numbered as follows:

1.	2.	3.
4.	5.	6.
7.	8.	9.
10.	11.	12.

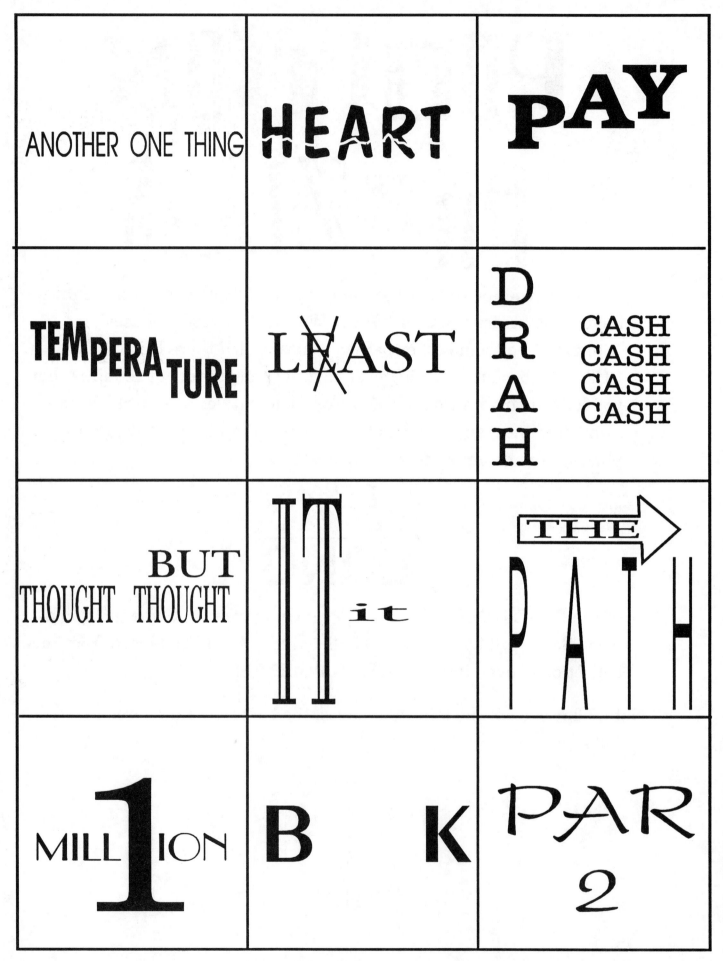

ANOTHER ONE THING

HEART

PAY

TEMPERATURE

LEAST

D R A H

CASH
CASH
CASH
CASH

BUT THOUGHT THOUGHT

IT it

THE PATH

MILL 1 ION

B K

PAR 2

FOOLING	NEA$R N$EAR NE$AR	CHANCE
MUSICALLY	END	Born Born
S, T I	MORE MORE MORE MORE MORE MORE	ONCE 8:00 AM
COLLAR HOT	STEP STEP STEP STEP	1111

I Q	GROUND LONDON	B B M M U U H H T T
SERMON MOUNT	TIMES	MONKEY RUOY
FLAT	RAKED	T I•M E
JUNE JUNE JUNE JUNE JUNE	T U CROWD	ON

<table>
<tr>
<td>NO NO
—————
RIGHT</td>
<td>FIRING FIRING FIRING</td>
<td>HEARTEN</td>
</tr>
<tr>
<td>H A P P I N E S S</td>
<td>BATTLE</td>
<td>SHOTGUN</td>
</tr>
<tr>
<td>DR. DO</td>
<td>BE BUSH AT</td>
<td>JAW
SILVER</td>
</tr>
<tr>
<td>G O O D B Y E</td>
<td>C C C C C C</td>
<td>JUST</td>
</tr>
</table>

ACT	SADDLE	OPINION OPINION
Reality E C A F	WALL writings	MINUTE HOUR
CH AN CE	BBBBBB	2TO
NI BUMP GHT	TIMING TIM ING	

LAP LAP LAP he he he	13579... COME	TLUASREMOS
|/ |/ AR NIGHT MOR /|\ /|\	PPPPPP EARTH	PLAY WORDS
PTT	AB... ♥	TUNNEL LIGHT
FEW MENTION FEW MENTION	Ci ii	YOUR 1111 LIFE

NEVER OLD LEARN OLD LEARN	BARS BARS BARS BARS BARS BARS BARS BARS BARS (LIFE)	HOME ――― RANGE
ONE ONE ONE	SP⊗OT (SNAKE X)	GRASS (SNAKE)
KEEP YOUR I BALL	1. GLANCE 2. 3. GLANCE	T A EVERYTHING EVERYTHING C T
SH GET APE	ON THE THE	E M I T

1. THOUGHT 2. IT	FA *Red* CE	**BED**
DEAD BODY MY	D O W N S P L I T	KIDNEY LUNG **HOME** HEART
AB **OUT**	NOTICE	STORY N / E / S
J U S T	**GOOD LAST GOOD LAST**	I E C EXCEPT

STAND
I

STAND I	K K *Words* C C *Words* U U *Words* T T *Words* S S	**ONCE** **ONCE** **ONCE** **ONCE**
BUSINES	MONO IT TONY	by LITTLE
G M E N S I S	DOG THE	GET GET IT GET GET
MORE IT IT THANi	KNOW IT NO	DAB

14

<table>
<tr><td>REA WITH SON</td><td>Y Y Y MEN</td><td>i i i
BAGS</td></tr>
<tr><td>*cut*
rest</td><td>IMPROVEMENT
IMPROVEMENT
IMPROVEMENT
IMPROVEMENT
IMPROVEMENT

IMPROVEMENT
IMPROVEMENT
IMPROVEMENT
IMPROVEMENT</td><td>THOUGHT AN</td></tr>
<tr><td>B SICK ED</td><td>M CE
M CE
M CE</td><td>STANDING
MISS</td></tr>
<tr><td>IDOL</td><td>LOOK ULEAP</td><td>O
N
A
I
P</td></tr>
</table>

A cu M	aMISS	WOMEN WOMEN WOMEN
CENTURY (↶)	E E A A R R T T H H	GOOD, BETTER...
(INCOME)	Scissors Scissors	OFTEN OFTEN NOT OFTEN
THINNING	DAYTHE	BO JACK X

PAT / **THE**	SEALED X	**AI** *LOVE* **R**
WINKS WINKS	**PILF**	
BE ᵀᴱᴳ D	**X** **TOAST**	S S S S B B B B A A A A R R R R G G G G
ᴼᶠ THE	$\dfrac{\mathcal{E}\ \mathcal{Z}}{iiiiii}$	IT TI

EA it's R E out AR	FLAT ONES (upside down)	PICT RE PICT RE PICT RE
MAD MAD MAD MAD MAD MAD (circling) U	WHERE WHERE WHERE WHERE WHERE WHERE ――――――― RAINBOW	GLO HAND VE
SUM 2 2 (reversed)	TRASH TRASH TRASH TRASH TRASH TRASH	WASHINGTON WILMINGTON
CUSTOMS	OH MY ACHING (upside down)	SC AL E

ONCE ONCE ONCE ONCE ALL ALL ALL ALL	ONE ONE ONE ONE ONE ONE	LOOKING
HAND MOUTH MOUTH	1. CHANCE 2. 3. CHANCE	kid ♡
TIME	FAIR	GONEWIND
QUITE	LAID	GO BROKE BROKE BROKE BROKE

WISH ★	ANOTHERTHING	**A** MOMENT
STAND / TRY 2	L R U C (vertical) BIBLE	G O I N G / G R A I N (vertical)
JUST 144 ICE	A BCDEFGHIJKLM NOPQRSTUUUU VWXYZ	SMALL · LARGE · A LITTLE
WHI ONCE LE	QUARTERSQUARTERSQUARTERS	FATE

SELF (with X over it)	N I P (vertical)	CHEEK / CHEEK (mirrored)
LOSS WORDS WORDS WORDS WORDS WORDS	__NHAPPY	SH KEEP APE
WEAR / LONG	OUT LUNCH LUNCH	ROUND / ME
"THAT" "THAT"	FEWFARFEW	BLOOD WATER

OVER AND ――――― AGAIN	**M** **I** **N** **D** NOT **M** **I** **N** **D**	NO F_N
LOOK ME E·Y E	BUMP HEAD	ANGLE ANGLE ANGLE
VISIT T I M E VISIT	HITTING HITTING HITTING HITTING **BELT**	GNIKCAB
	1. Thing 2. 3. Thing 4. 5. 6. Thing 7.	mal mal mal mal t e

SCHOOL SCHOOL

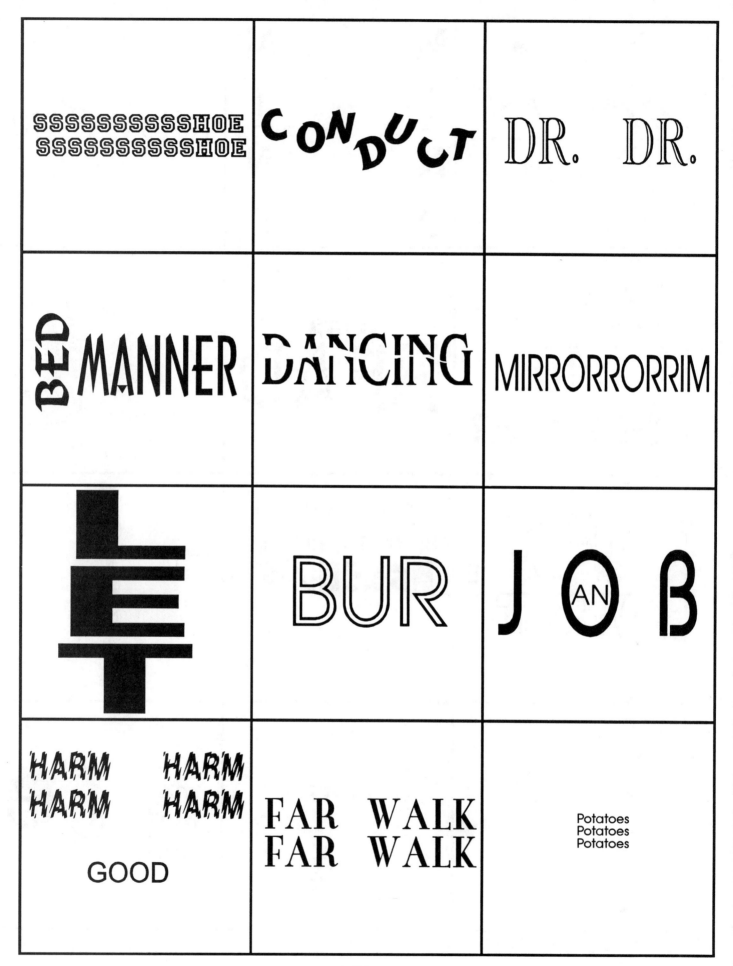

SSSSSSSSSSSHOE SSSSSSSSSSSHOE	CONDUCT	DR. DR.
BED MANNER	DANCING	MIRRORRORRIM
L E T	BUR	J O (AN) B
HARM HARM HARM HARM GOOD	FAR WALK FAR WALK	Potatoes Potatoes Potatoes

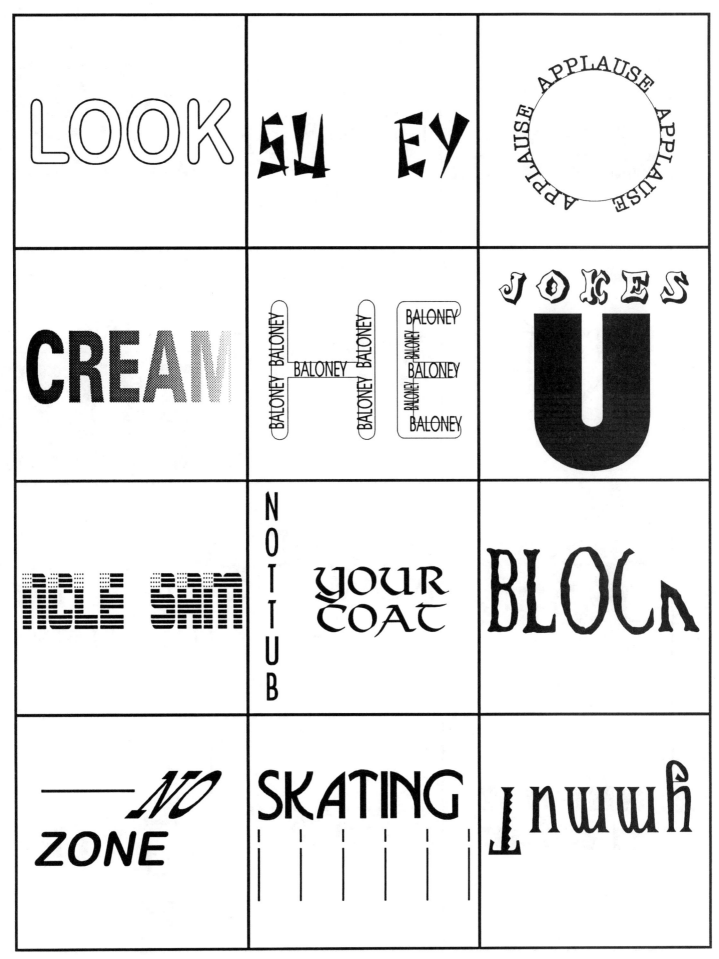

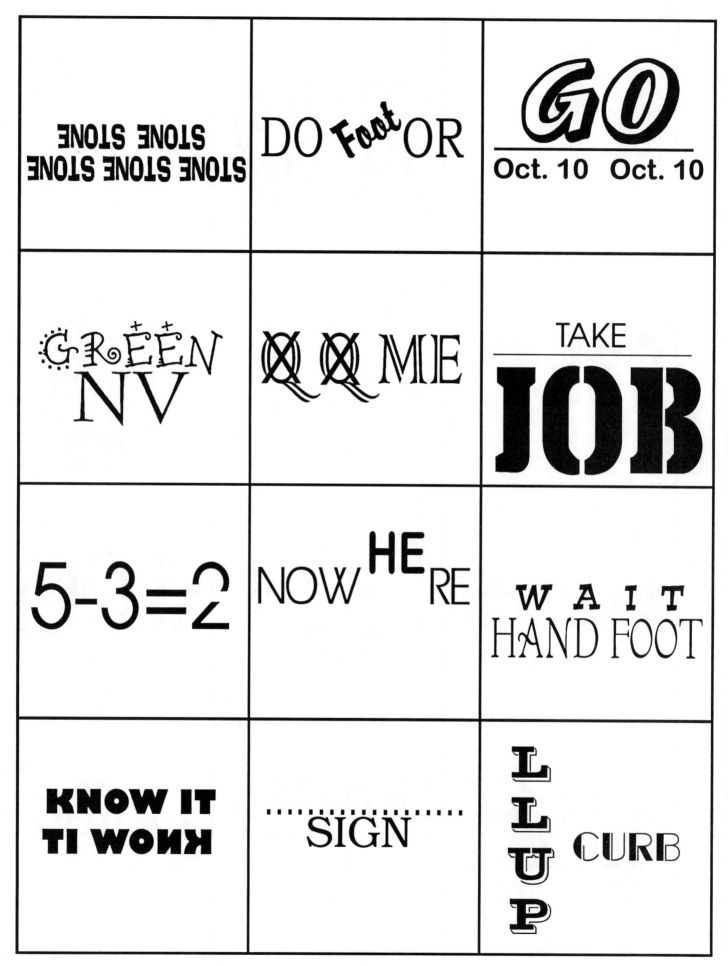

STONE STONE STONE STONE STONE STONE *(inverted)*	DO Foot OR	**GO** / Oct. 10 Oct. 10
GREEN NV	QQ ME	TAKE **JOB**
5-3=2	NOW **HE** RE	**WAIT** HAND FOOT
KNOW IT TI WONK *(mirrored)*	·········· SIGN ··········	L L U P CURB

26

BOPPER

CARDS
CARDS
CARDS
CARDS **U**

Y
N
N
U
S

S H O W E R S

O RDINARY

K COLC
K COLC

US MADE **A**

THE
tHE
THE

X MISSISSIPPI
X AMAZON
X RHINE
NILE

U 1 S

NME IN

NO X QQ

it it it it

F A L L	IMPOSSIBL	C OU R T SETTLEMENT
FOOT SHOE FOOT	ABCDEFG HIJK MN OPQRSTU VWXYZ	ECLIPSE
RECESS	SLEEPING JOB	MARKET
UNOTU	UP UP PAIN	LIE

STEP PETS PETS	T RN	BEANS BEANS BEANS BEANS BEANS BEANS BEANS BEANS BEANS BEANS BEANS BEANS BEANS BEANS BEANS BEANS BEANS BEANS
GIVE GIVE GIVE GIVE GET GET GET GET	VAWAITIN	T E GrO
From 2	Painting 123 456 789	POSED X
HEADAACHE	1,CHANCE,000 (1,000,000)	ORDER

LE GALLY	MUTINY BOUNTY	A TIMESPARE
ME_O_K	THEAdriveTRE	DAY DAY DAY DAY
AGENT AGENT	CHIMP	WAYS WAYS WAYS GO
Fiddler / ROOF	PAID I'M WORKED	my frog THROAT

FAT
FIRE

JOBS IN JOBS

END

FREE ALL ALL ALL ALL

FEET FEET

N N N N N N

ƎlԀԀⱯ

I SING
CAKE

ACCIDENT

MINDMIND

STICk

ICE

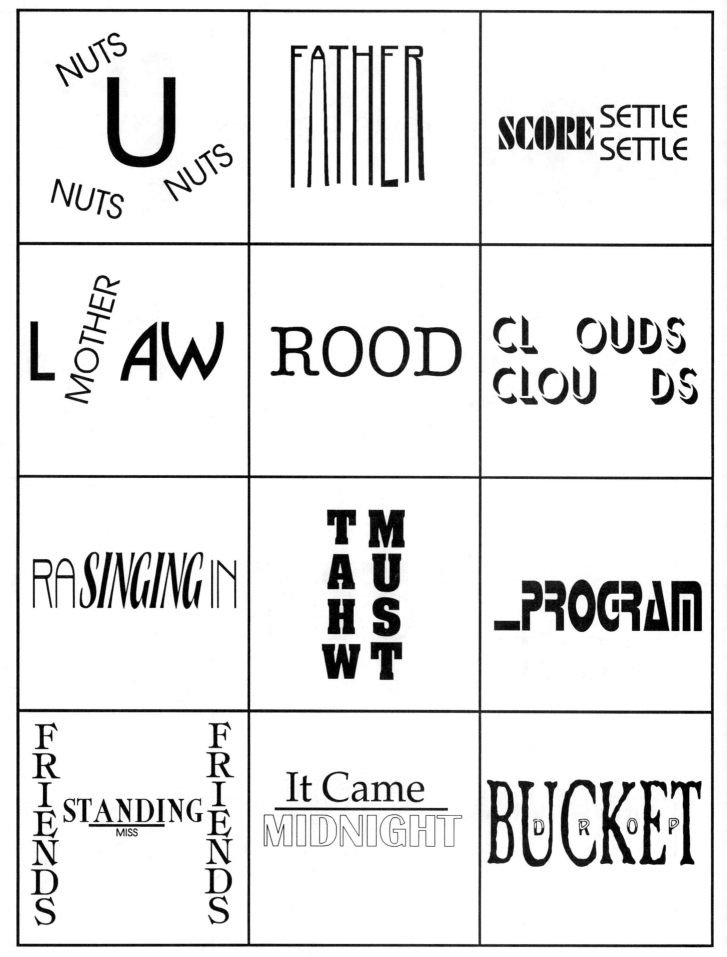

NUTS U NUTS NUTS NUTS

FATHER

SCORE SETTLE SETTLE

L MOTHER AW

ROOD

CL OUDS CLOU DS

RA SINGING IN

T M
A U
H S
W T
T

_PROGRAM

FRIENDS STANDING MISS FRIENDS

It Came
MIDNIGHT

BUCKET DROP

PANTS	NOW IN HERE	EV EN
NOON T	NUR 4TH	TISTITCHME
2345 67890	TES	DOLLAR
(	LO HEAD VE LO HEELS	TRANS MISSION

BUkickT	SMOKE SMOKE SMOKE	TIME
EMOTIONS EMOTIONS EMOTIONS	X Favorite	Jack Horner SAT
GO OUT	COUNT	Sleeping ∟
change	SHAKING SHAKING SHAKING SHAKING SHAKING SHAKING SHAKING	First

FIRST

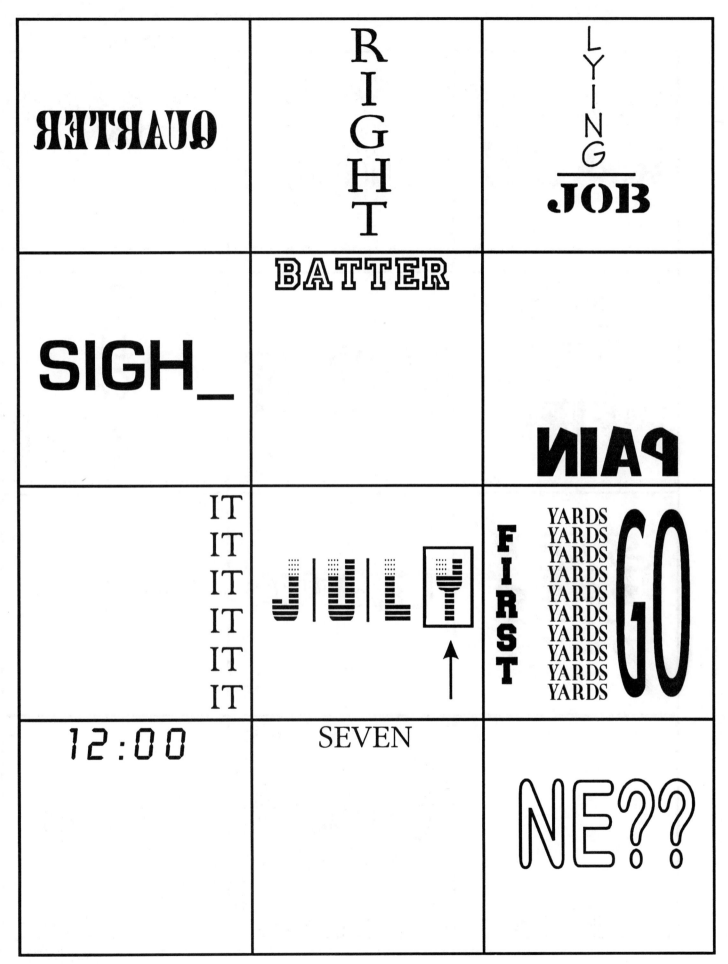

QUARTER *(reversed)*

RIGHT

LYING
——
JOB

SIGH_

BATTER

PAIN *(upside down)*

IT
IT
IT
IT
IT
IT

JULY ↑

FIRST

YARDS
YARDS
YARDS
YARDS
YARDS
YARDS
YARDS
YARDS
YARDS
YARDS

GO

12:00

SEVEN

NE??

KACE	THOdeepUGHT	DAY
🌐 FIRE	EMIT	THGIT
STEP PETS PETS	UPIT	
BRIDGE	DOOUT	TIME

LIGHTS LIGHTS

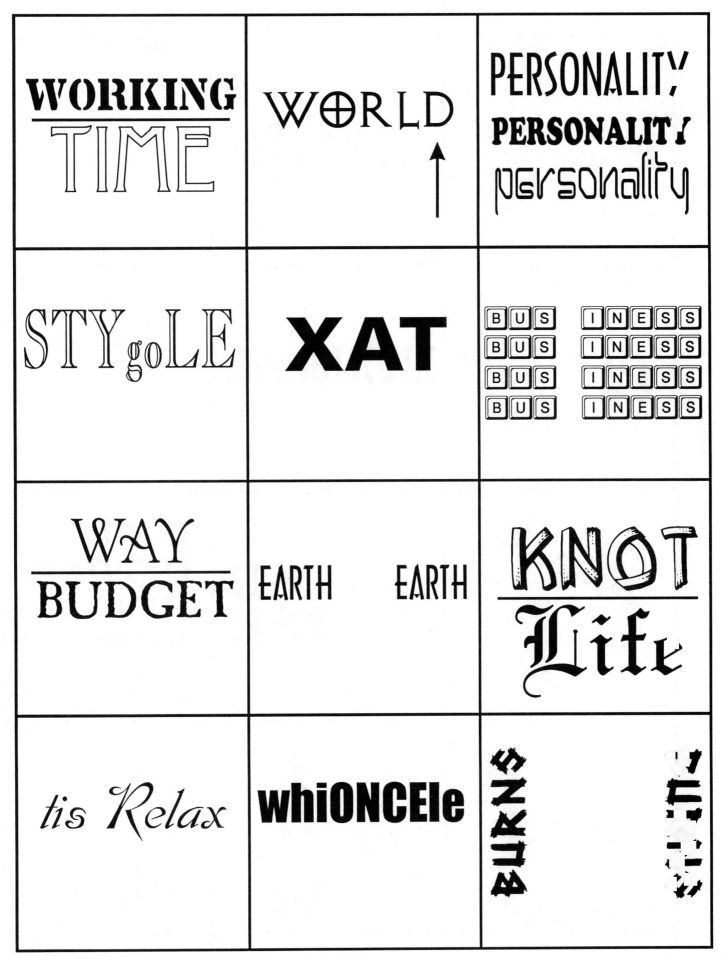

WORKING / TIME

W⊕RLD ↑

PERSONALITY
PERSONALITY
personality

STY go LE

XAT

BUS INESS
BUS INESS
BUS INESS
BUS INESS

WAY / BUDGET

EARTH   EARTH

KNOT / Life

tis Relax

whiONCEle

BURNS   BURNS

T E Stomach	tiLEVARTme	
12" 1'	RIDINGesroh	THINGS Things things GNIVOM
EVENTS EVENTS	STEP FAR FAR	NIGHTMARE NIGHTMARE NIGHTMARE NIGHTMARE NIGHTMARE
Talking 5280' 60 SECONDS	T A H W T A H W	WILL WAY WILL WAY WILL WAY

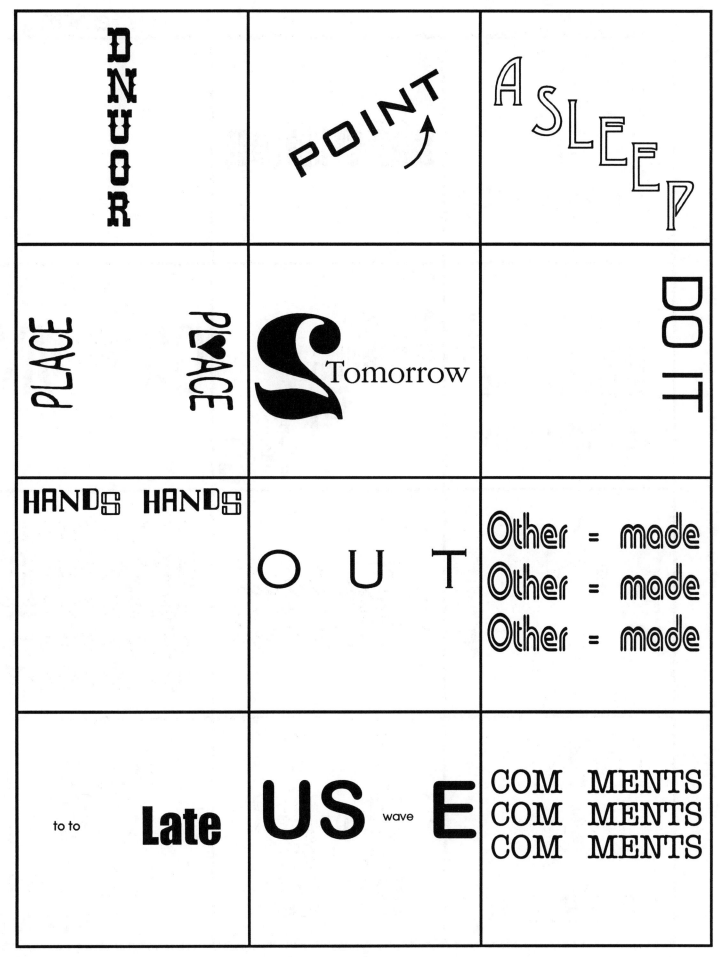

ROUND

POINT

ASLEEP

PLACE   PLACE

S Tomorrow

DO IT

HANDS   HANDS

O U T

Other = made
Other = made
Other = made

to to   Late

US wave E

COM   MENTS
COM   MENTS
COM   MENTS

bubble
bubble
bubble

BATCHELOR

STANDARD
conditions
conditions

FEE
du Lmp
du Imp
N
G

DR playing AY

O
F
F

O
F
F

Customer
Customer

LOTSputtingOF
TIME

T
I
S

COUorderRT

GO

STAND

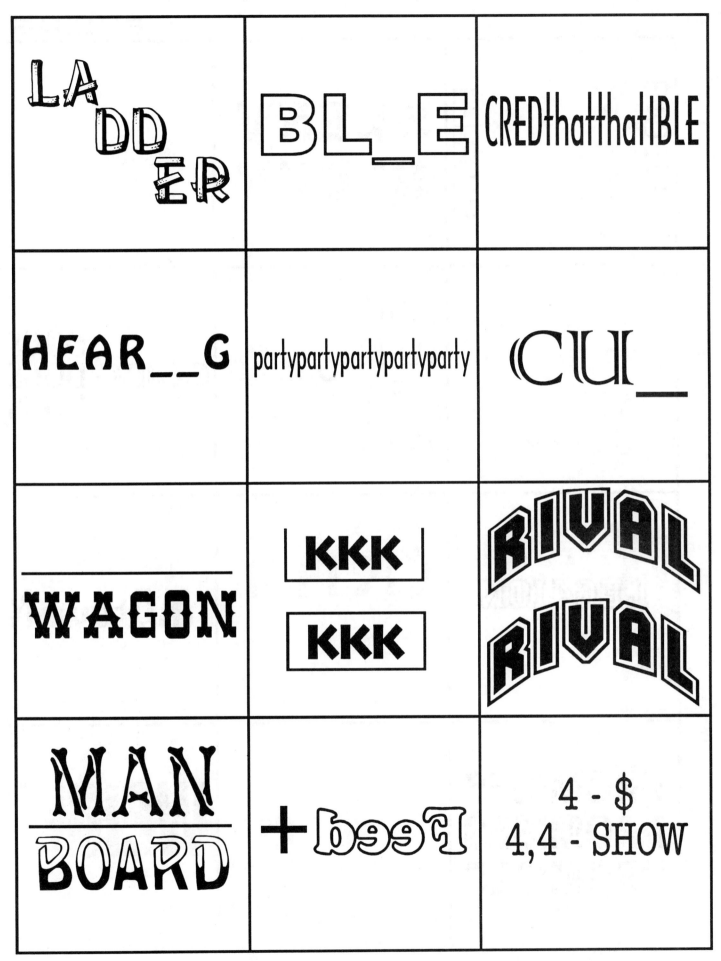

EFFECTS	EFFECTS	SLEEV SLEEV	
	romantic	ASK ASK ASK ASK — Oct. 10	GOING DOGS DOGS DOGS
LEG4ION	SISTER		MArownN
PROMISES PROMISES PROMISES	STOP		WEIGHT

WI FE ↑	Step TIME	some fresh air some fresh air some fresh air some fresh air
UP / DOWN	GROUND / RAILROAD	HANDS HEART
TO / BYE BUY BY BYE	The hands of time	→ Dentist Office Car Garage Optometrist Office Psychologist Office
Pancakes Pancakes Pancakes Pancakes Pancakes Pancakes	EYE EYE stomach	TABLE / PAID

Last NO NO	G MORNING I T T E G	NOW NOW NOW NOW NOW *Ever*
SOON TELL SOON TELL	CONandCLUSION	→ MOST MOST MOST → MOST MOST
WEATHER / a	LOlostVE	the people
WAY / GETTING	OUT / Limb	AupIR

44

T T T I I I S S S	KKJUSTKK	
PLY PLY PLY	SURF SURF	TIME GO
GROUND Feet Feet Feet Feet Feet Feet	POL4ICY	PUT E X A M
WAYS WAYS	September October November December January February	SSSSSSSSSS MATCH

twinS twinS	MOI'MOD *Love* *Love* *Love* *Love*	
CONSTRUCTION **IT'S**	*RE held GARD*	AM NOON PM
4 ROAD	Months Months Months Months Months Months LIVE LIVE	**COFFEE**
00:00 uuuu	WOOD WOOD WOOD WOOD WO **WALK** OD	PRIORITY

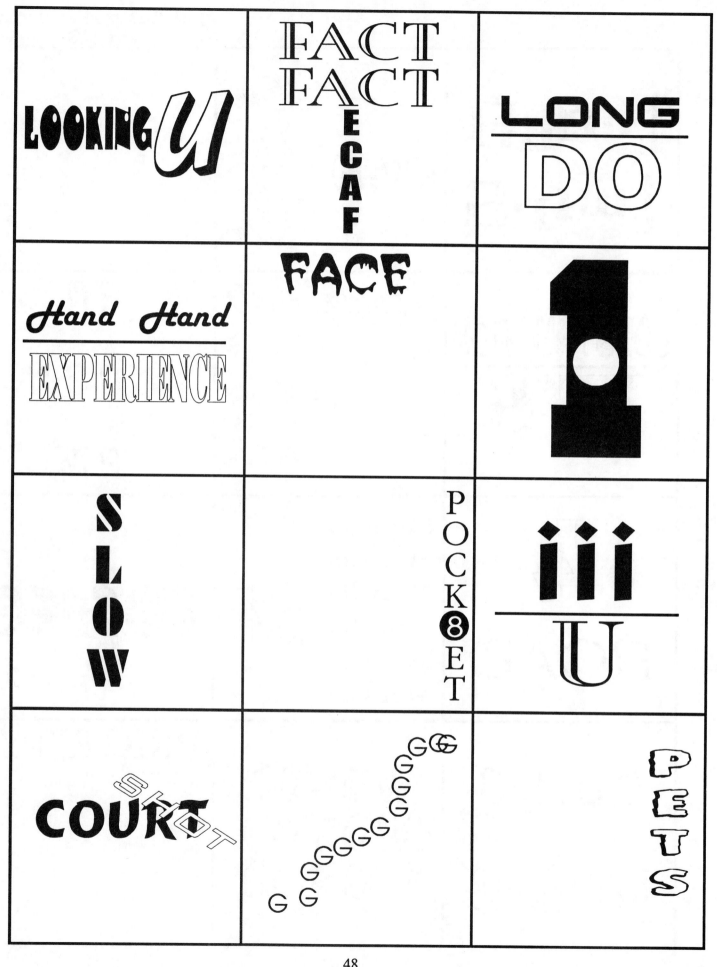

	PERFECT PERFECT PERFECT PERFECT PERFECT PERFECT PERFECT PERFECT PERFECT PERFECT PERFECT PERFECT PERFECT PERFECT PERFECT PERFECT PERFECT PERFECT	
$\dfrac{CCCCC}{\textbf{BASEBALL}}$	FORdeepEST	**CORNE** **CORNE**
RULE RULE	$\dfrac{\text{HEAVY}}{\text{EKAM}}$	$\dfrac{\text{ƎNIN}}{The}$
IT IT IT IT ABCDEFGHIJKLMNOPQRST_VWXYZ ABCDEFGHIJKLMNOPQRST_VWXYZ	TOWthrowEL	STEIN ↑

49

TOUCH	NIGHTNIGHTNIGHT	cr 1 owd crow 1 d c 1 rowd crow 1 d cro 1 wd
RISE ME NT ME NT	SHOW GAME	PLEASURE BUSINESS
R U N N E R	EEEL	K K K K K K K K K K FINISH
KEEP *Jones Jones*	SLAM	NET NET NET NET NET NET NET NET NET NET NET NET NET NET NET

PAYMENT
HOUSE

TIME

PIGGY
RIDE

DRIVEDRIVEDRIVEDRIVEDRIVE

shall
COME

ATHALON
ATHALON
ATHALON

TIDE

FIELD
↑

Prison prison prison prison prison.

FISHINGFISHINGFISHING

E A V E   E A V E

REC0RᵈEVENT	BLpigANKpigET	NIGHT NIGHT
S I T (SIT) TUHS	Plate PETS	ᴚUNNING
BAR BAR	S S I I D D E E (SIDE SIDE)	eee life eee
WOOD WOOD WOOD WOOD WOOD BABE WOOD WOOD WOOD	playing BOY BOY	golf

52

POINTPOINTPOINT	CORPORATE	
Serve / HAND	Stroke (reversed)	EVENLATEING
	NIGHT	BOGIE BOGIE
BLOW		
Flip Flip (reversed)	00:00 OUT OUT	PAGE

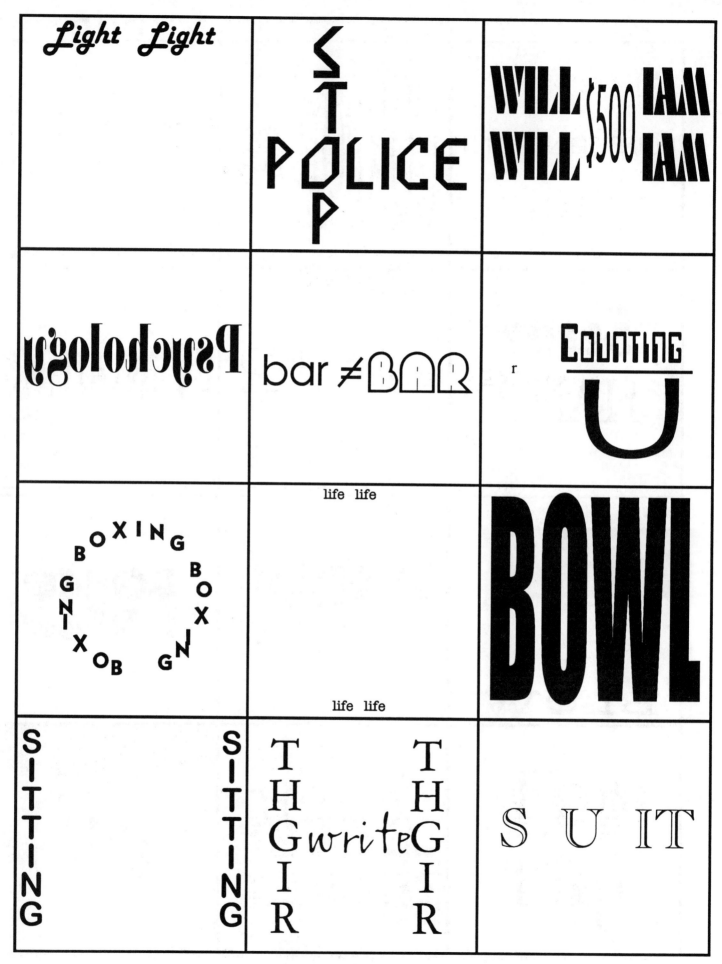

wood wood wood wood	iron iron iron iron iron	PAlivingST
punishment → PUNISHMENT	JUMP	SH★W
PHOT<u>O</u>	DAY Lee Lee	TENpunDED
<u>OUT</u> Date	CCC TICKET TICKET	MILD | WILD WALK

WARM	1. Log	STAGE
evil ↑ EVIL	Cheer ↑	NAIDEMOC (vertical)
NAUSEA NAUSEA NAUSEA	NEfriendED	HOOD / LOOK
BEST	Heaven Heaven Heaven Heaven Heaven Heaven → Heaven	1. Way 2. Weigh 3. Whey

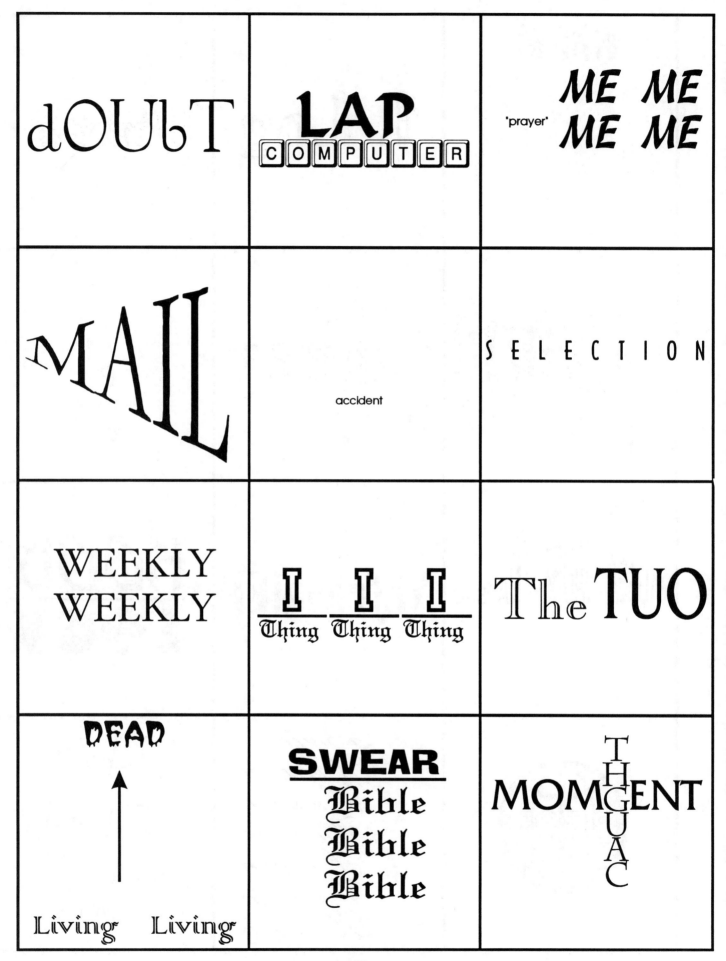

dOUbT

LAP
COMPUTER

'prayer' *ME ME ME ME*

MAIL

accident

SELECTION

WEEKLY WEEKLY

I I I
Thing Thing Thing

The TUO

DEAD
↑
Living   Living

SWEAR
Bible
Bible
Bible

MOMENT (THGUAC)

Iright**I**	L I M O S I N E	ROU◆GH
by **AND**	TIMES T.I.M.ES TIMES	iHITi
HA IR	1996 1997 1998 **AWAY** 1999	COMECOME · NOW/ME
TIturpNE	mouse	RUCKUS RUCKUS RUCKUS

pearlspearlspearlspearls	**PICTURE**	CHOICES CHOICES CHOICES
MUSTARD	GOING YOUR WORD	SCHOOL JOB
groPOOLund	IFLAND IF IFC	GET doggie
ROLLER beanbeanbeanbean		LIcrisisFE

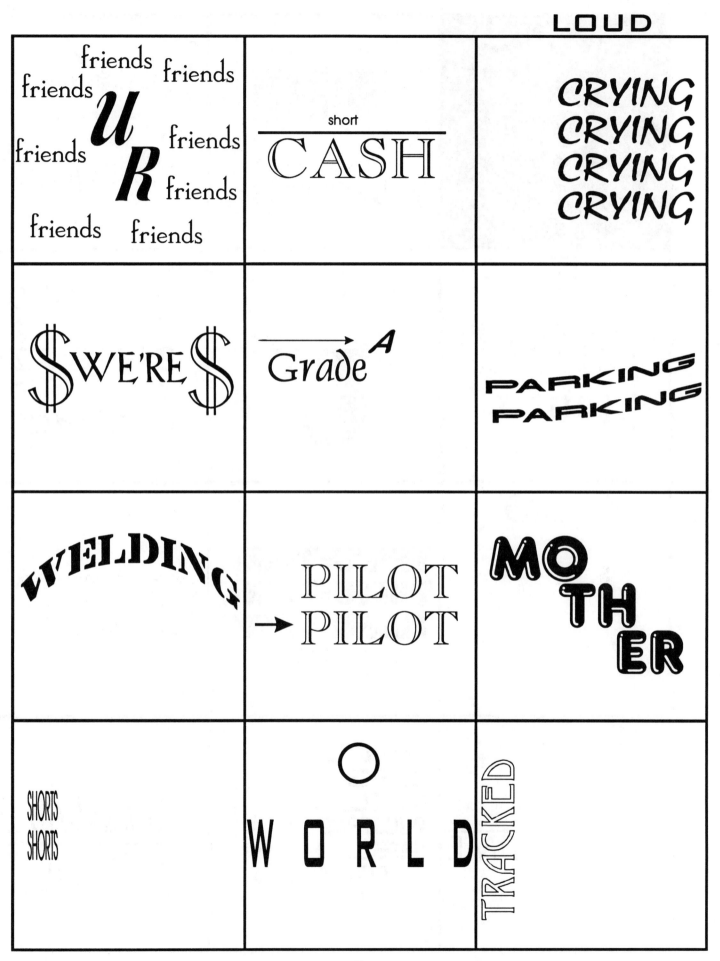

friends friends friends
friends U R friends
friends
friends friends

short
CASH

CRYING
CRYING
CRYING
CRYING

$WE'RE$

Grade A

PARKING
PARKING

WELDING

→ PILOT
PILOT

MO TH ER

SHORTS
SHORTS

O
WORLD

TRACKED

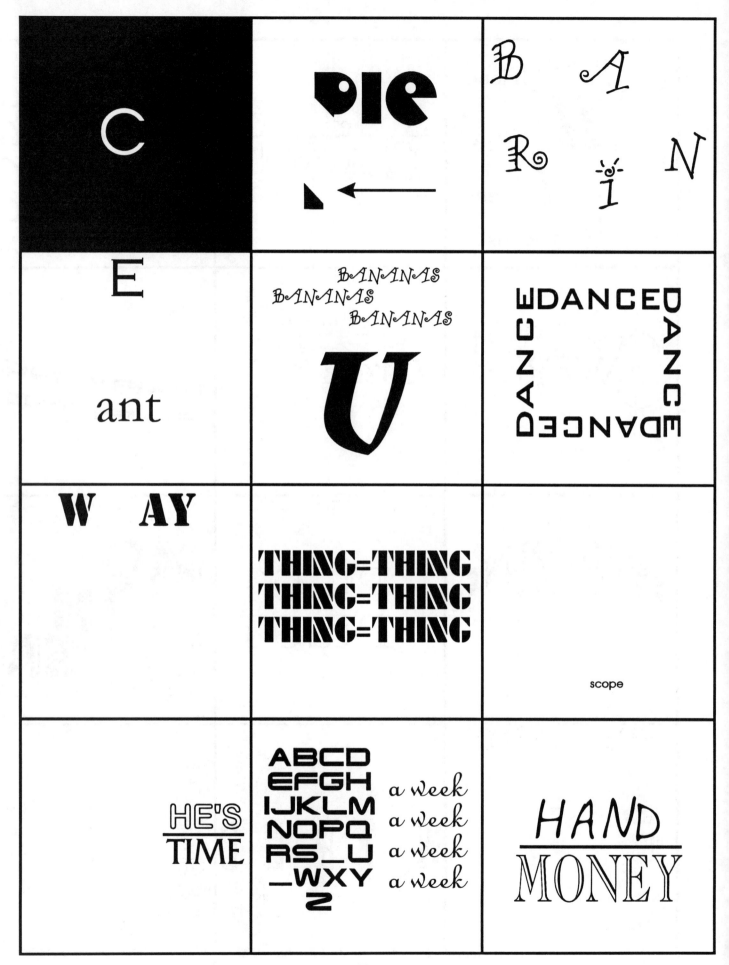

C

bIe ←

B A R I N

E

ant

BANANAS
BANANAS
BANANAS
U

DANCED DANCE
DANCE DANCED

W AY

THING=THING
THING=THING
THING=THING

scope

HE'S
TIME

ABCD
EFGH
IJKLM
NOPQ
RS_U
_WXY
Z

a week
a week
a week
a week

HAND
MONEY

B E D	3. Blame 4. Blame	**D** **A** **O** **R**
TENgoodSIONS	DANCE DANCE → DANCE	**WALK**
FILE *EcabT*	LIGHTER	**CANYON**
FREQUENCY	**CLUB**	2. THOUGHTS 2. THOUGHTS 2. THOUGHTS 2. THOUGHTS **it**

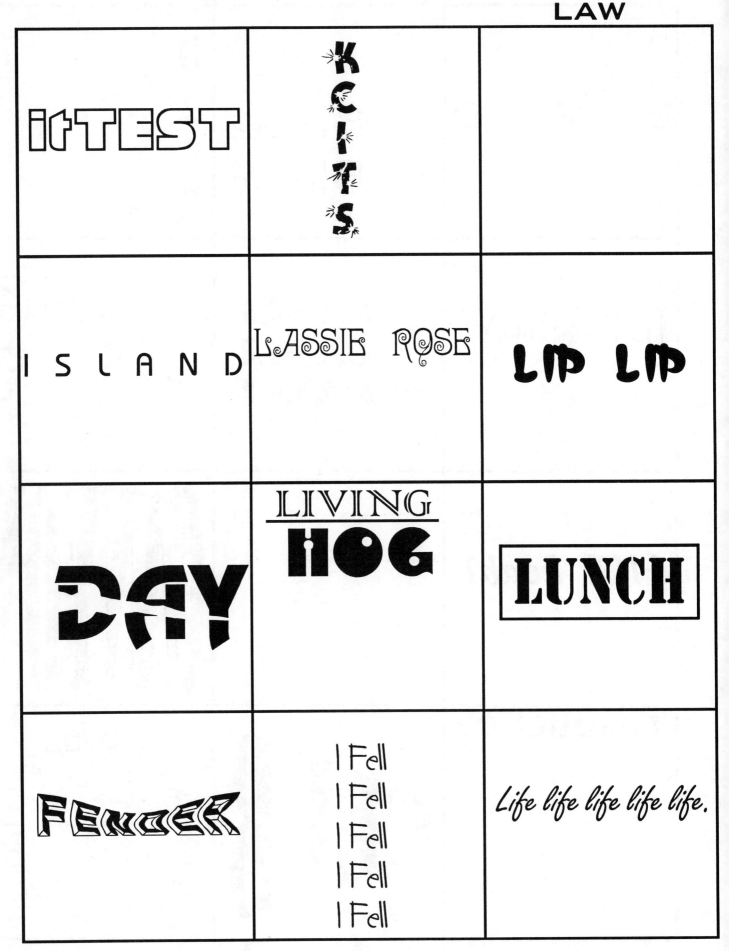

itTEST

KCITS

ISLAND

LASSIE ROSE

LIP LIP

DAY

LIVING
HOG

LUNCH

FENDER

I Fell
I Fell
I Fell
I Fell
I Fell

Life life life life life.

STUCK STUCK ME ME ME ME	minute minute	WATER WATER
BERMUDA BERMUDA BERMUDA BERMUDA	Theodore Roosevelt naked	COME —— IN
HAbirdND = BU2SH	RACE | CLOCK	ChanceChance ↑
uRIDE	SHOT	P ▶ ▶

65

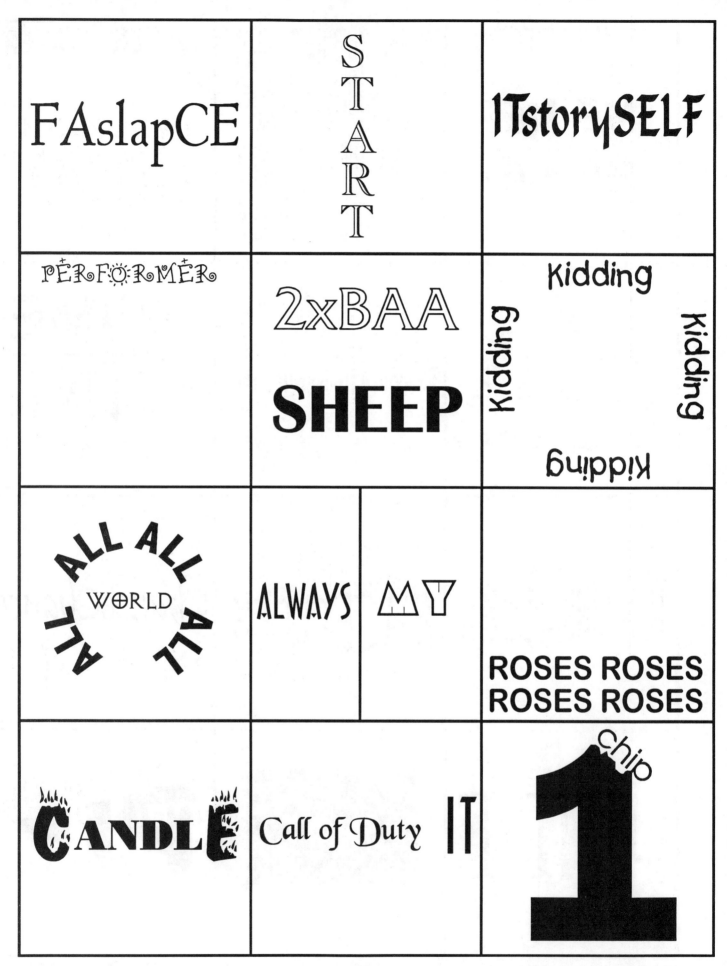

66

STOP

$.10

BASED
TRUE STORY

BBBB begin

YƎ⅃⅃A

RADIO
OIᗡAЯ

HANDS HANDS
HANDS HANDS

DECK

KNI BUMP GHT

Life

LIVE LIVE

DDDD days

DDDD nights

MIN BACK UTES
MIN BACK UTES
MIN BACK UTES
MIN BACK UTES
MIN BACK UTES

ƎƆAℲ **March**

DI ACID GESTION

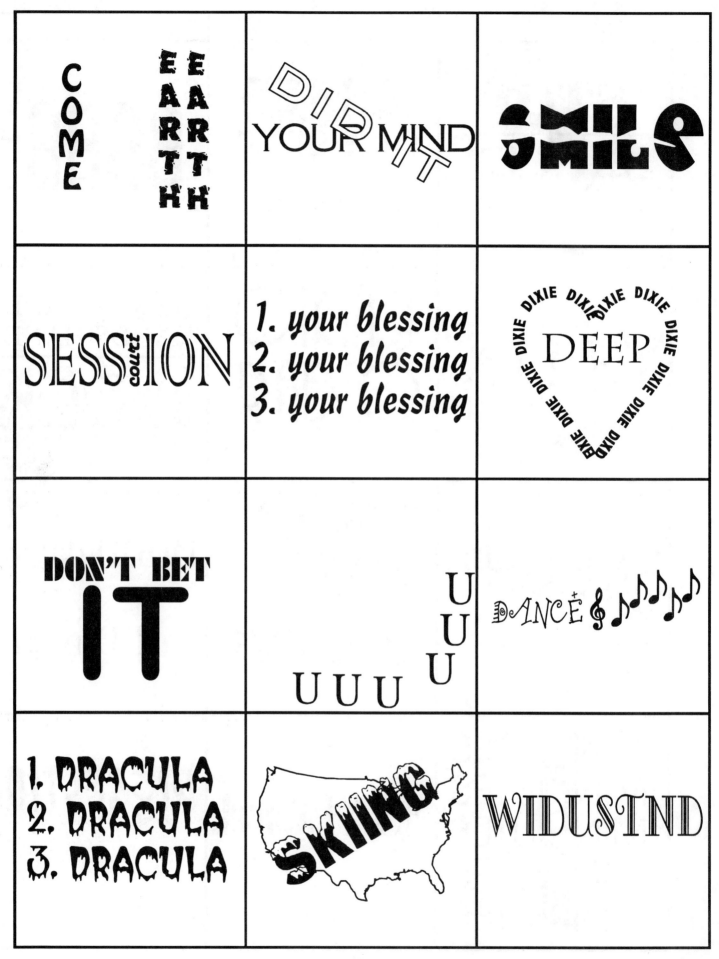

EAT	HOUR HOUR HOUR HOUR HOUR HOUR HOUR HOUR HOUR HOUR HOUR → HOUR	A EVERYTHING Z
A 1. Thing M 2. Thing 3. Thing	EARTH	FIRE FIRE
HE'S life	CHOLESTEROL	STAND / icu
→ EDUCATION EDUCATION	TROUIMBLE	T REASON REASON

THINK THINK THINK THINK THINK THINK **IT**

GET

FOULED FOULED FOULED

YOURACT

GET GET GET GET GET

spider

he'shimself

MACKERAL

Tuesd

STEP
—————
FART

T
E
G
Bed

COMMANDMENTS COMMANDMENTS COMMANDMENTS COMMANDMENTS COMMANDMENTS COMMANDMENTS COMMANDMENTS COMMANDMENTS COMMANDMENTS COMMANDMENTS	COAST	HE ○↑ RE
THAT'S	BAD BAD	ROAD ↑
IT'S	U just S	→ MOHICANS MOHICANS MOHICANS
house PRAIRIE	SPLOSTACE	TURN TURN TURN

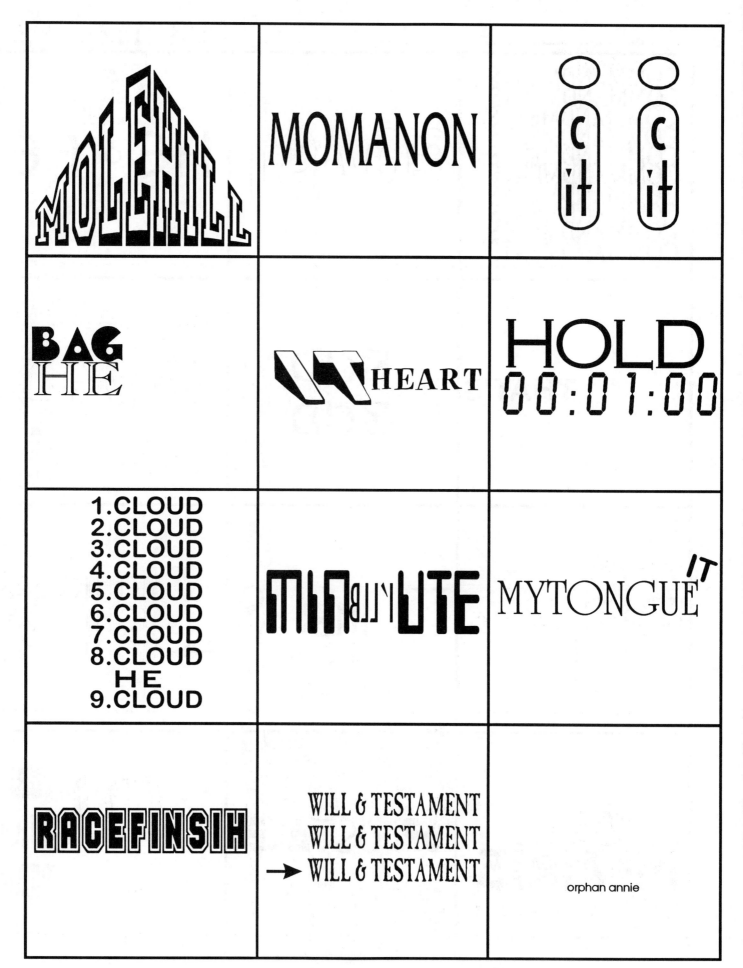

MOLEHILL

MOMANON

Ci t · Ci t

BAG
HE

HEART

HOLD
00:01:00

1.CLOUD
2.CLOUD
3.CLOUD
4.CLOUD
5.CLOUD
6.CLOUD
7.CLOUD
8.CLOUD
HE
9.CLOUD

MINBURYUTE

MYTONGUE IT

RACEFINSIH

WILL & TESTAMENT
WILL & TESTAMENT
→ WILL & TESTAMENT

orphan annie

74

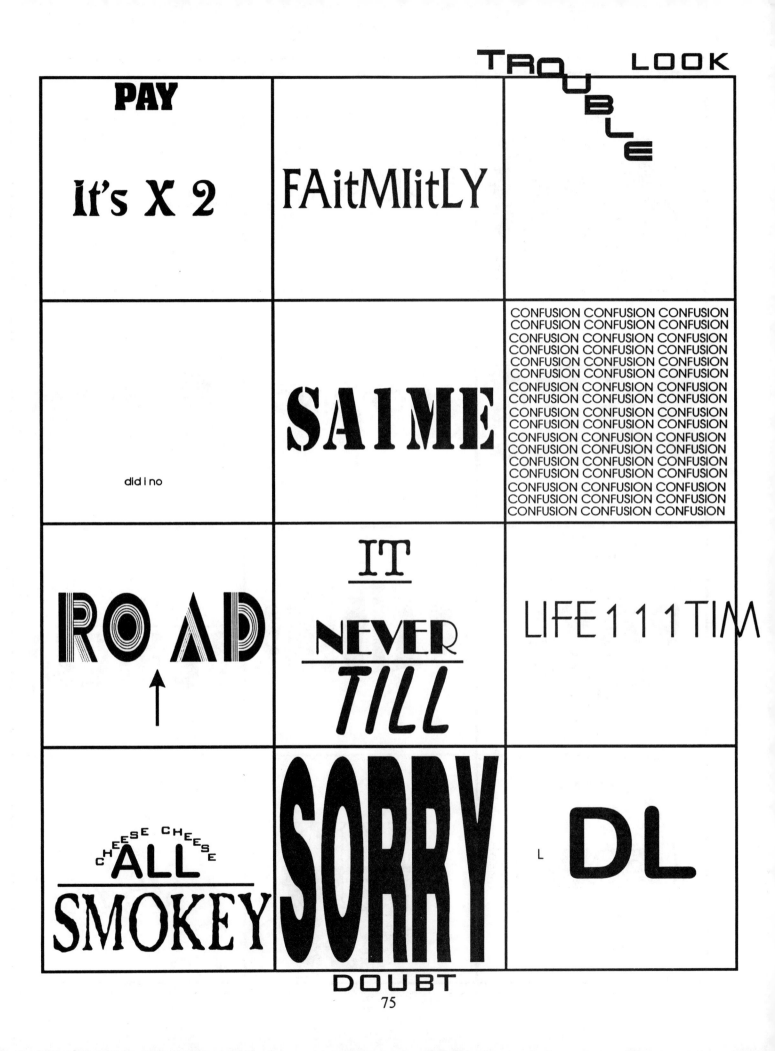

PAY

It's X 2

FAitMIitLY

did i no

SA1ME

CONFUSION CONFUSION CONFUSION
CONFUSION CONFUSION CONFUSION
CONFUSION CONFUSION CONFUSION
CONFUSION CONFUSION CONFUSION
CONFUSION CONFUSION CONFUSION
CONFUSION CONFUSION CONFUSION
CONFUSION CONFUSION CONFUSION
CONFUSION CONFUSION CONFUSION
CONFUSION CONFUSION CONFUSION
CONFUSION CONFUSION CONFUSION
CONFUSION CONFUSION CONFUSION
CONFUSION CONFUSION CONFUSION
CONFUSION CONFUSION CONFUSION
CONFUSION CONFUSION CONFUSION
CONFUSION CONFUSION CONFUSION
CONFUSION CONFUSION CONFUSION

RO AD

IT
NEVER
TILL

LIFE 1 1 1 TIM

CHEESE CHEESE
CHEESE
ALL
SMOKEY

SORRY

L DL

H₂ UR O	SPRssING	FIELD
EARS	SHOP↑PING	SANTA HISWAY
RAKE coal coal	RAISINS	right BROTHER
ROSIE	LT U	SUGAR Please

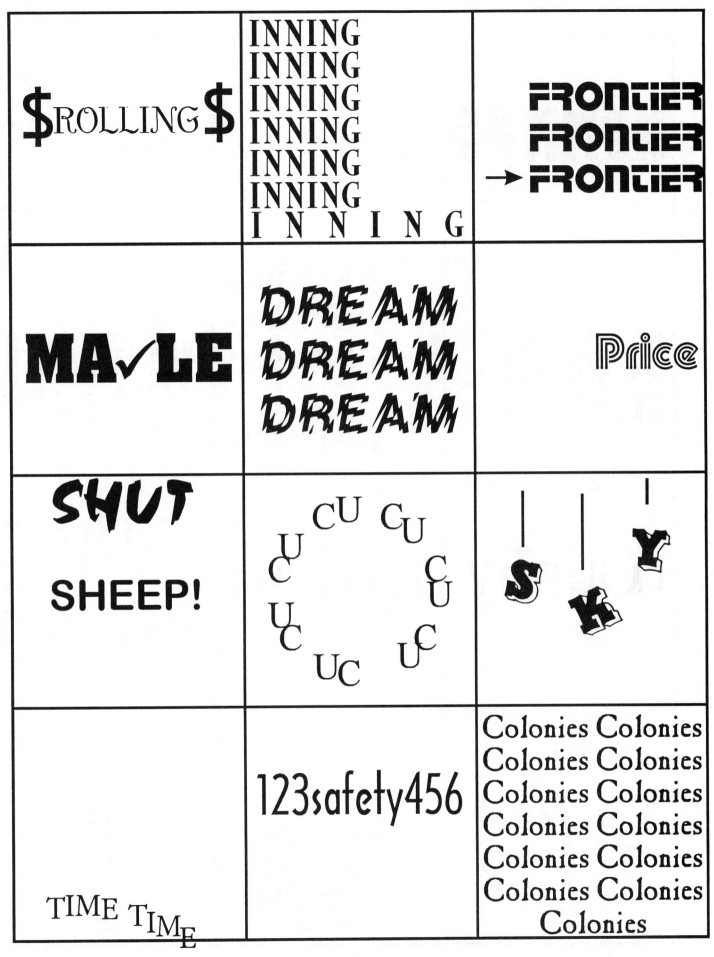

$ROLLING$

INNING
INNING
INNING
INNING
INNING
INNING
I N N I N G

FRONTIER
FRONTIER
→ FRONTIER

MA✓LE

DREAM
DREAM
DREAM

Price

SHUT

SHEEP!

CU CU
U CU
U CU
U CU
UC UC

S K Y

123safety456

Colonies Colonies
Colonies Colonies
Colonies Colonies
Colonies Colonies
Colonies Colonies
Colonies Colonies
Colonies

TIME TIME

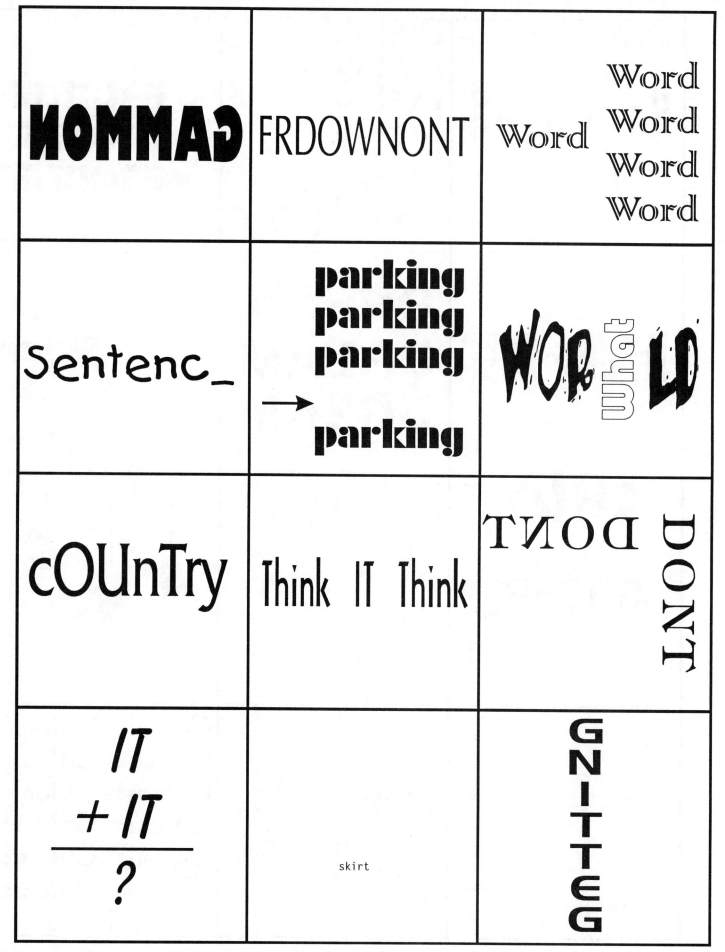

GAMMON (upside down)	FRDOWNONT	Word Word Word Word Word
Sentenc_	parking / parking / parking → / parking	WOR what LD
cOUnTry	Think IT Think	DONT DONT (upside down)
IT + IT / ?	skirt	GNITTEG (upside down)

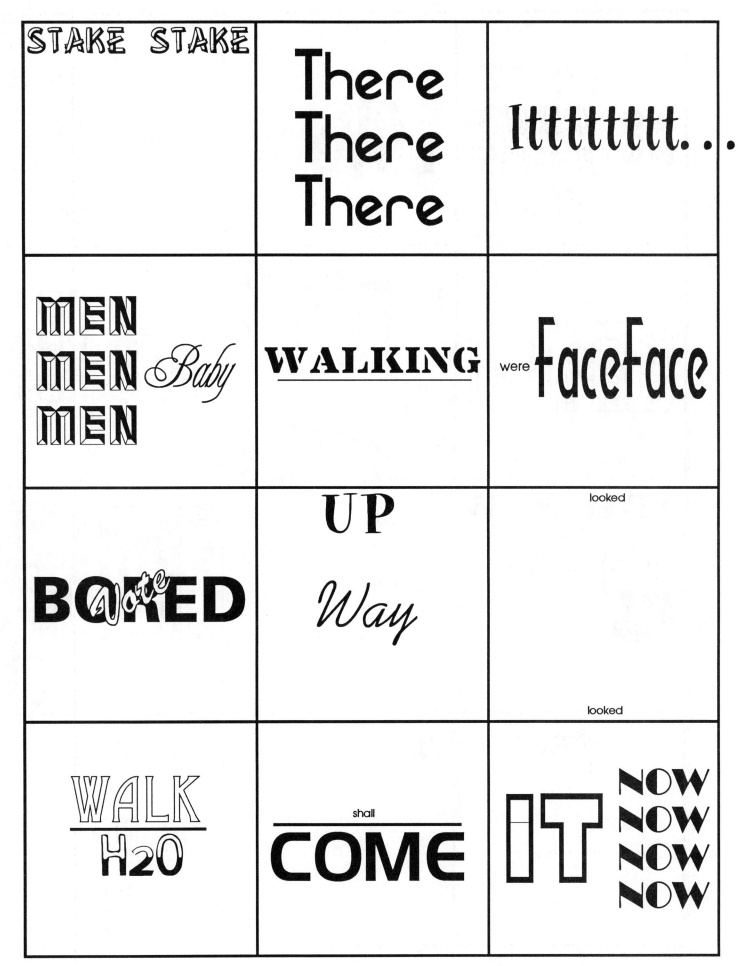

STAKE STAKE

There
There
There

Itttttttt...

MEN
MEN *Baby*
MEN

WALKING

were FaceFace

B**Vote**RED

UP
Way

looked

looked

WALK
H2O

shall
COME

IT NOW
NOW
NOW
NOW

BIG **BIG** *HIS BRITCHES* *HIS BRITCHES* *HIS BRITCHES* *HIS BRITCHES*	**LOVE**	WEL⊗COME
ELEPHANT	I T I T I T I I I I I	**RU** REEL REEL REEL REEL
NOW NOW **ALL**	SMART INTELLIGENT WISE	**BROTHER** **U**
CHEER	**IT**	
	UR	TEL U RLIGENT

80

Yearly ✓	*Dressed Dressed Dressed* **PlaceSTOP** **PlaceWAIT** **GO**	print
KEEP SMILING	Life 38, 39, 40	Hmm Thought Thought
DICE DICE	FAIR T T T T	i IT IT try IT **IT**
crycrycrycryBANK	Folks Folks Folks Folks	WELL NOW NOW NOW NOW

THAT'S **U**	ip↗	STRIKE STRIKE STRIKE
THINK	GARCARCARAGE GARCARCARAGE GARCARCARAGE	NIGHTmorning
FRECKLEhairhare	WAKE suzie	**21U**
m**UR**ind m**UR**ind m**UR**ind	**M** make R selves	GARBAGE

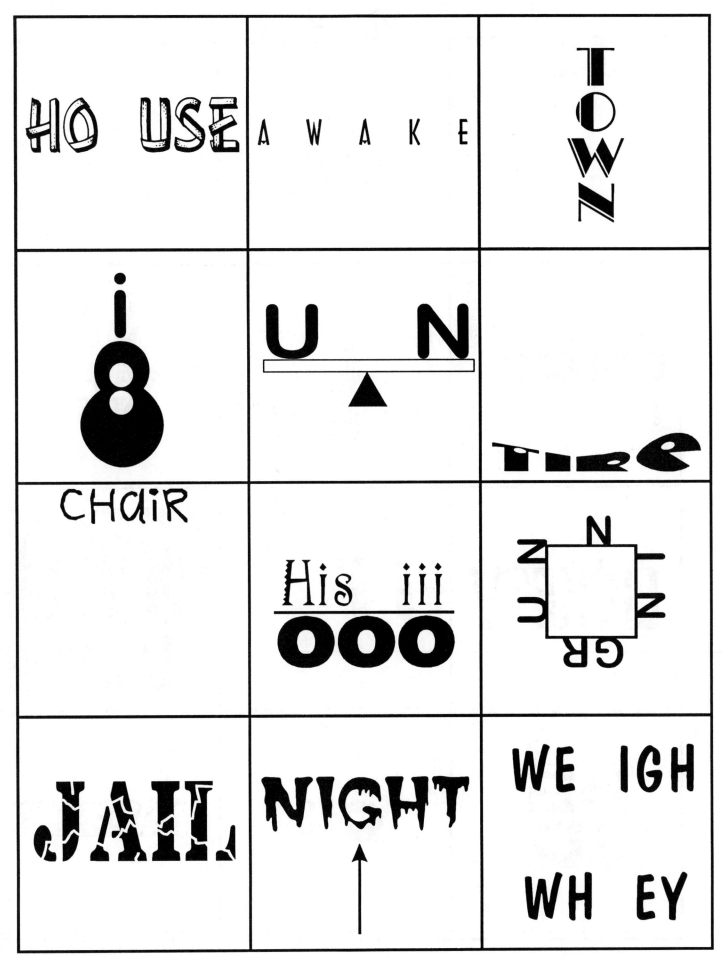

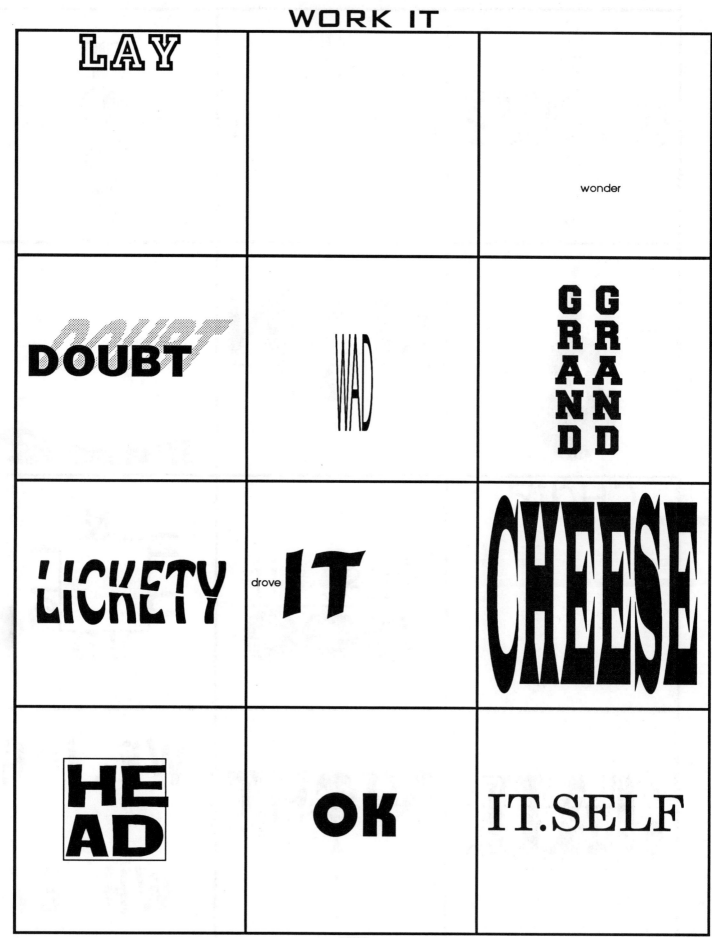

LAY		wonder
DOUBT (DOUBT)	WAD	GRAND GRAND
LICKETY	drove IT	CHEESE
HE AD	OK	IT.SELF

came

OVATION

HO
HO
+HO
―――

SESAME

CY   CY

$\frac{111}{444}$

G
N
I
W   K
A   L

ИІИІ Н

HISTORYHISTORY

joke

WHO   WHO
FIRST

VAD ERS

book

85

ROAD	MIND MATTER	LIP *TOE* LIP
ƎƆИA⅃פ	DRESSED bit	L O *FALLING* V E
KEET KEET	ho RN	BUD GET ▲
JOB I'M JOB	PHOTOGRAPHY	DIPPING

SAFE ƨORRY	ME AL ME AL ME AL ME AL **DAY**	**ODD odd**
● > I + T	**F~~I~~LES F~~I~~XES F~~I~~LES**	HOURS HOURS
HEATHEATHEATHEAT	FORTUNE	N L I E
PFRFFCT	**KNEE LIGHTS**	**SOM**ething

CANCELLED

DEATHLIFE

Chest

R
K CLOCK O
C NIGHT NIGHT

PUR SE
ALITY

KNOW

RAIN
RAIN RAIN
SINGING
RAIN RAIN

FIRE
Grace

FLY

BOYWORLD

1. World
2. World
3. World...

BASEBALL

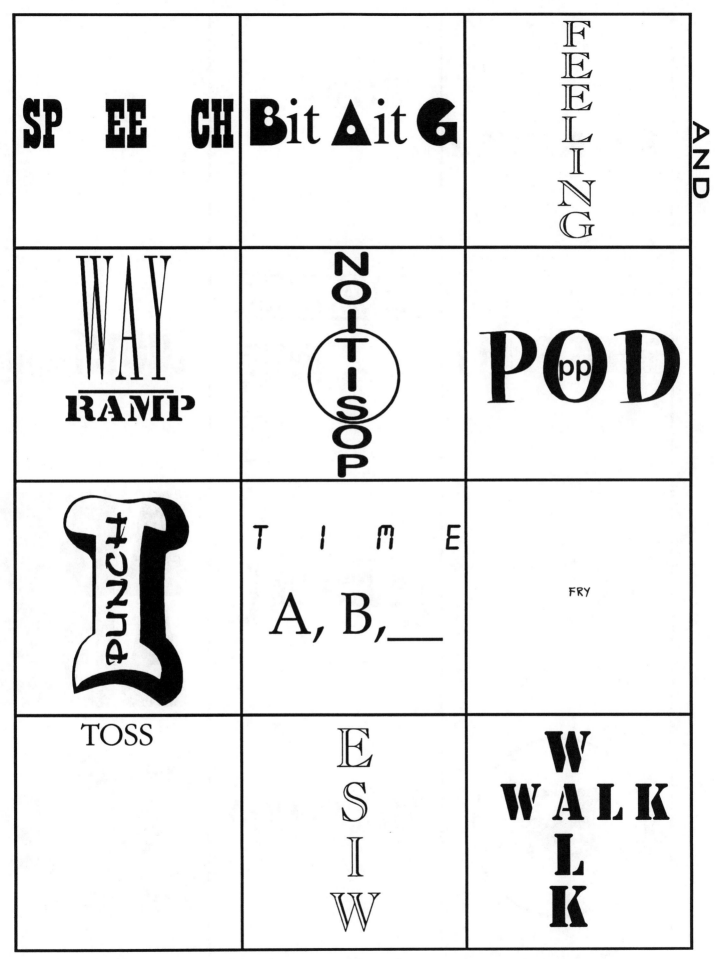

SP EE CH   Bit Ait G   FEELING   AND

WAY / RAMP   NOITISOP   POD pp

PUNCH   TIME   A, B,___   FRY

TOSS   E S I W   W WALK L K

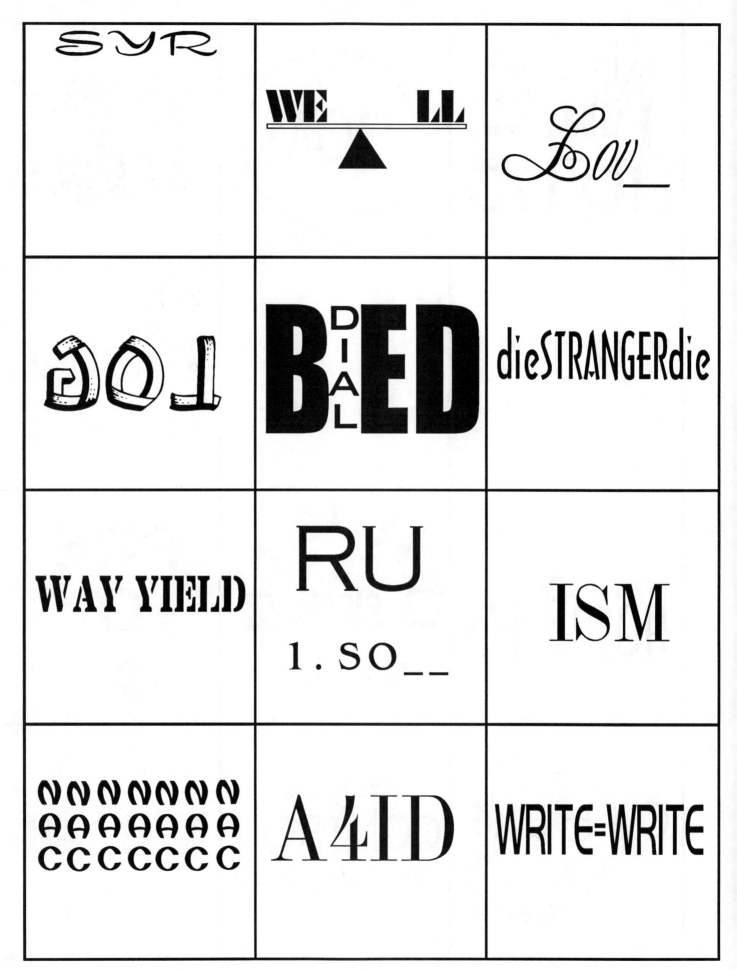

SYR

WE LL ▲

Lov__

ꓒOT

B DIAL ED

dieSTRANGERdie

WAY YIELD

RU
1. SO __

ISM

NNNNNNNN
AAAAAAAA
CCCCCCC

A4ID

WRITE=WRITE

92

ЯAcarGE

TION

SADDLE
SADDLE

H|E|A|D

noonSUNDAY

CLEANING
kiD
kiD

lbs. lbs. lbs. lbs. lbs
WEIGHT

HEAD

SHOOT SHOOT

X8
TERM

222
ARIZONA

LAB OR

D D I N E W G	¢ -MURDER	O O, O,
COPY	DECISION DECISION	WILSON
DEAL	BUCKLE SAFE SAFE T SAFE SAFE	Oct. Nov. Dec. DO
OVER OVER	EA π R EA π R	Sunday Monday Tuesday schedule

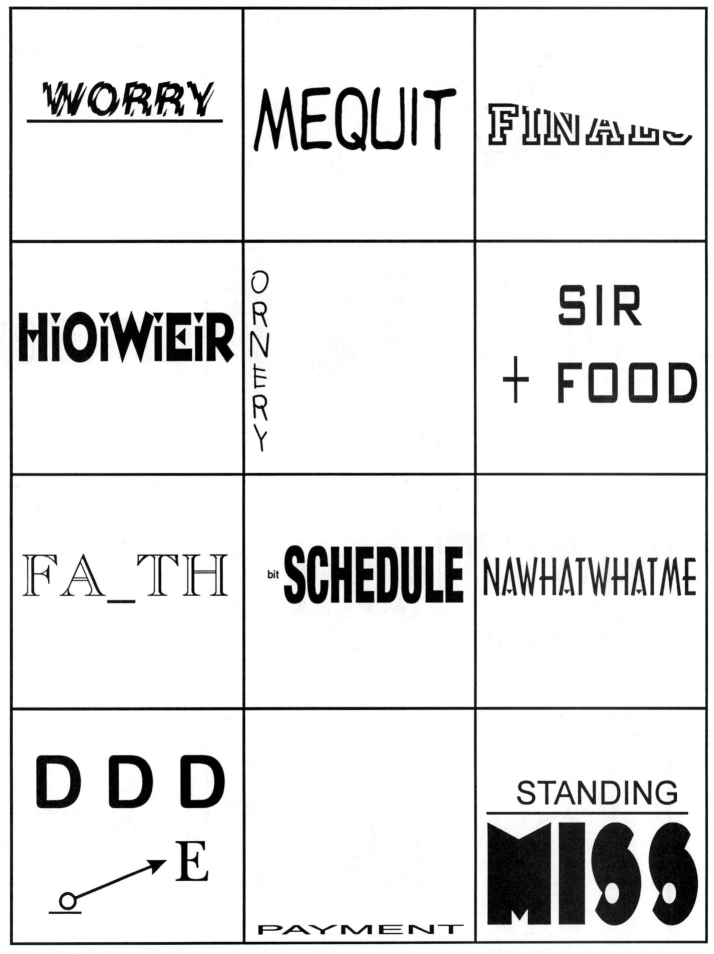

<u>WORRY</u>	MEQUIT	FINALS
HiOiWiEiR	ORNERY	SIR + FOOD
FA_TH	bit SCHEDULE	NAWHATWHATME
D D D / →E	PAYMENT	STANDING / MISS

U ALL S **NOW**	TURNED SIDE	SOIL
IT'S IT'S IT'S TIME IT'S IT'S IT'S	**JET**	HOROBOD
MAST	CRACKED Y DAY S DAY E	
333	UP	DES DES

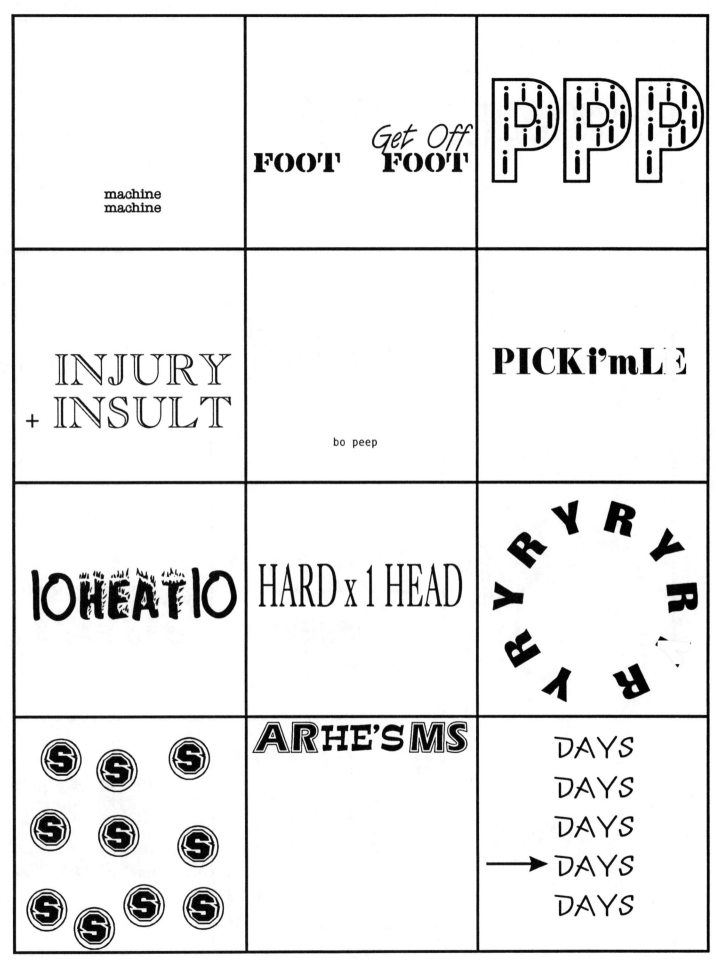

INSURCARANCE

SURE
SURE
SURE
SURE

bit
PRICED

CEsssRE

meALL

ANGEL

FOOT FOOT FOOT

SAFE
1ST

OUTER_

GOING AROUND

WALKING

DICE
-DICE

2. OUT 1 1	TURNED A A A A *Loan*	New Leaf
model	GRA 1'VE	T 2222
CALORIE DIET	TH hang ERE	E Y E
DRUG ————— DOE DOE	RIDING	__, 2, 3 No No No

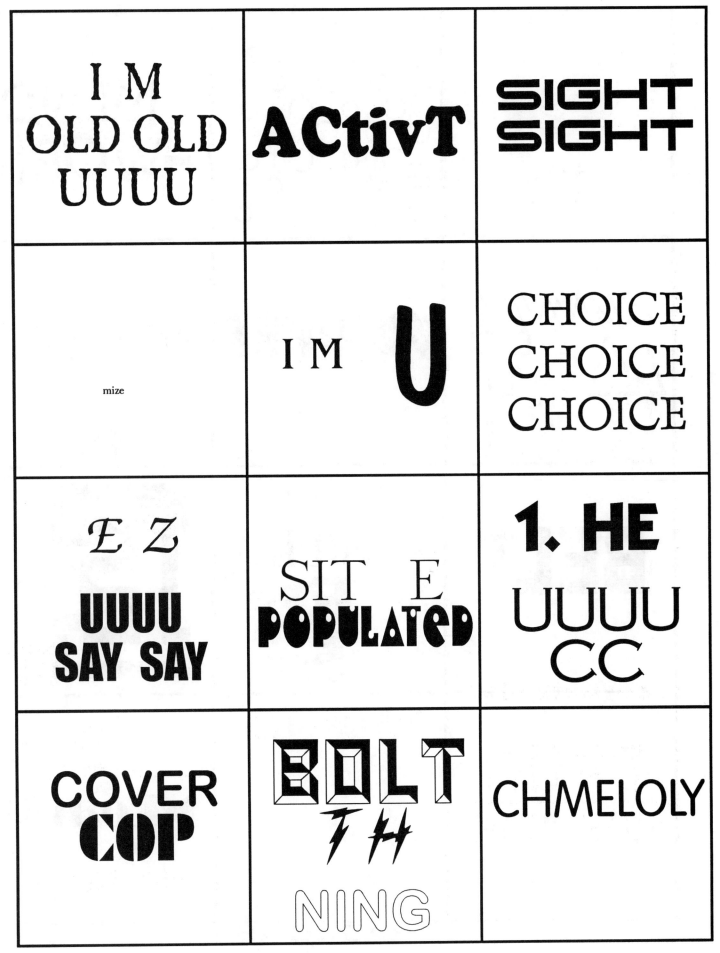

I M OLD OLD UUUU	ACtivT	SIGHT SIGHT
mize	I M U	CHOICE CHOICE CHOICE
E Z UUUU SAY SAY	SIT E POPULATED	1. HE UUUU CC
COVER COP	BOLT T H NING	CHMELOLY

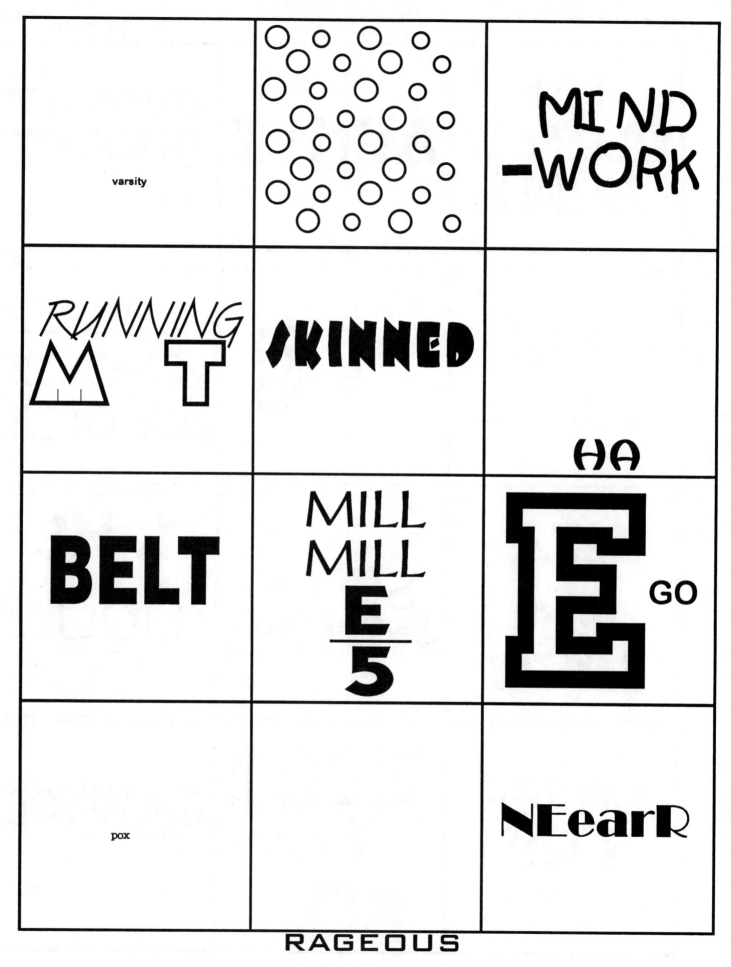

varsity

MIND
-WORK

RUNNING
M T

SKINNED

HA

BELT

MILL
MILL
E
—
5

E GO

pox

NEearR

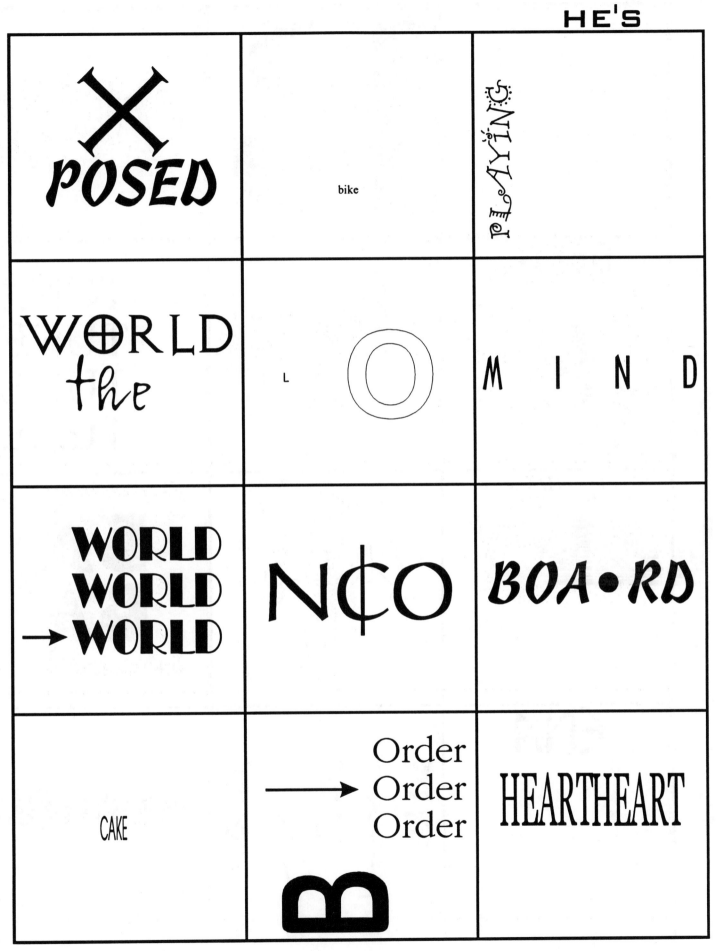

X POSED

bike

PLAYING

WORLD the

L O

M I N D

WORLD
WORLD
→ WORLD

NCO

BOA•RD

CAKE

Order
→ Order
Order

B

HEARTHEART

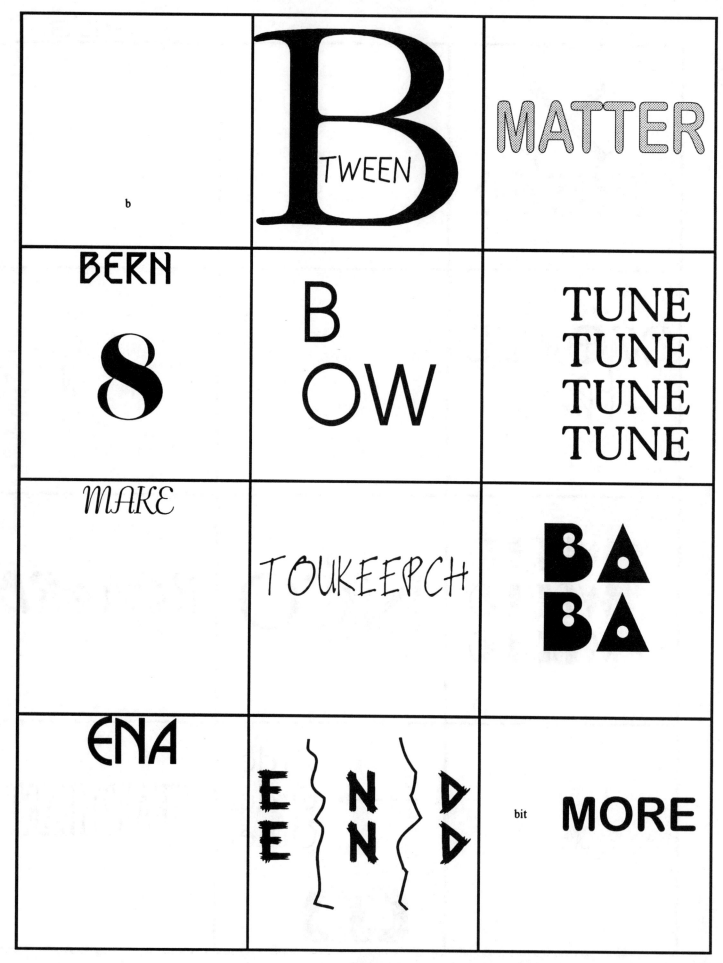

b

B TWEEN

MATTER

BERN

8

B
OW

TUNE
TUNE
TUNE
TUNE

MAKE

TOUKEEPCH

BA
BA

ENA

EE NN DD

bit MORE

D	✓	✓IT
TOLD U AND AGAIN	LEAN WARD WARD	_SHIP
SHAVE	H S A W Dinner	AGEBeauty
NICCUGHT	HOUR HOUR OPEN	apolis sota

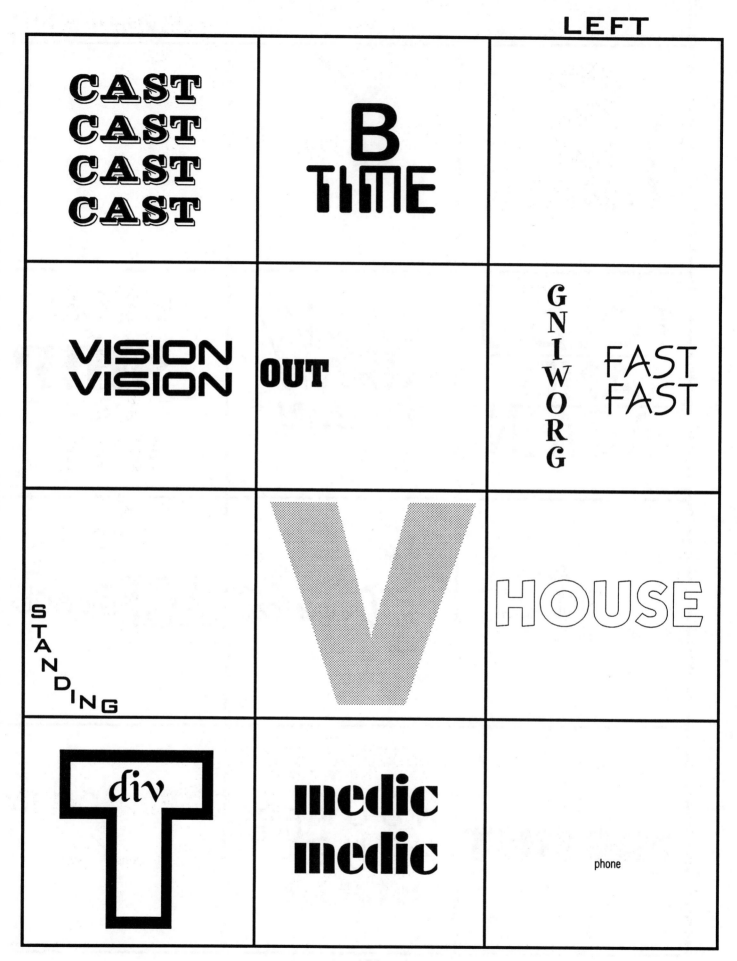

CAST
CAST
CAST
CAST

B
TIME

VISION
VISION

OUT

GNIWORG

FAST
FAST

STANDING

V

HOUSE

T div

medic
medic

phone

STIMATE	**Tone**	
NOON	FEATURE FEATURE	**GOOD GOOD BB TRUE**
c s **TA**	**TIVALNE**	**C** *erra*
STAR	**MUCH MUCH SOON SOON**	**STFRANKEIN**

TAKING
MAJOR

FUNOR

CHiLD
B

NOTCH

E

R
SEM

K
C
I
P
TRUCK

JUeRE

ƎVOM

H
S
I
B

HACATT

CUrrrrrrrrrBE

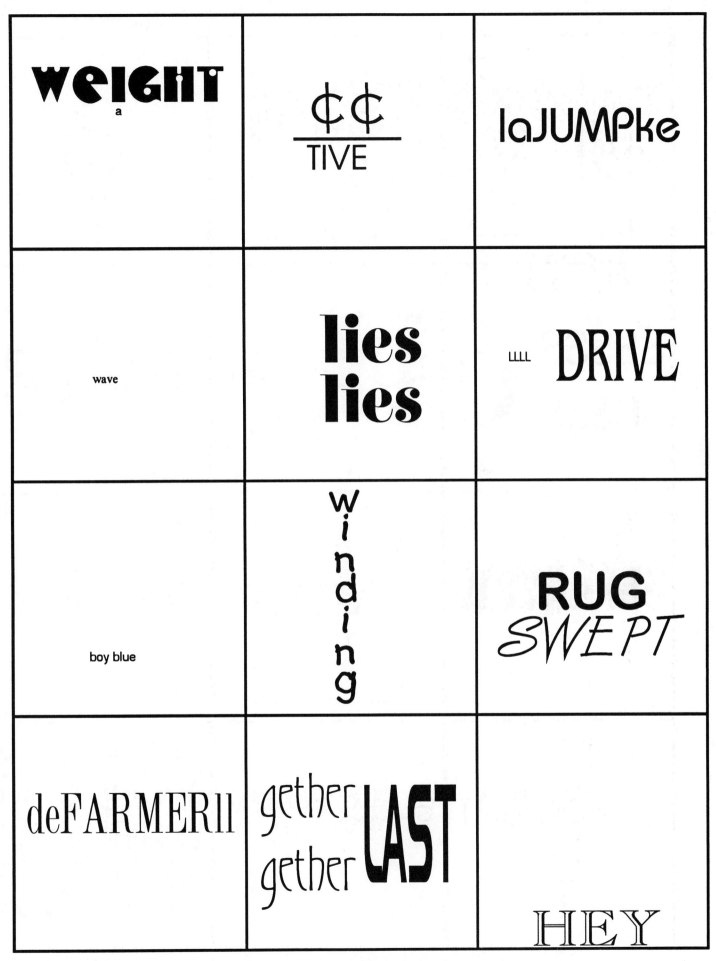

WEIGHT a	$\dfrac{\text{¢¢}}{\text{TIVE}}$	laJUMPke
wave	lies lies	LLLL DRIVE
boy blue	w i n d i n g	RUG SWEPT
deFARMERll	gether LAST gether	HEY

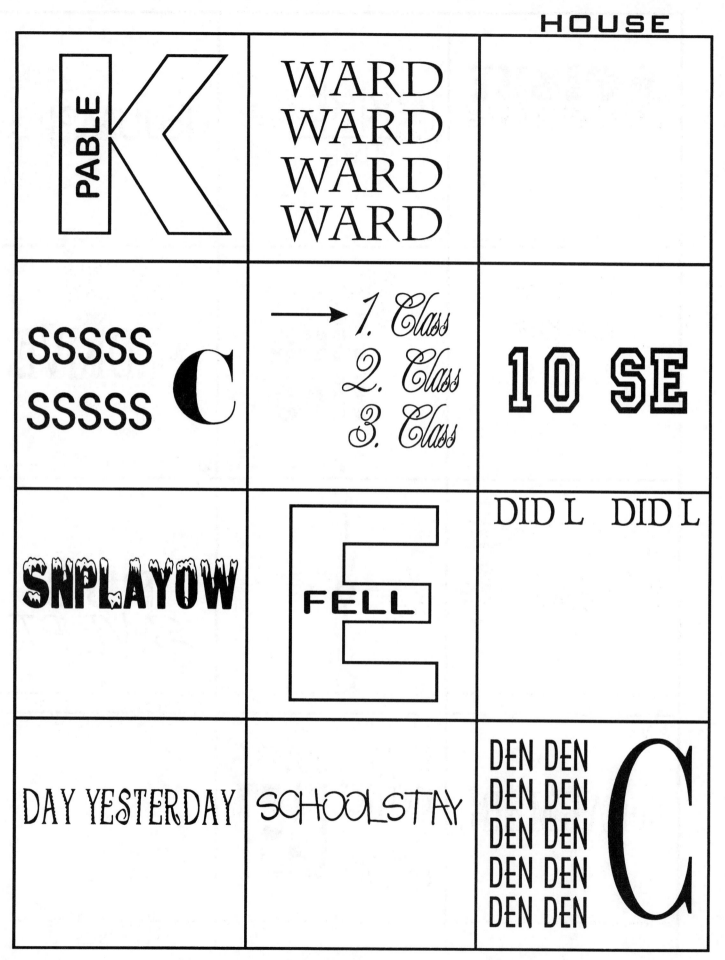

PABLE **K**

WARD
WARD
WARD
WARD

SSSSS
SSSSS **C**

→ *1. Class*
2. Class
3. Class

10 SE

SNPLAYOW

FELL **E**

DID L   DID L

DAY YESTERDAY

SCHOOLSTAY

DEN DEN
DEN DEN
DEN DEN
DEN DEN
DEN DEN **C**

ENDSENDS	HIGH High ↑	Good ZERO ZERO ZERO ZERO
ceps ceps ceps ceps	Pay / TIME	H S U P H S U P
UPDOWN INOUT	Dki	Never / TIME
ever ever ever ever day	DU HE IS MPS DU MPS	SCHOOL

DROP

CR PEACHES EAM
PEACHES

HOPE HOPE

EVERYTHING
Hamburger

R
RR
E
Y
M

pig pig pig

PICK ME

TOWN

chinchin

THAT
BUTTON

FOUR FOUR
FOUR FOUR

dipper

POSWIMOL

SWA

112

MIRLOOKROR (mirrored)	ATUNE	Looking Looking *MEAT U*
♪♪♪♪♪♪ (musical notes)	rent rent rent rent	
CHOW (vertical)	**MUCH MUCH EAT EAT**	**OFF** (inverted)
COVER COVER **HIDING**	chicken	**FULL** *whuh*

DRAWER	BEB BEB	BAD *wolf*
twinkle twinkle ★	SITTING FENCE	**S** SCHOOL
i SLEPT	GO IT IT IT IT	RACE
WAG TRAIN	DIPPER	2 DRiNk DRiNk DRiNk DRiNk DRiNk

CYCLE CYCLE CYCLE	GO VACATION	STAY NIGHT
bear	TRO ur UBLE	$\dfrac{1}{1}$
DRESS DINNER DINNER DINNER DINNER	DINNER TABLE	LEM PIE DDDD SERT
TURN LIGHT	HIC	BIRD

BROTHER sister	2ndØ	AGE -B, U, T
I M 1,2,3,... **U**	**PEN** sword	G HISTORY
U WIN + U LOOSE +	DISK	B BOW W
Calm*STORM*	ACTI ON	IM IN AG AT ION

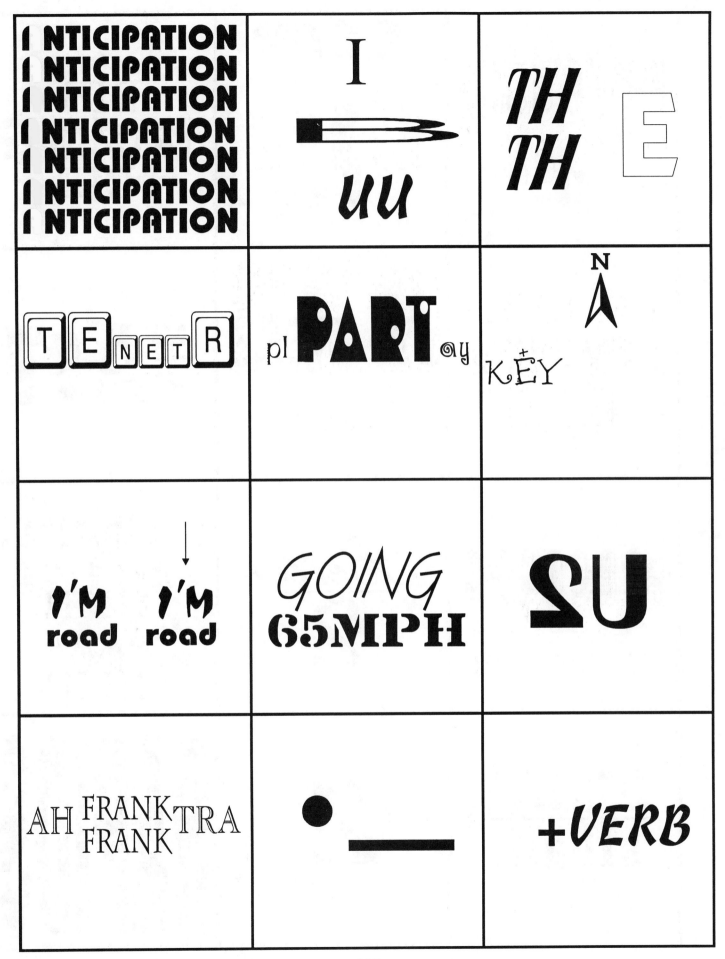

LET Gone Gone / B Gone Gone

GENE L

DIE TROUBLE DIE

FallSpring

MY behind WORK

FAST

NNNN / sick medicine

Better 2

i NNNN i / a / TH TH / AAAA / TH TH

DENIM / all all

X

RAPIDS

T A B L E	I D L Job	MANY MANY LOVE LOVE time time
NERVE MY NERVE	¢ EEEEEEEE LLLLLLLL	H A T
PUNCH ——	TREE	X spensive
HE'S libbing +libbing *it*	AIR ∈ —— ER	LORUVE

119

HA / LULU HUH Y e	& DDD M OW 10 10 10 10 10	CL — …J,K,_,M,N,…
	BOY N I duh Ho	hill → HILL
Care A B N C	GUAY GUAY	TOR / TOE E O TEAR
CUH / D uh	LAND	DOE nesia

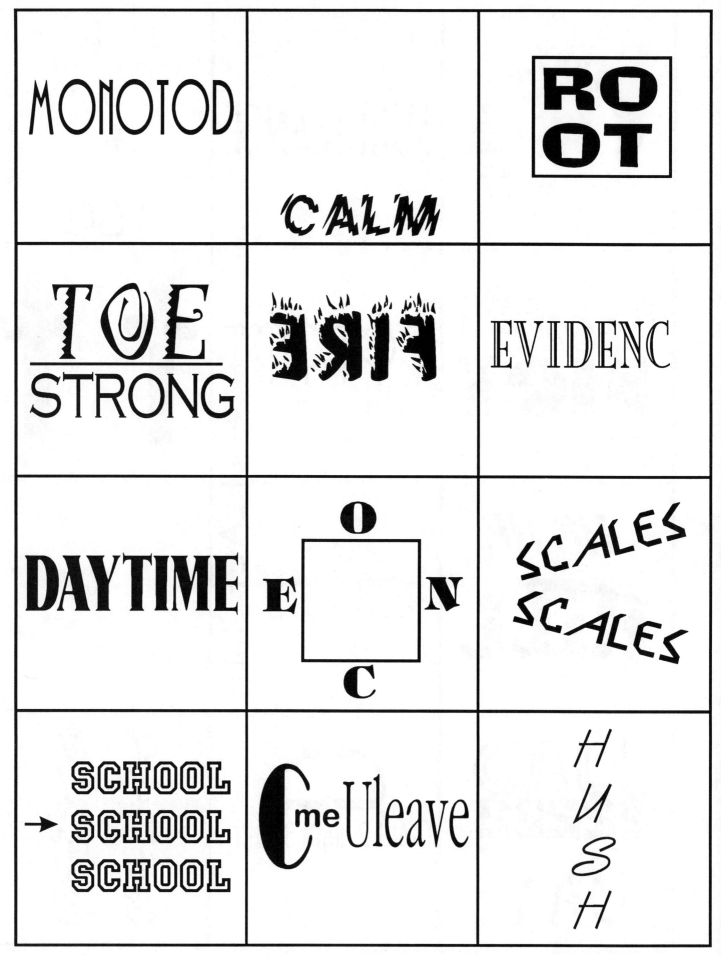

MONOTOD

CALM

RO
OT

TOE
STRONG

FIRE

EVIDENC

DAYTIME

O
E   N
C

SCALES
SCALES

→ SCHOOL
SCHOOL
SCHOOL

C me Uleave

H
U
S
H

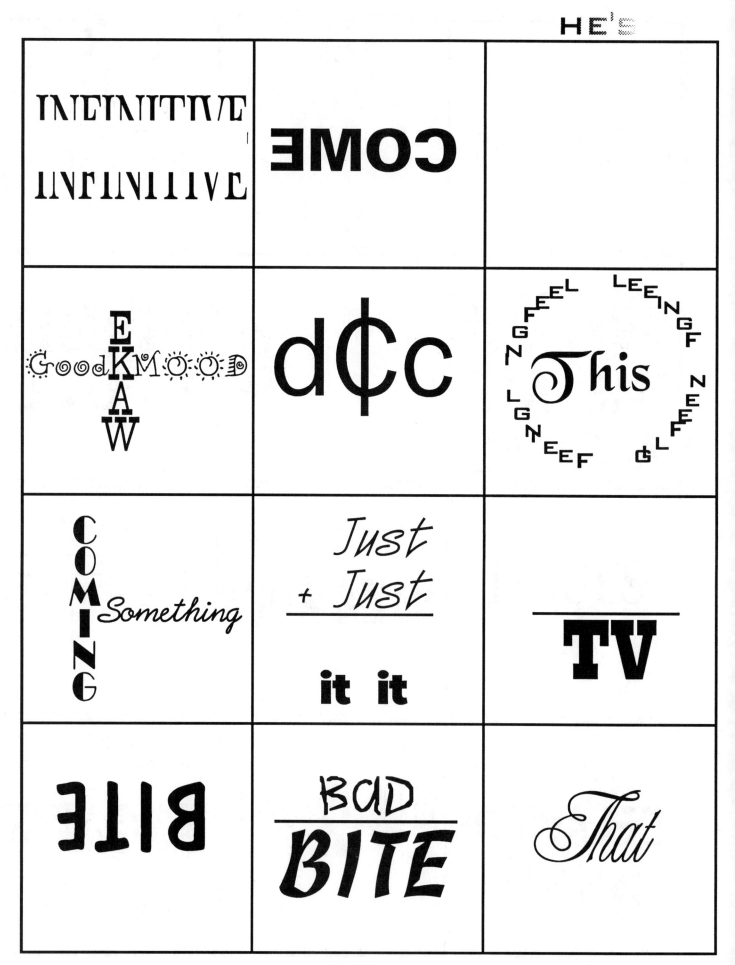

DOUBLE	ARM DEODERANT	IT IT WHELMING
SN☃OW -ING	OFFICE	ME AL △
reason DOUBT DOUBT	co144me	BA$$NK
CARD L SssS	Who What 1ST 2ND	DEW U L E E F IT IT

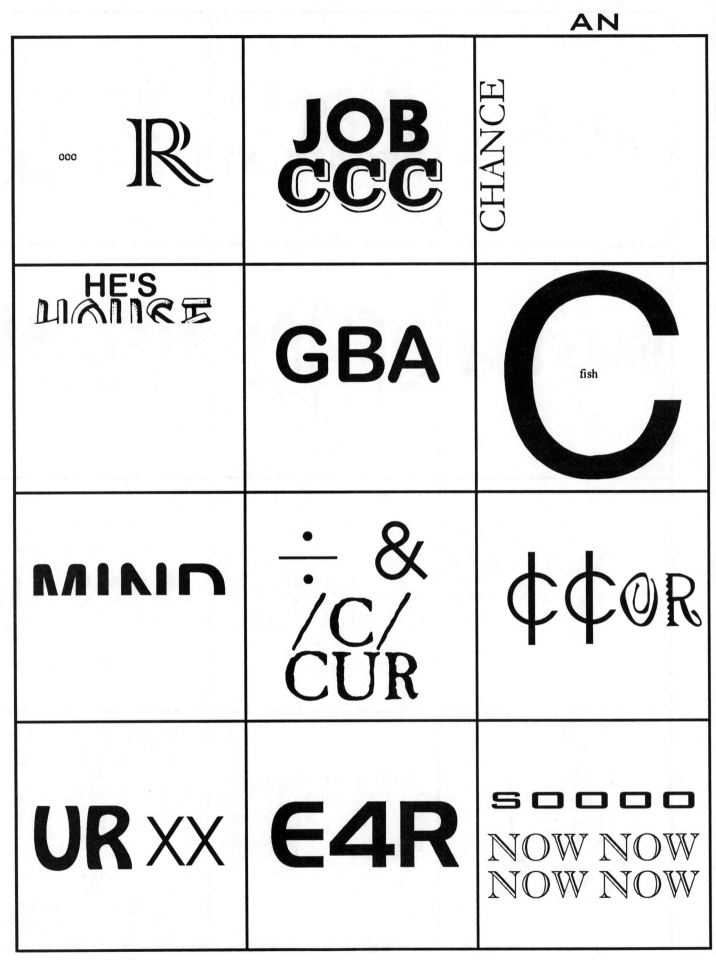

ccc R	JOB CCC	CHANCE
HE'S HOUSE	GBA	C fish
MIND	÷ & /C/ CUR	¢¢¢OR
UR xx	E4R	soooo NOW NOW NOW NOW

RO fork **AD**	LO end OK SE end E SIGHT	BITTEN *Shy Shy*
Bedtime It's	**DICE** **DICE**	READ
Blo C use	I'm WORLD	Taken Taken Taken Taken Taken
START START START START START START START START START		STAY TALE

128

PRESSURE / DOWN	TES	LOW / HEAD
Job MAN MAN MAN MAN	ZERO	BOON D DOCK / BOON O DOCK / BOON W / BOON N DOCK
ALL world	GNIKOOL ᘮ ᘮ	00:00 Play Play
XY__ Neighbor Neighbor	Farmer Farmer / ALL ALL	Bridge Bridge / Bridge

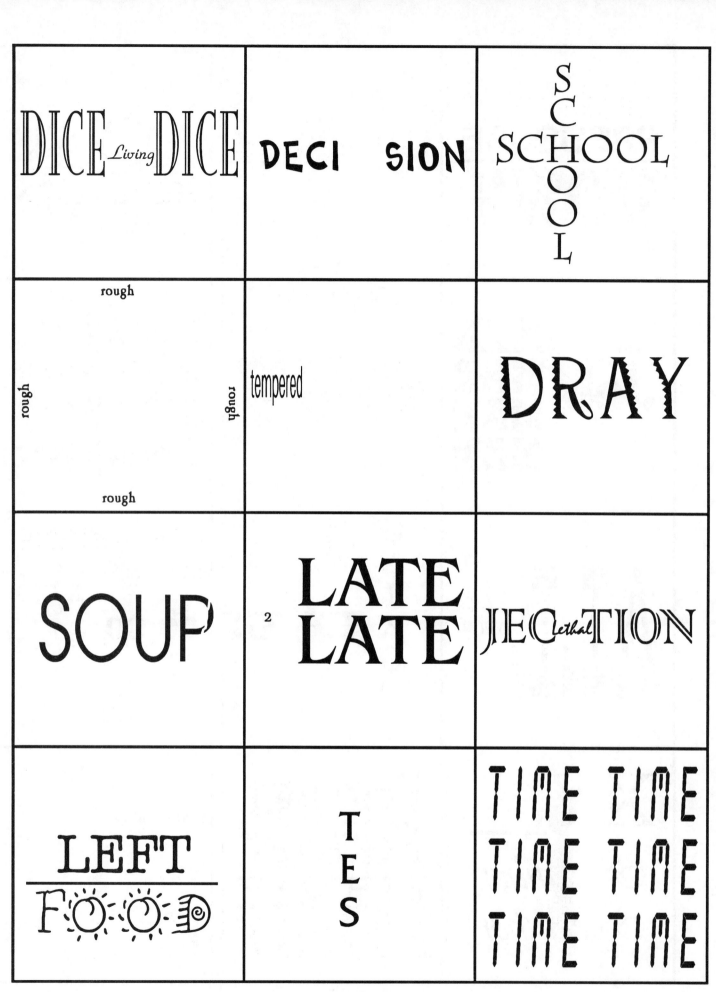

PINEAPPLE CAKE	MOV 4 IE	12" $\frac{Of\_}{12"}$
TIME ↑	OUT	YOUR BOAT YOUR BOAT YOUR BOAT
SEPT cu EMBER	DIRECTION DIREC Step TION	EXPECTATIONS EXPECTATIONS E V I L
i	MIN u D MI u ND M u IND	

BREAK

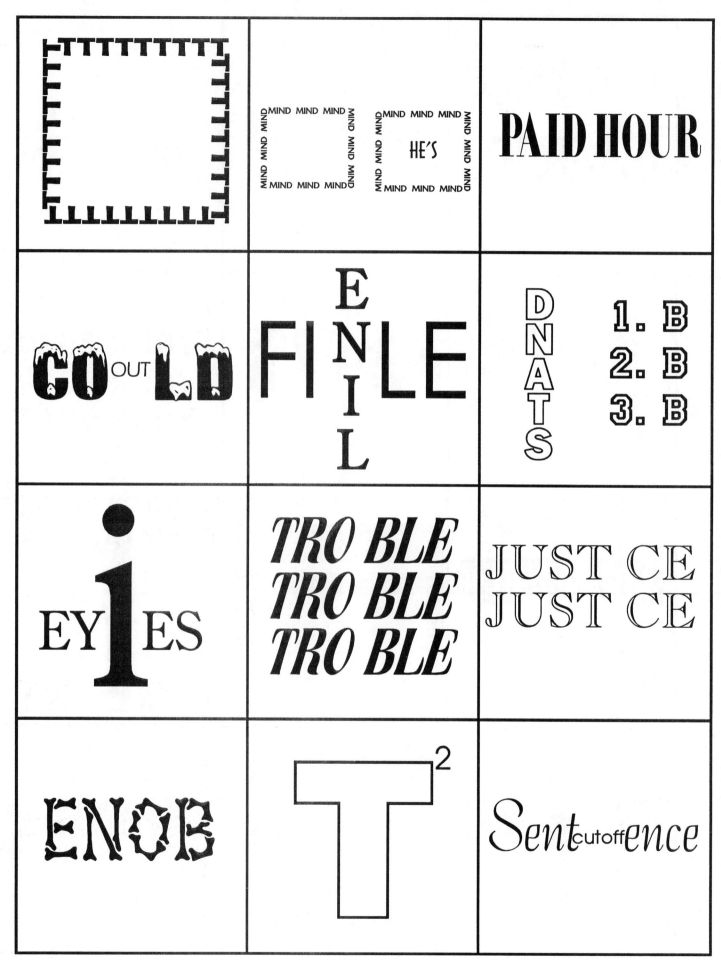

MIND MIND MIND MIND MIND MIND

HE'S

PAID HOUR

CO OUT LD

F E N I L L E

D N A T S

1. B
2. B
3. B

EY **i** ES

TRO BLE
TRO BLE
TRO BLE

JUST CE
JUST CE

ENOB

T²

Sent cutoff ence

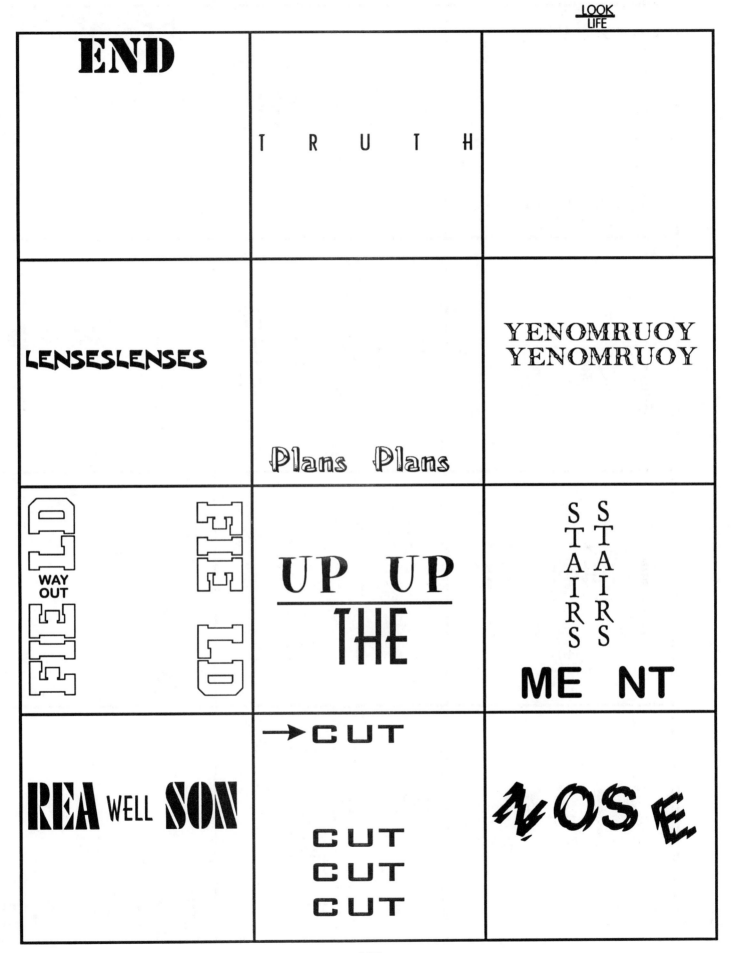

END

T RUTH

LENSESLENSES

Plans Plans

YENOMRUOY
YENOMRUOY

FIELD
WAY OUT
FIE LD

UP UP
THE

STAIRS STAIRS
ME NT

REA WELL SON

→CUT

CUT
CUT
CUT

NOSE

JUMP JUMP	PLY **IN**	**BREAKING**
$\dfrac{\text{Best}}{\textbf{ALL}}$	→ 1. TIME 2. EMIT 3. TIME	*Moving*
GNIKLAT	M Y L E G S	→ **LEE** **LEE** **LEE**
I'LL BE *(reversed)*	Yourself K C I P	**PITCHER**

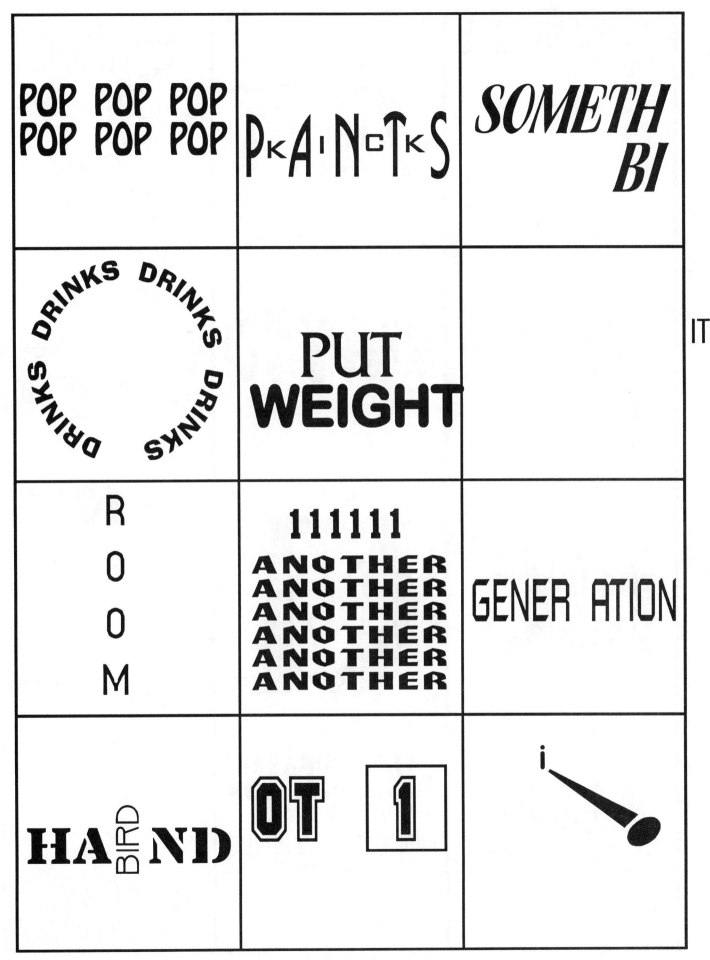

POP POP POP POP POP POP	P K A I N C T K S	SOMETH BI
DRINKS DRINKS DRINKS DRINKS DRINKS DRINKS	PUT WEIGHT	IT
R O O M	111111 ANOTHER ANOTHER ANOTHER ANOTHER ANOTHER ANOTHER	GENER ATION
HA BIRD ND	OT 1	i

KISS MAKE

$\sqrt{\text{ALL EVIL}}$

Quack
Cluck
Peep
Chirp

LOOK KOOL U CROSS

WATER

T LIVE

ICE³

U BC

TNT

BEND / DRAW DRAW

MOUN *friends* TAINS
EMPIRE STATE *friends* BUILDING

SIDE

oLD

1,2,3,4,5,.... THOUGHT

RULES RULES RULES

AEIO_

SEATDRIVER (reversed)

HEAD SHOULDERS

R E S T

Moving Moving

L NCH
L NCH

WALLUP

Law ON

TAKE
———
BID

HOT HANDLE
HOT HANDLE

137

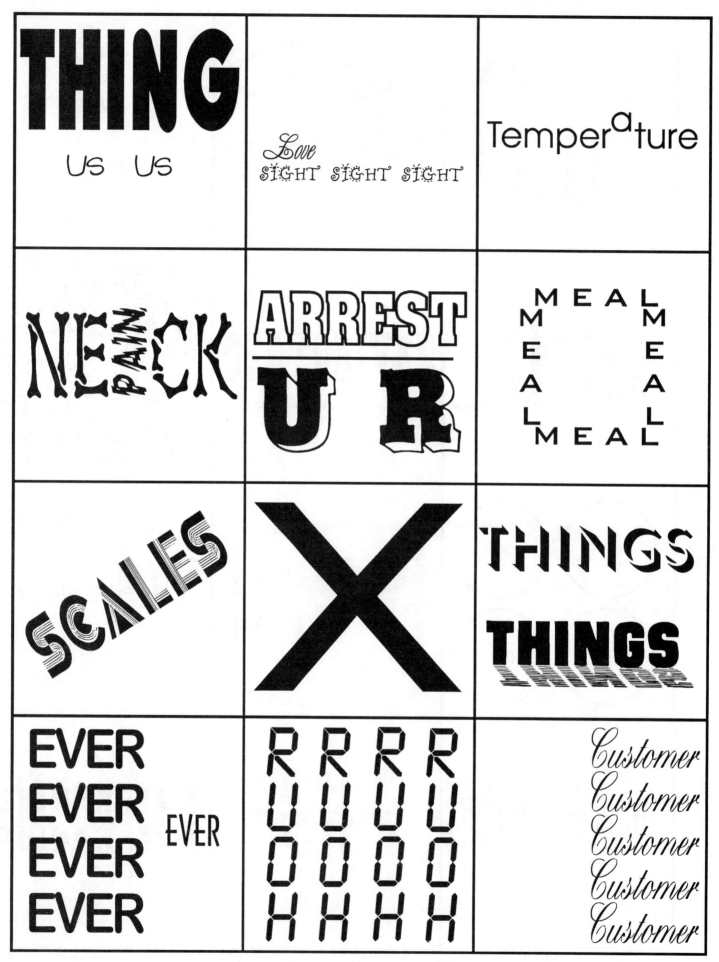

THING
Us   Us

Love
SIGHT SIGHT SIGHT

Temper^ature

NE PAIN CK

ARREST
U R

M E A L
M E A L
M E A L
M E A L

SCALES

X

THINGS
THINGS

EVER
EVER
EVER   EVER
EVER

R R R R
U U U U
O O O O
H H H H

Customer
Customer
Customer
Customer
Customer

ROGER
AND

CRY CRY
SHOULDER

HUMOR

•That's

SCISAB
SCISAB

Eggs Eggs
EASY

Jumping END END END

$$\frac{O}{Ph.D \ M.A. \ B.A.}$$

HAY
HAY
HAY
HAY
NEEDLE
HAY
HAY

THIRIGHTNGS

COUGH

ROCK

140

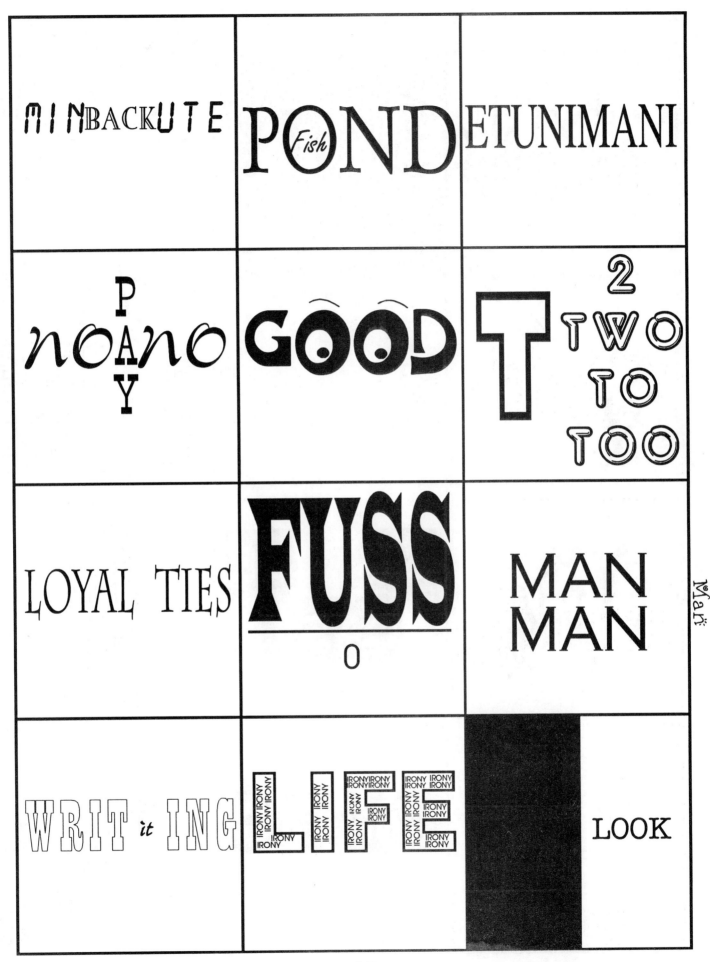

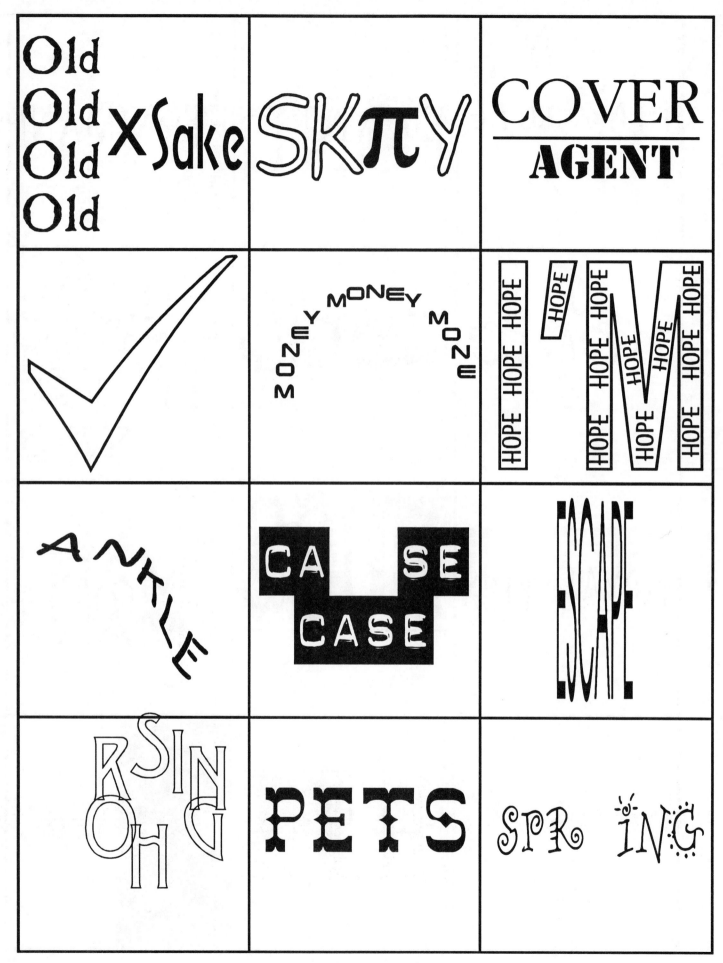

M	GEN_ƎRAL	N / E / S / W (with D's around W)
EE E	+ KING	RE MI FA SOL LA TI
NE1410S	24 HOURS	Feeling / WORLD
servicesmile	R.P.I.	WETHER

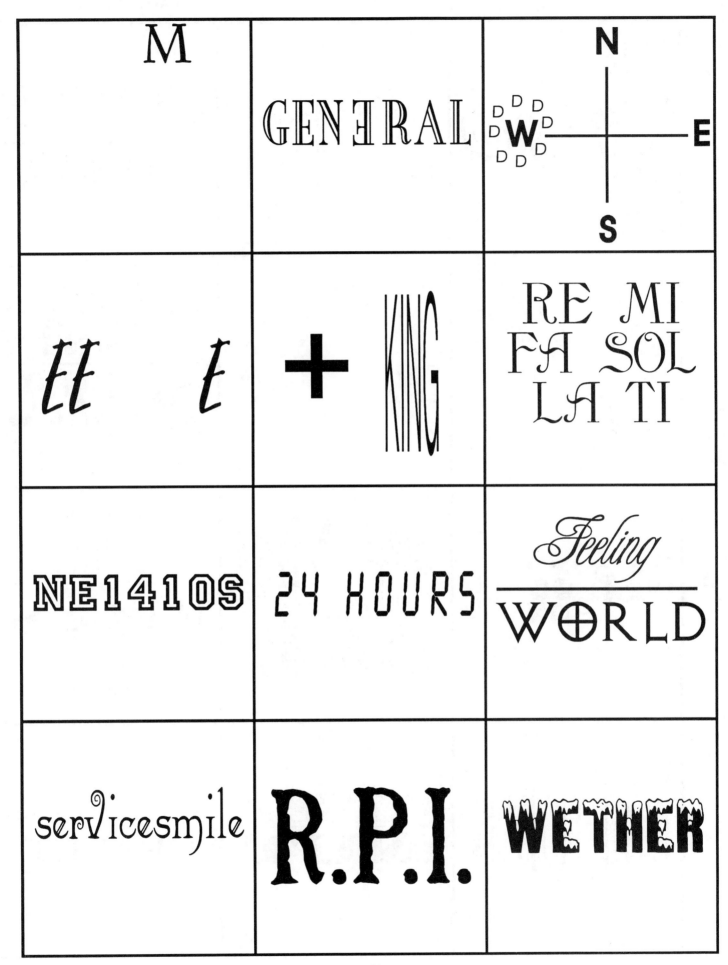

THROAT	*FATHER* *FATHER* *FATHER* *FATHER*	CATCH
FUR FUR FUR FUR	✔ BOOK	*dress* *dress* + *dress*
DAD	**CUT** **the rest**	*Your Heart* **fall**
BEANS (U R)	EVER EVER EVER EVER **U** miss	E A G L E

C (boy)	E (arrows)	
HE|AD	GOODNESS GOODNESS —— NEST	PEN I'M NY
GET —— BORED	MUCH MUCH EXPOSURE	WEIGH —— PRICED
WING	ESTIMATE —— THE COST	U hope R F have UN

146

AXE (inverted) **GRIND** **GRIND**	THE THE (reversed) Drawing Board	**GET** *BANDWAGON*
u can **1,2,3....** **IT**	your **B** bonnet	**BOTTOM BOTTOM**
WO wolf **OL**	me me me CRYING SPILT MILK	CAN'T DO CAN'T DO CAN'T DO
→**DOG** **DOG** **DOG** **DOG**	DOG HE'S HOUSE	DO 12" OR

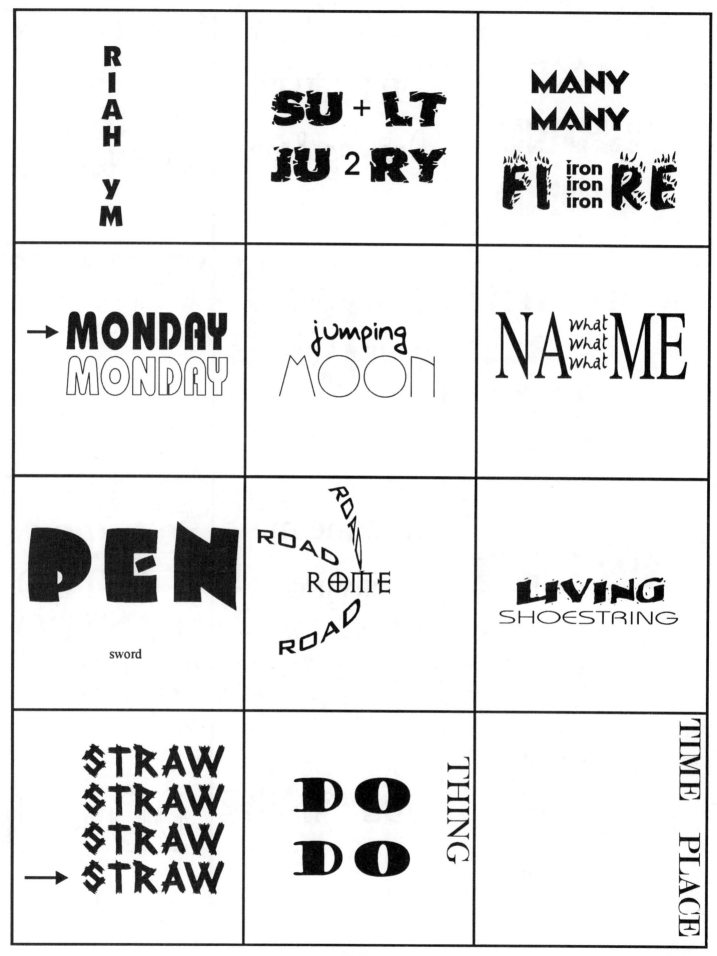

POSITION PUZZLES

PUZZLES

ANSWERS

Page 12

1. NEVER TO OLD TO LEARN
2. LIFE BEHIND BARS
3. HOME ON THE RANGE
4. NO ONE IS PERFECT
5. X MARKS THE SPOT
6. SNAKE IN THE GRASS
7. KEEP YOUR EYE ON THE BALL
8. WITH OUT A SECOND GLANCE
9. EVERYTHING IN TACT
10. GET IN SHAPE
11. ON THE DOUBLE
12. TIME'S UP

Page 13

1. NO SECOND THOUGHT ABOUT IT
2. RED IN THE FACE
3. A KING SIZED BED
4. OVER MY DEAD BODY
5. SPLIT RIGHT DOWN THE MIDDLE
6. HOME IS WHERE THE HEART IS
7. OUT AND ABOUT
8. SHORT NOTICE
9. WEST SIDE STORY
10. JUST AROUND THE CORNER
11. TOO GOOD TO LAST
12. I BEFORE E EXCEPT AFTER C

Page 14

1. I UNDERSTAND
2. TOO STUCK UP FOR WORDS
3. JUST FOR ONCE
4. UNFINISHED BUSINESS
5. IT BREAKS THE MONOTONY
6. LITTLE BY LITTLE
7. MESSING AROUND
8. THE UNDER DOG
9. FORGET IT
10. MORE TO IT THAN MEETS THE EYE
11. NO TWO WAYS ABOUT IT
12. BAD BACK

Page 15

1. WITHIN REASON
2. THREE WISE MEN
3. BAGS UNDER THE EYES
4. CUT ABOVE THE REST
5. ROOM FOR IMPROVEMENT
6. AN AFTER THOUGHT
7. SICK IN BED
8. THREE BLIND MICE
9. MISS UNDERSTANDING
10. FALLEN IDOL
11. LOOK BEFORE YOU LEAP
12. UPRIGHT PIANO

Page 16

1. SEE YOU IN THE MORNING
2. A NEAR MISS
3. LITTLE WOMEN
4. TURN OF THE CENTURY
5. DOWN TO EARTH
6. THE BEST IS YET TO COME
7. HIGHER INCOME BRACKET
8. A PAIR OF SCISSORS
9. MORE OFTEN THAN NOT
10. THINNING ON TOP
11. THE END OF THE DAY/THE FOLLOWING DAY
12. JACK IN THE BOX

Page 17

1. PAT ON THE BACK
2. SEALED WITH A KISS
3. LOVE IS IN THE AIR
4. FORTY WINKS
5. BACK FLIP
6. CHICKEN OUT
7. GET BACK IN BED
8. EGGS ON TOAST
9. UP FOR GRABS
10. SMALL OF THE BACK
11. EASY ON THE EYES
12. SPLIT IT TWO WAYS

Page 18

1. IN ONE EAR OUT THE OTHER
2. FLAT ON ONES BACK
3. YOU OUGHT TO BE IN THE PICTURES
4. MAD ABOUT YOU
5. SOMEWHERE OVER THE RAINBOW
6. HAND IN GLOVE
7. SOMEONE TO TURN TO
8. A PILE OF TRASH
9. IN TWO PLACES AT THE SAME TIME
10. A BREAK IN CUSTOMS
11. OH MY ACHING BACK
12. SCALE DOWN

Page 19

1. TWO SCRAMBLED EGGS
2. ROBIN HOOD
3. CASH ON DELIVERY
4. UPSET OVER NOTHING
5. A LOT OF IT GOING AROUND
6. DOWN AND OUT
7. UP AND AT 'EM
8. KNOCK ON WOOD
9. SHAPE UP OR SHIP OUT
10. ENDLESS SUPPLY
11. HEAD IN THE SAND
12. YOU TURN ME ON BABY

Page 20

1. FOR ONCE AND FOR ALL
2. NO ONE IS RIGHT
3. ON THE OUTSIDE LOOKING IN
4. HAND TO MOUTH
5. NO SECOND CHANCE
6. A KID AT HEART
7. FILLING TIME
8. FAIR AND SQUARE
9. GONE WITH THE WIND
10. QUITE RIGHT
11. LAID BACK
12. GO FOR BROKE

Page 21

1. WISH UPON A STAR
2. ONE THING AFTER ANOTHER
3. A TOUCHING MOMENT
4. TRY TO UNDERSTAND
5. CURL UP WITH A GOOD BOOK
6. GOING AGAINST THE GRAIN
7. A GROSS INJUSTICE
8. ONLY A ROSE FOR YOU
9. A LITTLE ON THE LARGE SIZE
10. ONCE IN AWHILE
11. CLOSE QUARTERS
12. A TWIST OF FATE

Page 22

1. SELF CENTERED
2. PIN UP
3. TURN THE OTHER CHEEK
4. LOSS FOR WORDS
5. UNHAPPY WITH OUT YOU
6. KEEP IN SHAPE
7. LONG UNDERWEAR
8. OUT TO LUNCH
9. THIS ROUND IS ON ME
10. SAY THAT AGAIN
11. TOO FEW AND FAR BETWEEN
12. BLOOD IS THICKER THAN WATER

Page 23

1. OVER AND OVER AGAIN
2. NOT IN YOUR RIGHT MIND
3. NO FUN WITHOUT YOU
4. LOOK ME SQUARE IN THE EYE
5. A BUMP ON THE HEAD
6. TRIANGLE
7. LONG TIME BETWEEN VISITS
8. NO HITTING BELOW THE BELT
9. BACKING UP
10. SCHOOLS OUT
11. SOMETHING'S MISSING
12. FORMAL TEA PARTY

Page 24

1. A PAIR OF TENNIS SHOES
2. DISORDERLY CONDUCT
3. PARADOX
4. BEDSIDE MANNER
5. BREAK DANCING
6. TWO WAY MIRROR
7. A BIG LET DOWN
8. RUB THE WRONG WAY
9. AN INSIDE JOB
10. MORE HARM THAN GOOD
11. TOO FAR TO WALK
12. SMALL POTATOES

Page 25

1. A BLANK LOOK
2. CHOP SUEY
3. ROUND OF APPLAUSE
4. VANISHING CREAM
5. HE'S FULL OF BOLOGNA
6. THE JOKES ON YOU
7. UNCLE SAM WANTS YOU
8. BUTTON UP YOUR OVER COURT
9. A CHIP OFF THE OLD BLOCK
10. A NO PASSING ZONE
11. SKATING ON THIN ICE
12. UPSET TUMMY

Page 26

1. LEAVE NO STONE UNTURNED
2. FOOT IN THE DOOR
3. GO ON A DOUBLE DATE
4. GREEN WITH ENVY
5. EXCUSE ME
6. TAKE ON A BIG JOB
7. SPLIT THE DIFFERENCE
8. HE CAME OUT OF NOWHERE
9. WAIT ON HAND AND FOOT
10. KNOW IT FORWARD AND BACK
11. SIGN ON THE DOTTED LINE
12. PULL UP TO THE CURB

Page 27

1. TEENY BOPPER
2. THE CARDS ARE STACKED UP AGAINST YOU
3. SUNNYSIDE UP
4. SCATTERED SHOWERS
5. NOTHING OUT OF THE ORDINARY
6. SET THE CLOCKS BACK
7. MADE IN THE USA
8. THE GOOD THE BAD THE UGLY
9. ONE MORE RIVER TO CROSS
10. ONE AMONG US
11. ENEMY WITHIN
12. NO EXCUSE FOR IT

Page 28

1. FALL APART
2. ALMOST IMPOSSIBLE
3. OUT OF COURT SETTLEMENT
4. THE SHOE IS ON THE OTHER FOOT
5. NOEL
6. PARTIAL ECLIPSE
7. SHORT RECESS
8. SLEEPING ON THE JOB
9. SLUMP IN THE MARKET
10. NOT IN USE
11. DOUBLED UP IN PAIN
12. LITTLE WHITE LIE

Page 29

1. ONE STEP FORWARD , 2 STEPS BACK
2. NO U TURN
3. FULL OF BEANS
4. FORGIVE AND FORGET
5. WAIT IN VAIN
6. GET UP AND GO
7. FROM TOP TO BOTTOM
8. PAINTING BY NUMBERS
9. OVEREXPOSED
10. A SPLITTING HEADACHE
11. ONE CHANCE IN A MILLION
12. SIDE ORDER

Page 36

1. CAKE MIX
2. DEEP IN THOUGHT
3. DAY IN DAY OUT
4. SET THE WORLD ON FIRE
5. TURN BACK TIME
6. UP TIGHT
7. ON STEP FORWARD, TWO STEPS BACK
8. PUT UP WITH IT
9. LIGHTS OUT
10. LOW BRIDGE
11. DO WITH OUT
12. TIMES RUNNING OUT

Page 37

1. WORKING OVERTIME
2. END OF THE WORLD
3. MULTIPLE PERSONALITIES
4. GO IN STYLE
5. TAX RETURN
6. OPEN FOR BUSINESS
7. WAY OVER BUDGET
8. WORLDS APART
9. NOT ON YOUR LIFE
10. SIT BACK AND RELAX
11. ONCE IN AWHILE
12. SIDE BURNS

Page 38

1. UPSET STOMACH
2. TRAVEL BACK IN TIME
3. HIDE OUT
4. ONE FOOT BEFORE THE OTHER
5. RIDING HORSE BACK
6. MOVING UP TO BIGGER AND BETTER THINGS
7. TURN OF EVENTS
8. ONE STEP TO FAR
9. RECURRING NIGHTMARE
10. TALKING A MILE A MINUTE
11. WHAT'S UP
12. WHERE THERE'S A WILL THERE'S A WAY

Page 39

1. ROUND UP
2. TURNING POINT
3. FALLING ASLEEP
4. HEARTS IN THE RIGHT PLACE
5. BACK TO THE FUTURE
6. DO IT RIGHT
7. HANDS UP
8. SPREAD OUT
9. MADE FOR EACH OTHER
10. TOO LITTLE TOO LATE
11. MICROWAVE IN USE
12. PARTING COMMENTS

Page 40

1. TINY BUBBLES
2. BACHELOR PARTY
3. EATING OUT
4. SUB STANDARD CONDITIONS
5. FEELING DOWN IN THE DUMPS
6. PLAYING IN THE BACKYARD
7. OFF SIDES
8. REPEAT CUSTOMERS
9. PUTTING IN LOTS OF OVERTIME
10. SIT UP STRAIGHT
11. ORDER IN THE COURT
12. GO AND STAND IN THE CORNER

Page 41

1. STEP LADDER
2. BLUE WITHOUT YOU
3. THAT'S INCREDIBLE
4. SLIGHT HEARING LOSS
5. PARTY LINE
6. SHORT CUT
7. COVERED WAGON
8. OPEN AND SHUT CASE
9. ARCH RIVALS
10. MAN OVERBOARD
11. POSITIVE FEEDBACK
12. ONE FOR THE MONEY TWO FOR THE SHOW

Page 48

1. HERE'S LOOKING AT YOU
2. FACE UP TO THE FACTS
3. LONG OVERDUE
4. HANDS ON EXPERIENCE
5. FACE LIFT
6. HOLE IN ONE
7. SLOW DOWN
8. EIGHT BALL IN THE SIDE POCKET
9. ALL EYES ARE ON YOU
10. CROSS COURT SHOT
11. G STRING
12. STEP RIGHT UP

Page 49

1. SIDE OUT
2. NO ROOM FOR ERROR
3. COUNT ME OUT
4. BASEBALL SEASON
5. DEEP IN THE FOREST
6. CUTTING CORNERS
7. GROUND RULE DOUBLE
8. HEAVY ON THE MAKE UP
9. ON THE BACK NINE
10. IT'S NO USE
11. THROW IN THE TOWEL
12. EINSTEIN

Page 50

1. TOUCH DOWN
2. NIGHTLINE
3. THERE'S ONE IN EVERY CROWD
4. HIGH RISE APARTMENTS
5. PRE GAME SHOW
6. MIXING BUSINESS WITH PLEASURE
7. LONG DISTANCE RUNNER
8. EASEL
9. 10K RACE
10. KEEP UP WITH THE JONESES
11. GRAND SLAM
12. NOTHING BUT NET

Page 51

1. YOU ARE OUT
2. DOWN PAYMENT ON A HOUSE
3. CHECK OUT TIME
4. PIGGY BACK RIDE
5. LINE DRIVE
6. WE WILL OVERCOME
7. TRIATHALON
8. HIGH TIDE
9. CENTER FIELD
10. A PRISON SENTENCE
11. FISHING LINE
12. EAVES DROPPING

Page 52

1. RECORD BREAKING EVENT
2. PIGS IN A BLANKET
3. ALL NIGHT STAKE OUT
4. SIT DOWN AND SHUT UP
5. STEP UP TO THE PLATE
6. RUNNING BACK
7. PARALLEL BARS
8. STANDING SIDE BY SIDE
9. A LIFE OF EASE
10. BABE IN THE WOODS
11. PLAYING WITH THE BIG BOYS
12. MINIATURE GOLF

Page 53

1. THREE POINT LINE
2. CORPORATE DOWNSIZING
3. DUG OUT
4. OVERHAND SERVE
5. BACK STROKE
6. LATE IN THE EVENING
7. LOW BLOW
8. NIGHT SHIFT
9. DOUBLE BOGIE
10. DOUBLE BACK FLIP
11. NO TIME OUTS LEFT
12. TURN THE PAGE

Page   66

1 . A SLAP IN THE FACE
2 . A STANDING START
3 . A STORY IN ITSELF
4 . A TOP PERFORMER
5 . BAA BAA BLACK SHEEP
6 . ALL KIDDING ASIDE
7 . ALL AROUND THE WORLD
8 . ALWAYS BY MY SIDE
9 . BED OF ROSES
10 . BURN THE CANDLES AT BOTH END
11 . BEYOND THE CALL OF DUTY
12 . CHIP ON ONE'S SHOULDER

Page   67

1 . STOP ON A DIME
2 . BASED ON A TRUE STORY
3 . BEFORE WE BEGIN
4 . BACK ALLEY
5 . TWO WAY RADIO
6 . ALL HANDS ON DECK
7 . A BUMP IN THE NIGHT
8 . ONE LIFE TO LIVE
9 . FORTY DAYS AND FORTY NIGHT
10 . BACK IN FIVE MINUTES
11 . ABOUT FACE FORWARD MARCH
12 . ACID INDIGESTION

Page   68

1 . COME DOWN TO EARTH
2 . DID IT CROSS YOUR MIND
3 . CRACK A SMILE
4 . COURT IS IN SESSION
5 . COUNT YOUR BLESSINGS
6 . DEEP IN THE HEART OF DIXIE
7 . DON'T BET ON IT
8 . DRIVE YOU UP THE WALL
9 . DANCE TO THE MUSIC
10 . COUNT DRACULA
11 . CROSS COUNTRY
12 . DUST IN THE WIND

Page   69

1 . EAT YOUR HEART OUT
2 . ELEVENTH HOUR
3 . EVERYTHING FROM A TO Z
4 . FIRST THING IN THE MORNING
5 . FOUR CORNERS OF THE EARTH
6 . GREAT BALLS OF FIRE
7 . HE'S LARGER THAN LIFE
8 . HIGH CHOLESTEROL
9 . I SEE YOU UNDERSTAND
10 . HIGHER EDUCATION
11 . I'M IN TROUBLE
12 . IT STANDS TO REASON

Page   70

1 . IT GETS WORSE AND WORSE
2 . ALL GREEK TO ME
3 . BE ON THE LOOK OUT
4 . IT'S FOR KEEPS
5 . ALL IN ALL
6 . BATTERIES NOT INCLUDED
7 . AN ALL STAR PLAYER
8 . FOR GOODNESS SAKE
9 . BUT IN ANY EVENT
10 . BURN UP THE ROAD
11 . ALL IN THE FAMILY
12 . FIRST COME, FIRST SERVED

Page   71

1 . EYES IN THE BACK OF MY HEAD
2 . GENIE IN A BOTTLE
3 . GO THROUGH THE MOTIONS
4 . HAND IT OVER NOW
5 . GOOD TO THE LAST DROP
6 . HE'S ALWAYS IN TROUBLE
7 . I DON'T UNDERSTAND IT AT ALL
8 . HE'S BACK IN THE SADDLE AGAIN
9 . YOU ARE EXACTLY RIGHT
10 . HERE'S TO YOU
11 . I'M IN IT OVER MY HEAD
12 . JACK IN THE BOX

Page 72

1. THINK ABOUT IT
2. GET OUT OF HERE
3. IT'S ALL FOULED UP
4. GET YOUR ACT TOGETHER
5. GET IN A SINGLE FILE LINE
6. ITSY BITSY SPIDER
7. HE'S BESIDE HIMSELF
8. HOLY MACKEREL
9. START OFF THE DAY RIGHT
10. STEP ON THE GAS
11. KEEP OUT
12. GET UP ON THE WRONG SIDE OF THE BED

Page 73

1. TEN COMMANDMENTS
2. THE COAST IS CLEAR
3. I'M OUT OF HERE
4. THAT'S EXACTLY RIGHT
5. THAT'S TOO BAD
6. THE END OF THE ROAD
7. IT'S NOT EVEN CLOSE TO BEING RIGHT
8. JUST BETWEEN US
9. LAST OF THE MOHICANS
10. LITTLE HOUSE ON THE PRAIRIE
11. LOST IN SPACE
12. NO LEFT TURN

Page 74

1. MAKE A MOUNTAIN OUT OF A MOLE HILL
2. MAN IN THE MOON
3. I CAN SEE IT IN THE EYES
4. HE'S LEFT HOLDING THE BAG
5. HOLD IT CLOSE TO THE HEART
6. HOLD ON A MINUTE
7. HE'S ON CLOUD NINE
8. I'LL BE BACK IN A MINUTE
9. IT'S ON THE TIP OF MY TONGUE
10. IT'S A RACE TO THE FINISH
11. LAST WILL AND TESTAMENT
12. LITTLE ORPHAN ANNIE

Page 75

1. IT'S TIME TO PAY UP
2. IT RUNS IN THE FAMILY
3. LOOK OUT, TROUBLE'S COMING
4. LITTLE DID I KNOW
5. IT'S ONE IN THE SAME
6. MASS CONFUSION
7. MIDDLE OF THE ROAD
8. NEVER OVER TILL IT'S OVER
9. ONCE IN A LIFETIME
10. ON TOP OF OLD SMOKEY ALL COVERED WITH CHEESE
11. NO ROOM FOR DOUBT
12. WHEEL AND DEAL

Page 76

1. YOU ARE IN HOT WATER
2. PARIS IN THE SPRING
3. OUT IN LEFT FIELD
4. PIERCED EARS
5. SHOPPING CENTER
6. SANTA'S ON HIS WAY
7. RAKE OVER THE COALS
8. PLUMP RAISINS
9. RIGHT ON, BIG BROTHER
10. RING AROUND THE ROSIE
11. PUT IT (ALL) BEHIND YOU
12. PRETTY PLEASE WITH SUGAR ON TOP

Page 77

1. ROLLING IN THE MONEY
2. SEVENTH INNING STRETCH
3. THE FINAL FRONTIER
4. THE CHECK IS IN THE MAIL
5. SHATTERED DREAMS
6. THE PRICE IS RIGHT
7. THE SILENCE OF THE LAMBS
8. SEE YOU AROUND
9. THE SKY IS FALLING
10. TIME IS RUNNING OUT
11. SAFETY IN NUMBERS
12. THE THIRTEEN COLONIES

Page 78

1. BACKGAMMON
2. DOWN IN FRONT
3. WORD FOR WORD
4. INCOMPLETE SENTENCE
5. EMPTY PARKING SPACE
6. WHAT IN THE WORLD
7. OUT IN THE COUNTRY
8. THINK TWICE ABOUT IT
9. DON'T BACK DOWN
10. IT DOESN'T ADD UP
11. MINISKIRT
12. GETTING STOOD UP

Page 79

1. THE STAKES ARE HIGH
2. THEY'RE ALL THE SAME
3. THERE'S NO END TO IT
4. THREE MEN AND A BABY
5. WALKING ON A THIN LINE
6. WE WERE FACE TO FACE
7. VOTE ACROSS THE BOARD
8. UP, UP AND AWAY
9. WE LOOKED HIGH AND LOW
10. WALK ON WATER
11. WE SHALL OVERCOME
12. THIS IS IT FOR NOW

Page 80

1. TOO BIG FOR HIS BRITCHES
2. TUNNEL OF LOVE
3. WELCOME CENTER
4. WHITE ELEPHANT
5. IT'S WIDE OPEN
6. ARE YOU FOR REAL
7. ALL RIGHT UP TO NOW
8. WORDS OF WISDOM
9. BIG BROTHER IS WATCHING YOU
10. CHEER UP
11. YOU ARE NOT EVEN CLOSE TO IT
12. YOU ARE INTELLIGENT

Page 81

1. YEARLY CHECKUP
2. ALL DRESSED AND NO PLACE TO GO
3. SMALL PRINT OR THE FINE PRINT
4. KEEP ON SMILING
5. LIFE BEGINS AT FORTY
6. HMM, ON SECOND THOUGHT
7. THE DICE ARE HOT
8. FAIR, FAT, AND FORTY
9. EYE IT, TRY IT, BUY IT
10. CRY ALL THE WAY TO THE BANK
11. DIFFERENT STROKES FOR DIFFERENT FOLKS
12. WELL BYE FOR NOW

Page 82

1. THAT'S UP TO YOU
2. TURNIP
3. THREE STRIKES AND YOUR OUT
4. THINK BIG
5. TWO CARS IN EVERY GARAGE
6. THE MORNING AFTER THE NIGHT BEFORE
7. TWO HAIRS PAST A FRECKLE
8. WAKE UP, LITTLE SUZY
9. TWO TO ONE AGAINST YOU
10. YOU ARE ALWAYS ON MY MIND
11. WE MAKE EM OURSELVES
12. GARBAGE IN, GARBAGE OUT

Page 83

1. A HOUSE DIVIDED OR HOUSE BROKEN
2. WIDE AWAKE
3. DOWNTOWN
4. I OVER ATE
5. UNBALANCED
6. FLAT TIRE
7. HIGH CHAIR
8. DARK CIRCLES UNDER HIS EYES
9. RUNNING AROUND THE BLOCK
10. JAIL BREAK
11. MIDNIGHT
12. SPLIT TWO WAYS

Page 84

1. LAY UP
2. WORK IT OUT
3. SMALL WONDER
4. SHADOW OF DOUBT
5. TIGHT WAD
6. GRAND STANDS
7. LICKETY SPLIT
8. WE DROVE RIGHT BY IT
9. THE BIG CHEESE
10. BLOCK HEAD
11. WE CAME OUT OKAY
12. AN END IN ITSELF

Page 84

1. STANDING OVATION
2. TALLY HO
3. OPEN SESAME
4. CYCLONES
5. CLOSE QUARTERS
6. JAY WALKING
7. BOTTOM OF THE NINTH
8. HISTORY REPEATS ITSELF
9. A SIDE-SPLITTING JOKE
10. WHO'S ON FIRST
11. SPACE INVADERS
12. LITTLE BLACK BOOK

Page 86

1. BLACK TOP ROAD
2. MIND OVER MATTER
3. TIP TOE THROUGH THE TULIPS
4. A BACKWARD GLANCE
5. A LITTLE BIT UNDER DRESSED
6. FALLING IN LOVE
7. PARAKEETS
8. LITTLE BIG HORN
9. BALANCED BUDGET
10. I'M IN BETWEEN JOBS
11. BLACK AND WHITE PHOTOGRAPHY
12. SKINNY DIPPING

Page 87

1. BETTER SAFE THAN SORRY
2. 3 SQUARE MEALS A DAY
3. ODD COUPLE
4. THE WHOLE IS GREATER THAN THE SUM OF IT
5. X FILES
6. 48 HOURS
7. HEAT WAVE
8. WHEEL OF FORTUNE
9. LINE UP ALPHABETICALLY
10. ALMOST PERFECT
11. NEON LIGHTS
12. START OF SOMETHING BIG

Page 88

1. CANCELLED CHECK
2. LIFE AFTER DEATH
3. SUNKEN CHEST
4. ROCK AROUND THE CLOCK TONIGHT
5. SPLIT PERSONALITY
6. IT'S A NO NO
7. SINGING IN THE RAIN
8. GRACE UNDER FIRE
9. HIGH FLY
10. BOY MEETS WORLD
11. WORLD SERIES
12. BASEBALL DIAMOND

Page 89

1. PARTS OF SPEECH
2. IT'S IN THE BAG
3. FELLING DOWN AND OUT
4. HIGHWAY ON-RAMP
5. SIT IN ONE POSITION
6. TWO PEAS IN A POD
7. PUNCH IN THE EYE
8. LONG TIME NO SEE
9. SMALL FRY
10. TOSS UP
11. WISE UP
12. CROSS WALK

Page 90

1. TOP OF THE NINTH
2. A LONG LETTER FROM HOME
3. LIGHTNING
4. HARMONIZE
5. FULL BACK, HALF BACK, QUARTER BACK
6. WORD TO THE WISE
7. SMALL FORTUNE
8. BUS TERMINALS
9. DARK AGES
10. ENCIRCLE
11. SOON AFTER THAT
12. WITCH DOCTOR

Page 91

1. NYLON HOSE
2. DOMINO
3. PARTIALLY
4. PAINLESS OPERATION
5. SIDEWALK
6. STAYING AHEAD OF THE GAME
7. END UP IN THE HOSPITAL
8. WORKING AROUND THE CLOCK
9. PREADOLESCENTS
10. ONE AFTER ANOTHER
11. IN COMPLETE CONTROL
12. FLASH LIGHT

Page 92

1. SYRUP
2. WELL BALANCED
3. ENDLESS LOVE
4. BACKLOG
5. LAID UP IN BED
6. STRANGER IN PARADISE
7. YIELD RIGHT OF WAY
8. ARE YOU LONESOME WITH OUT ME?
9. CAPITALISM
10. 7-UP CANS
11. FOREIGN AID
12. EQUAL RIGHTS

Page 93

1. CAR IN REVERSE (GEAR)
2. LOTION
3. BLAZING SADDLES
4. HEAD QUARTERS
5. SUNDAY AFTERNOON
6. CLEANING UP AFTER THE KIDS
7. 5 POUNDS OVERWEIGHT
8. BONE HEAD
9. PARACHUTE
10. EXTERMINATE
11. TUCSON, ARIZONA
12. DIVISION OF LABOR

Page 94

1. WEDDING RING
2. SENSELESS MURDER
3. LAST ROUND UP
4. COPYRIGHT
5. SPLIT SECOND DECISION
6. FLIP WILSON
7. SHADY DEAL
8. BUCKLE UP FOR SAFETY
9. 3 MONTHS OVERDUE
10. LEFT OVERS
11. PIONEERS
12. 3 DAYS BEHIND SCHEDULE

Page 95

1. WORRY OVER NOTHING
2. QUIT FOLLOWING ME
3. SEMI-FINALS
4. EISENHOWER
5. DOWN RIGHT ORNERY
6. SURPLUS FOOD
7. BLIND FAITH
8. A LITTLE BIT BEHIND SCHEDULE
9. WHAT'S IN A NAME
10. 3-D MOVIE
11. LOW DOWN PAYMENT
12. A BIG MISUNDERSTANDING

Page 102

1 . JUNIOR VARSITY
2 . OZONE
3 . MINDLESS WORK
4 . RUNNING ON EMPTY
5 . THICK SKINNED
6 . ALOHA
7 . BLACK BELT
8 . TWO MILLION FIVE
9 . BIG EGO
10 . SMALL POX
11 . OUTRAGEOUS
12 . INNER EAR

Page 103

1 . UNDEREXPOSED
2 . MINIBIKE
3 . HE'S OUTSIDE PLAYING
4 . THE UNDER WORLD OR ON TOP OF THE WORLD
5 . WHEELBARROW
6 . EXPANDING THE MIND
7 . THIRD WORLD
8 . INNOCENT
9 . BULLETIN BOARD
10 . SHORTCAKE
11 . BELAY THAT ORDER
12 . HEART TO HEART

Page 104

1 . BELITTLE
2 . IN BETWEEN
3 . GRAY MATTER
4 . HIBERNATE
5 . ELBOW
6 . FORTUNE
7 . MAKE UP
8 . KEEP IN TOUCH
9 . TUBA
10 . HYENA
11 . SPLIT ENDS
12 . A LITTLE BIT MORE

Page 105

1 . DECIDE
2 . A CHECKUP
3 . CHECK IT OUT
4 . TOLD YOU OVER AND OVER AGAIN
5 . LEAN OVER BACKWARDS
6 . SPACESHIP
7 . A CLOSE SHAVE
8 . WASH UP BEFORE DINNER
9 . AGE BEFORE BEAUTY
10 . SEE YOU AT MIDNIGHT
11 . OPEN AFTER HOURS
12 . MINNEAPOLIS, MINNESOTA

Page 106

1 . FORECAST
2 . BE ON TIME
3 . LEFT OUT
4 . DOUBLE VISION
5 . LEFT OUT
6 . GROWING UP TOO FAST
7 . STANDING IN A CORNER
8 . GRAVY
9 . WHITE HOUSE OR LIGHT HOUSE
10 . DIVINITY
11 . PARAMEDICS
12 . MICROPHONE

Page 107

1 . UNDERESTIMATE
2 . MONOTONE
3 . OUTSPOKEN
4 . HIGH NOON
5 . DOUBLE FEATURE
6 . TOO GOOD TO BE TRUE
7 . SIESTA
8 . VALENTINE
9 . HIGH SIERRA
10 . FALLING STAR
11 . TOO MUCH TO SOON
12 . FRANKENSTEIN

Page   108

1 . MAJOR UNDERTAKING
2 . INFERNO
3 . BEHOLD A CHILD
4 . TOP NOTCH
5 . LEFTY
6 . SEMINAR
7 . PICKUP TRUCK
8 . INJURY
9 . MOVE BACK
10 . BISHOP
11 . CAT IN THE HAT
12 . INCUBATOR

Page   109

1 . A LITTLE UNDERWEIGHT
2 . UNDERSENSITIVE
3 . JUMP IN A LAKE
4 . MICROWAVE
5 . PARALYZE
6 . FOUR WHEEL DRIVE
7 . LITTLE BOY BLUE
8 . WINDING DOWN
9 . SWEPT UNDER THE RUG
10 . THE FARMER IN THE DELL
11 . TOGETHER AT LAST
12 . HALO

Page   110

1 . INCAPABLE
2 . FORWARD
3 . OUTHOUSE
4 . TENNESSEE
5 . FIRST CLASS
6 . TENNESSEE
7 . PLAY IN THE SNOW
8 . FELONY
9 . HI DIDDLE DIDDLE
10 . THE DAY BEFORE YESTERDAY
11 . STAY AFTER SCHOOL
12 . TENDENCY

Page   111

1 . MAKING ENDS MEET
2 . JUNIOR HIGH
3 . GOOD FOR NOTHING
4 . FORCEPS
5 . OVERTIME PAY
6 . PUSH UPS
7 . OPPOSITES ATTRACT
8 . MIXED UP KID
9 . NEVER ON TIME
10 . FOREVER AND A DAY
11 . HE IS DOWN IN THE DUMPS
12 . HIGH SCHOOL DROP OUT

Page   112

1 . PEACHES AND CREAM
2 . HIGH HOPES
3 . A HAMBURGER WITH EVERYTHING ON IT
4 . MERRY GO ROUND
5 . THREE LITTLE PIGS
6 . PICK ME UP DOWN TOWN
7 . DOUBLE CHIN
8 . THAT IS RIGHT ON THE BUTTON
9 . FOUR SQUARE
10 . LITTLE DIPPER
11 . SWIMIN' POOL
12 . SWALLOW

Page   113

1 . LOOK IN A MIRROR
2 . A TUNE UP
3 . LOOKING HIGH AND LOW
4 . A TUNE UP
5 . FOR RENT
6 . MEET YOU AT THE TOP
7 . CHOW DOWN
8 . TOO MUCH TO EAT
9 . BACK OFF
10 . HIDING UNDER THE COVERS
11 . CHICKEN LITTLE
12 . WONDERFUL

Page 114

1. TOP DRAWER
2. BUNK BEDS
3. BIG BAD WOLF
4. TWINKLE TWINKLE LITTLE STAR
5. SITTING ON A FENCE
6. BACK TO SCHOOL
7. I OVERSLEPT
8. GO FOR IT
9. A CLOSE RACE
10. WAGON TRAIN
11. BIG DIPPER
12. ONE TO MANY DRINKS

Page 115

1. TRICYCLE
2. GO ON VACATION
3. STAY OVERNIGHT
4. BABY BEAR
5. YOU ARE IN BIG TROUBLE
6. ONE ON ONE
7. DRESS UP FOR DINNER
8. DINNER IS ON THE TABLE
9. LEMON PIE FOR DESSERT
10. TURN ON THE LIGHT
11. HICCUP
12. BIG BIRD OR BLACK BIRD

Page 116

1. BIG BROTHER, LITTLE SISTER
2. SECOND TO NONE
3. AGELESS, BEAUTY
4. I AM COUNTING ON YOU
5. THE PEN IS MIGHTIER THAN THE SWORD
6. GOING DOWN IN HISTORY
7. YOU WIN SOME, YOU LOOSE SOME
8. COMPACT DISK
9. CROSS BOW
10. THE CALM BEFORE THE STORM
11. A PIECE OF THE ACTION
12. STAGGERING THE IMAGINATION

Page 117

1. FULL OF ANTICIPATION
2. I BELONG TO YOU
3. TOOTH FAIRY
4. INTERNET
5. BIG PART IN A SMALL PLAY
6. KEY WEST
7. I'M ON THE ROAD AGAIN
8. GOING OVER THE SPEED LIMIT
9. BACK TO YOU
10. FRANK SINATRA
11. POINT BLANK
12. ADVERB

Page 118

1. LET BYGONES BE BYGONES
2. DENTAL HYGIENE
3. TROUBLE IN PARADISE
4. SPRING FORWARD, FALL BACK
5. A LITTLE BEHIND IN MY WORK
6. BREAKFAST
7. FORENSIC MEDICINE
8. BETTER HALF
9. AN EYE FOR AND EYE, A TOOTH FOR A TOOTH
10. DENIM OVERALLS
11. ANNEX
12. GRAND RAPIDS

Page 119

1. CORNER TABLE
2. IDEAL JOB
3. TOO MANY TO LOVE, TOO LITTLE TIME
4. MY NERVES ARE ON END
5. BICENTENNIAL
6. THREE CORNERED HAT
7. PUNCH LINE
8. TREE TOP
9. INEXPENSIVE
10. HE'S ADLIBBING IT
11. HONORARY
12. ARE YOU IN LOVE

Page 138

1 . THIS THING IS BIGGER THAN THE BOTH OF US
2 . LOVE AT FIRST SIGHT
3 . ARISE IN TEMPERATURE
4 . PAIN IN THE NECK
5 . YOU ARE UNDER ARREST
6 . SQUARE MEAL
7 . TIP THE SCALES
8 . SIGN OF THE TIMES
9 . SEEING THINGS IN A DIFFERENT LIGHT
10 . FOR EVER AND EVER
11 . FOR HOURS ON END
12 . THE CUSTOMER IS ALWAYS RIGHT

Page 141

1 . BACK IN A MINUTE
2 . SMALL FISH IN A LARGE POND
3 . BACK IN A MINUTE
4 . PAY THROUGH THE NOSE
5 . GOOD LOOKING
6 . TEA FOR TWO
7 . SPLIT ROYALTIES
8 . BIG FUSS OVER NOTHING
9 . ODD MAN OUT
10 . PUT IT IN WRITING
11 . LIFE IS FULL OF SMALL IRONIES
12 . LOOK ON THE BRIGHT SIDE

Page 139

1 . A SWARM OF BEES
2 . IN BLACK AND WHITE
3 . BOB UP AND DOWN
4 . FORTY WINKS
5 . TURN THE TABLES
6 . BIG SHOW OFF
7 . TWO BLACK EYES
8 . COAST TO COAST
9 . MUCH ADO ABOUT NOTHING
10 . ABANDON HOPE
11 . INCH BY INCH
12 . JUST BETWEEN YOU AND ME

Page 142

1 . FOR OLD TIMES SAKE
2 . PIE IN THE SKY
3 . UNDER COVER AGENT
4 . BLANK CHECK
5 . NOT ENOUGH MONEY TO GO AROUND
6 . I'M FULL OF HOPE
7 . TWISTED ANKLE
8 . OPEN AND SHUT CASE
9 . NARROW ESCAPE
10 . HORSING AROUND
11 . A STEP BACKWARDS
12 . SPRING BREAK

Page 140

1 . A SHOULDER TOP CRY ON
2 . A LITTLE LIGHT HUMOR
3 . ROGER OVER AND OUT
4 . THAT'S BESIDE THE POINT
5 . BACK TO BASICS
6 . TWO EGGS OVER EASY
7 . JUMPING TO CONCLUSIONS
8 . THREE DEGREES BELOW ZERO
9 . A NEEDLE IN A HAYSTACK
10 . ROCK BOTTOM
11 . RIGHT IN THE MIDDLE OF THINGS
12 . COUGH DROP

Page 143

1 . STICKEM UP
2 . ATTORNEY JOURNAL
3 . WEST INDIES
4 . TOO EASY
5 . POSITIVE THINKING
6 . SHORT ON DOUGH
7 . ANY ONE FOR TENNIS
8 . CALL IT A DAY
9 . FEELING ON TOP OF THE WORLD
10 . SERVICE WITH A SMILE
11 . A GRAVE ERROR
12 . BAD SPELL OF WEATHER

Page   144

1 . BEAR IN MIND
2 . THE UPS AND DOWNS OF LIFE
3 . TIGHT WAD
4 . MIXING BUSINESS WITH PLEASURE
5 . YOU'RE ON THE RIGHT TRACK
6 . CANNON BALL
7 . BOYSENBERRY
8 . YOU ARE A BEAUTIFUL GIRL
9 . ENROLL
10 . DEFENSE
11 . COCONUT SYRUP
12 . A SMALL COVER CHARGE

Page   145

1 . CUT THROAT
2 . FOREFATHERS
3 . KETCHUP
4 . FURROW
5 . CHECKBOOK
6 . ADDRESSES
7 . IT'S APPARENT
8 . A CUT ABOVE THE REST
9 . FOLLOW YOUR HEART
10 . YOU ARE FULL OF BEANS
11 . FOREVER MISSING YOU
12 . SPREAD EAGLE

Page   146

1 . BUOYANCY
2 . GORY
3 . A HANDOUT
4 . HEADQUARTERS
5 . HONEST TO GOODNESS
6 . I'M INNOCENT
7 . GET ON BOARD
8 . TOO MUCH OVEREXPOSURE
9 . WAY OVERPRICED
10 . RIGHT WING
11 . UNDERESTIMATE THE COST
12 . HOPIN' YOU'RE HAVIN' FUN

Page   147

1 . AN AXE TO GRIND
2 . BACK TO THE DRAWING BOARD
3 . GET ON THE BANDWAGON
4 . YOU CAN COUNT ON IT
5 . A BEE IN YOUR BONNET
6 . BOTTOMS UP
7 . A WOLF IN SHEEP'S CLOTHING
8 . NO USE CRYING OVER SPILT MILK
9 . NO CAN DO
10 . TOP DOG
11 . HE'S IN THE DOG HOUSE
12 . FOOT IN THE DOOR

Page   147

1 . MY HAIR IS STANDING ON END
2 . AD INSULT TO INJURY
3 . TOO MANY IRONS IN THE FIRE
4 . BLACK MONDAY
5 . JUMPING OVER THE MOON
6 . WHAT'S IN A NAME
7 . THE PEN IS MIGHTIER THAN THE SWORD
8 . ALL ROADS LEAD TO ROME
9 . LIVING ON A SHOESTRING
10 . THE LAST STRAW
11 . RIGHT THING TO DO
12 . RIGHT TIME, RIGHT PLACE

TWOsomes
THREEsomes
FOURsomes and MORE!

Here's a fun way to get the brain warmed-up! These quick word puzzles are based on well known people, places, or things that, in our culture, ...GO TOGETHER! I'll give you the first words, you see if you can supply the last. For example, can you finish this?

SNAP, CRACKLE & _____?

Did you say, POP?

You'll be surprised at how many of these you and your friends will know! These can also be good research or discussion starters!

Have FUN!

TWOsomes

1 . A and — E
2 . A and — P (stores)
3 . A fool and — his money (are soon parted)
4 . A wing and — a prayer
5 . Abercrombie and — Fitch
6 . Abraham and — Isaac
7 . Abott and — Costella
8 . Above and — beyond
9 . Aches and — pains
10 . Accidental death and — dismemberment
11 . Action and — adventure
12 . Adam and — Eve
13 . Aiding and — abetting
14 . Aim and — fire
15 . Aladdin and — the wonderful lamp
16 . Alive and — well
17 . All creatures great and — small
18 . All dressed up and — no where to go
19 . All for one and — one for all
20 . All set and — ready to go
21 . All the bells and — whistles
22 . All things bright and — beautiful
23 . All things wise and — wonderful
24 . All's well and — good
25 . All work and — no play ...
26 . Alpha and — omega
27 . Amos and — Andy
28 . An arm and — a leg
29 . An eye for an eye and — a tooth for a tooth
30 . An Officer and — a gentleman
31 . Androcles and — the Lion
32 . Antony and — Cleopatra
33 . Apples and — oranges
34 . Arm and — Hammer

35 . Armed and	dangerous
36 . Arms and	legs
37 . Art is long and	life is short
38 . Arts and	Crafts
39 . Arts and	Entertainment
40 . As I live and	breathe
41 . Ask a silly question and	you'll get a silly answer (lie)
42 . Ask and	it shall be given
43 . Ask me no questions and	I'll give you no lies
44 . A ,T and	T
45 . At sixes and	sevens
46 . Aunt and	uncle
47 . B and	B
48 . Bacon and	eggs
49 . Back and	forth
50 . Bag and	baggage
51 . Bang and	Olufsen
52 . Ball and	chain
53 . Barbie and	Ken
54 . Barnes and	Noble
55 . Barney Google and	Snuffy Smith
56 . Barnum and	Bailey
57 . Bartles and	James
58 . Baskin and	Robbins
59 . Bat and	ball
60 . Batman and	Robin
61 . Bausch and	Lomb
62 . Bean and	bacon
63 . Beatrice and	Romona
64 . Beauty and	the Beast
65 . Beavis and	Butthead
66 . Beck and	call
67 . Bed and	Breakfast
68 . Bedknobs and	Broomsticks
69 . Beldar and	Prymaat
70 . Ben and	Jerry's
71 . Bennie and	the Jets
72 . Benson and	Hedges
73 . Bert and	Ernie
74 . Betty and	Veronica

75 . Betty and	Wilma
76 . Between Scylla and	Charybdis
77 . Between the devil and	the deep blue sea
78 . Between a rock and	a hard place
79 . Big as life and	twice as natural
80 . Binney and	Smith
81 . Black and	Decker
82 . Black and	white
83 . Black and	blue
84 . Blond hair and	blue eyes
85 . Blondie and	Dagwood
86 . Blood and	fire
87 . Blood and	guts
88 . Bloom and	grow
89 . Bob Marley and	the Wailers
90 . Body and	soul
91 . Bonnie and	Clyde
92 . Booker T and	the MG's
93 . Boris and	Natasha
94 . Bow and	arrow
95 . Boys and	girls
96 . Bread and	butter
97 . Bread and	water
98 . Bread and	wine
99 . Bride and	groom
100 . Bright and	early
101 . Bright and	shiny
102 . Bright-eyed and	bushy tailed
103 . Brother and	sister
104 . Brute force and	ignorance
105 . Bull and	bear
106 . Burger and	fries
107 . Burns and	Allen
108 . Bush and	Quayle
109 . Butch Cassidy and	the Sundance Kid
110 . By and	by
111 . By and	large
112 . By faith and	love
113 . By fits and	starts
114 . By guess and	by golly

115 . By leaps and	bounds
116 . By sheer luck and	awkwardness
117 . Buy and	sell
118 . Cagney and	Lacey
119 . Cain and	Able
120 . Cake and	ice cream
121 . Callard and	Bowser
122 . Calvin and	Hobbes
123 . Carrot and	stick
124 . Cash and	carry
125 . Castor and	Pollux
126 . Cause and	effect
127 . Cats and	dogs
128 . Cease and	desist
129 . Chase and	Sanborn
130 . Checks and	balances
131 . Cheech and	Chong
132 . Cheese and	crackers
133 . Children and	fools (tell the truth)
134 . Children should be seen and	not heard
135 . Chip and	Dale
136 . Chips and	dip
137 . Chutes and	ladders
138 . Cleaned and	pressed
139 . Clear and	present danger
140 . Clinton and	Gore
141 . Cloak and	dagger
142 . Coat and	hat
143 . Coat and	tie
144 . Cold and	clammy
145 . Come and	get it
146 . Come and	go
147 . Come one and	all
148 . Comings and	goings
149 . Cookies and	cream
150 . Cops and	robbers
151 . Cornbeef and	cabbage (hashbrowns)
152 . Cowboys and	Indians
153 . Crash and	burn
154 . Cream and	sugar

155 . Cruel and	unusual (punishment)
156 . Cry and	you cry alone
157 . Cup and	saucer
158 . Curds and	whey
159 . Currier and	Ives
160 . Curriculum and	instruction
161 . Cut and	paste
162 . Cut and	dried
163 . D and	C (medical procedure)
164 . D and	B (Dunn & Bradstreet)
165 . D and	D (Dungeons and Dragons)
166 . Dammed if you do and	dammed if you don't
167 . Dark and	gloomy or dreary
168 . David and	Goliath
169 . David and	Basheba (or Jonathon)
170 . Day and	night
171 . Day in and	day out
172 . Dazed and	confused
173 . Death and	disease
174 . Decline and	fall
175 . Deep and	wide
176 . Deeper and	deeper
177 . Dick and	Jane
178 . Diet and	exercise
179 . Divide and	conquer
180 . Do's and	don'ts
181 . Dogs and	cats
182 . Dollars and	cents
183 . Don't drink and	drive
184 . Down and	dirty
185 . Down and	out
186 . Dr. Jeckyl and	Mr. Hyde
187 . Drugs and	alcohol
188 . Dry up and	blow away
189 . Dumb and	Dumber
190 . Dunn and	Bradstreet
191 . Dungeons and	dragons
192 . Eat out of house and	home
193 . Each and	every
194 . Early to bed and	early to rise

195 . Earth and	sky
196 . Easy come and	easy go
197 . Ephalumps and	Woozles
198 . Ernest and	Julio
199 . Every want and	desire
200 . Fair and	equitable
201 . Fair and	square
202 . Fame and	fortune
203 . Family and	friends
204 . Far and	distant
205 . Far and	away
206 . Fast and	furious
207 . Feed a cold and	starve a fever
208 . Felix and	Oscar
209 . Ferdinand and	Isabella
210 . Field and	Stream
211 . Fields have eyes and	woods have ears
212 . First and	foremost
213 . First and	ten
214 . Fish and	chips
215 . Fish and	game
216 . Fits and	starts
217 . Five and	dime
218 . Flesh and	blood
219 . Flowing with milk and	honey
220 . Folsam and	Jetsom
221 . Food and	drug (administration)
222 . Foot loose and	fancy free
223 . For all intents and	purposes
224 . For God and	the king
225 . Forever and	a day
226 . Forever and	ever
227 . Forgive and	forget
228 . Fork and	spoon
229 . Forty days and	forty nights
230 . Four and	20 blackbirds
231 . Four score and	seven years ago
232 . Fran and	Ollie
233 . Frank and	Earnest
234 . Frankincense and	myrrh

235 . Fred Flintsone and	Barney Rubble
236 . Fred and	Wilma
237 . Fred and	Ethel
238 . Fred Astaire and	Ginger Rogers
239 . Freddy and	the Dreamers
240 . Frederick and	Nelson
241 . Free and	easy
242 . Frick and	Frack
243 . Friends and	family
244 . Fun and	games
245 . Gainers and	losers
246 . Gains and	losses
247 . George Thorogood and	the Destroyers
248 . Gerry and	the Pacemakers
249 . Get up and	go
250 . Getting better and	better
251 . Gilbert and	Sullivan
252 . Give and	take
253 . Give and	go
254 . Give him an inch and	he'll take a mile
255 . Give one enough rope and	he'll hang himself
256 . Gladys Knight and	the Pips
257 . Gloom and	doom
258 . Goldilocks and	the three bears
259 . Good and	bad
260 . Good and	evil
261 . Goodyear Tire and	Rubber
262 . Green and	growing
263 . Green eggs and	ham
264 . Grilled cheese sandwich and	tomato soup
265 . Grin and	bear it
266 . Guns and	Roses
267 . Guys and	Dolls
268 . H and	R Block
269 . Hailstones and	Halibut bones
270 . Hale and	hearty
271 . Hall and	Oates
272 . Ham and	eggs
273 . Ham and	cheese
274 . Hamburgers and	hot dogs

275 .	Hamburgers and	french fries
276 .	Hammer and	sickle
277 .	Hammer and	nail
278 .	Hammer and	tongs
279 .	Hansel and	Gretel
280 .	Hard and	fast
281 .	Hat and	gloves
282 .	Have your cake and	eat it too
283 .	Haw and	gee
284 .	Hawks and	doves
285 .	Head and	Shoulders
286 .	Health and	fitness
287 .	Heart and	soul
288 .	Heart and	lung(s) (machine)
289 .	Heaven and	Hell
290 .	He's tall and	skinny
291 .	Heckle and	Jeckle
292 .	Hell and	high water
293 .	Hem and	haw
294 .	Here and	now
295 .	Hi and	Lois
296 .	Hide and	seek
297 .	High and	dry
298 .	High and	mighty
299 .	Highways and	biways
300 .	Hill and	Dale
301 .	Hit and	run
302 .	Hither and	yon
303 .	Hither and	thither
304 .	Hootie and	the Blowfish
305 .	Hook and	slice
306 .	Hope for the best and	prepare for the worst
307 .	Honest and	truthful
308 .	Horse and	carriage
309 .	Hot and	cold
310 .	Hot and	bothered
311 .	Hot and	steamy
312 .	Hue and	cry
313 .	Hue and	contrast
314 .	Huffing and	puffing

315 . Hugs and	kisses
316 . Hurry up and	wait
317 . Hustle and	bustle
318 . I can see for miles and	miles
319 . I'm a poet and	didn't know it
320 . In and	out
321 . Indiana Jones and	the Raiders of the Lost Ark
322 . Indiana Jones and	the Temple of Doom
323 . Indian Jones and	the Last Crusade
324 . In one ear and	out the other
325 . In sickness and	in health
326 . In this day and	age
327 . Ins and	outs
328 . Jack and	Jill
329 . Jack and	the beanstalk
330 . Jacob and	Essau
331 . James and	the Giant Peach
332 . Jason and	the Argronauts
333 . Jason and	the golden fleece
334 . Johnson and	Johnson
335 . Jonah and	the whale
336 . Joseph and	his brothers
337 . Joseph and	the coat of many colors
338 . Joseph and	the Amazing Technicolor Dreamcoat
339 . Jughead and	Archie
340 . Jump and	shout
341 . Just me and	you
342 . KC and	the sunshine band
343 . Kate and	Allie
344 . Keep your shop and	your shop will keep you
345 . Ketchup and	mustard
346 . Kid Creole and	the Coconuts
347 . Kind hearts and	coronets
348 . King and	Queen
349 . Kiss and	make-up
350 . Kiss and	tell
351 . Kit and	caboodle
352 . Knives and	fork
353 . Kool and	the Gang
354 . Labor and	Industry

355 . Ladies and	gentlemen
356 . Lady and	the Tramp
357 . Land of the free and	home of the brave
358 . Lashed and	thrased
359 . Last will and	testament
360 . Lathe and	plaster
361 . Latitude and	longitude
362 . Laurel and	Hardy
363 . Laugh and	the world laughs with you
364 . Laverne and	Shirley
365 . Law and	order
366 . Lean and	mean
367 . Learn to read and	write
368 . Leda and	the swan
369 . Lend your money and	lose your friends
370 . Let's not and	say we did
371 . Lewis and	Clark
372 . Life and	times
373 . Life and	death
374 . Life and	laughter
375 . Life is short and	time is swift
376 . Life isn't all beer and	skittles
377 . Light and	fluffy
378 . Little and	often (fills the purse)
379 . Live and	learn
380 . Live and	live
381 . Live and	let die
382 . Live long and	prosper
383 . Liver and	onions
384 . Loggins and	Messina
385 . Lois Lane and	Clark Kent
386 . Lock and	key
387 . Look and	see
388 . Look high and	low
389 . Look long and	hard
390 . Lords and	Ladies
391 . Lost and	found
392 . Loud and	clear
393 . Love and	affection
394 . Love and	war

395 . Love and	marriage
396 . Lucy and	Desi
397 . M &	M's
398 . Macaroni and	cheese
399 . MacNeil and	Lehrer
400 . Maggie and	Jiggs
401 . Maintenance and	operations
402 . Make ones bed and	lie in it too
403 . Marquette and	Joliette
404 . Mary and	Joseph
405 . Meat and	potatoes
406 . Merry Christmas and	happy New Year
407 . Merry Christmas to all and	to all a good night
408 . Mickey and	Minney
409 . Might and	main
410 . Milk and	cookies
411 . Moan and	groan
412 . Mom and	Dad (Pop)
413 . Mom and	apple pie
414 . More and	more
415 . Mork and	Mindy
416 . Mother and	father
417 . Mountains and	valleys
418 . My pride and	joy
419 . National Aeronautics and	Space Administration
420 . Near and	dear
421 . Neck and	neck
422 . Nelson and	Winthrop
423 . News and	commentary
424 . Nickel and	dime
425 . Nip and	tuck
426 . No pain,	no gain
427 . Noah and	the flood (the ark)
428 . Not here and	not now
429 . Nothing is certain is certain but death and	taxes
430 . Now and	then
431 . Nuts and	bolts
432 . Of mice and	men
433 . Off and	on
434 . Oil and	water (don't mix)

435 . Oil and	vinegar
436 . Old and	gray
437 . On a wing and	a prayer
438 . On and	on
439 . On pins and	needles
440 . On the up and	up
441 . Once and	for all
442 . One cannot love and	be wise
443 . One for the money and	two for the show
444 . One hand for yourself and	one for the ship
445 . One law for the rich and	another for the poor
446 . One for all and	all for one
447 . One if by land and	two if by sea
448 . Onward and	upward
449 . Open and	shut
450 . Open and	closed
451 . Out and	about
452 . Out of the frying pan and	into the fire
453 . Over and	out
454 . Over and	over
455 . Ozzie and	Harriet
456 . P's and	Q's
457 . Paper and	pencil (pen)
458 . Park and	ride
459 . Part and	parcel
460 . Paul McCartney and	Wings
461 . Paul Revere and	the Raiders
462 . Peace and	quiet
463 . Peace and	joy
464 . Peaches and	cream
465 . Peanut butter and	jelly
466 . Peas and	carrots
467 . Pebbles and	Bam Bam
468 . Pen and	pencil (ink)
469 . Penn and	Teller
470 . Penny wise and	pound foolish
471 . Peter and	the Wolf
472 . Pick and	choose
473 . Picks and	pans
474 . Piglet and	Pooh

475 . Pins and	needles
476 . Pitch and	yaw
477 . Play cat and	mouse
478 . Please and	thank you
479 . Plug and	play
480 . Pomp and	circumstance
481 . Port and	starboard
482 . Pork and	beans
483 . Positive and	negative
484 . Potatoes and	gravy
485 . Pratt and	Whitney
486 . Pride and	joy
487 . Pride and	prejudice
488 . Principal and	interest
489 . Pro's and	con's
490 . Proctor and	Gamble
491 . Profits and	loss
492 . Punch and	Judy
493 . Pure and	simple
494 . Push and	shove
495 . Push and	pull
496 . Puss and	boots
497 . Put two and	two together
498 . Quality and	quantity
499 . Questions and	answers
500 . Quick and	dirty
501 . R and	R
502 . R and	B
503 . R and	D
504 . Ragedy Ann and	Andy
505 . Rain cats and	dogs
506 . Rank and	file
507 . Rants and	raves
508 . Read it and	weep
509 . Relative and	absolute
510 . Ren and	Stimpy
511 . Research and	development
512 . Rest and	relaxation
513 . Rich and	famous
514 . Right or	left

515 . Rise and	fall
516 . Rise and	shine
517 . Road and	track
518 . Rock and	roll
519 . Rocks and	minerals
520 . Rocky and	Bullwinkle
521 . Roe and (vs)	Wade
522 . Roger, over and	out
523 . Rogers and	Hammerstein
524 . Romeo and	Juliet
525 . Roses are red and	violets are blue
526 . Rough and	ready
527 . Rough and	tumble
528 . Rough and	tough
529 . Run and	gun
530 . Run with the hare and	hunt with the hounds
531 . Rythm and	blues
532 . Safe and	sound
533 . Safe and	sane
534 . Sail the oceans and	seas
535 . Saint George and	the Dragon
536 . Sales and	marketing (or service)
537 . Salt and	pepper
538 . Samson and	Delilah
539 . Sanford and	Son
540 . Sarah plain and	tall
541 . Savings and	loans (association
542 . Scope and	sequence
543 . Scylla and	Charybdis
544 . Seals and	Crofts
545 . Search and	rescue
546 . Searching far and	wide
547 . Sears and	Roebuck
548 . Securities and	Exchange Commission
549 . Sense and	sensibility
550 . Separation of Church and	State
551 . Share and	share alike
552 . Shake and	bake
553 . Shake and	shiver
554 . Shirt and	tie

555 . Shoes and	socks
556 . Short and	stout
557 . Show and	tell
558 . Sick and	tired
559 . Siegfried and	Roy
560 . Silver and	gold
561 . Similies and	metaphors
562 . Simon and	Schuster
563 . Simon and	Simon
564 . Simon and	Garfunkel
565 . Sinbad and	the sailor
566 . Siouxsie and the	Banshees
567 . Sisckle and	Eibert
568 . Sit and	think
569 . Sit back and	relax
570 . Sit up and	beg
571 . Six of one and	half a dozen of another
572 . Skin and	bones
573 . Slice and	dice
574 . Slip and	fall
575 . Slip and	slide
576 . Sly and	the Family Stone
577 . Smith and	Wesson
578 . Smoke and	mirrors
579 . Snakes and	Ladders
580 . Snow White and	the seven dwarfs
581 . So on and	so forth
582 . Soap and	water
583 . Sodom and	Gomorrah
584 . Song and	dance
585 . Sonny and	Cher
586 . Sound and	fury
587 . Sow to the wind and	reap the whirlwind
588 . Space and	time
589 . Spaghetti and	meatballs
590 . Spare the rod and	spoil the child
591 . Speak of the devil and	he appears
592 . Speak softly and	carry a big stick
593 . Spic and	span
594 . Split pea and	ham

595 . Stand and	deliver
596 . Stand up and	be counted
597 . Standard and	Poor's
598 . Stars and	stripes
599 . Starsky and	Hutch
600 . States and	capitols
601 . Steak and	eggs
602 . Steak and	potatoes
603 . Steak and	lobster
604 . Sticks and	stones
605 . Stocks and	bonds
606 . Stop and	go
607 . Strong and	silent
608 . Suave and	debonair
609 . Sugar and	spice
610 . Sun and	moon
611 . Sweet and	sour
612 . Swimming and	diving
613 . Table and	chair
614 . Tango and	Cash
615 . Tar and	feather
616 . Tarzan and	Jane
617 . Tea and	Crumpets
618 . Tell the truth and	shame the devil
619 . Texas A &	M
620 . The birds and	the bees
621 . The blind men and	the elephant
622 . The Blue and	the Gray
623 . The Captain and	Tenile
624 . The cat and the	fiddle
625 . The cat's in the cradle and	the silver spoon
626 . The Fox and	the grapes
627 . The French and	Indian War
628 . The Ghost and	Mrs. Muir
629 . The Hatfields and	the McCoys
630 . The hero and	the crown
631 . The King and	I
632 . The merryman and	his maid
633 . The old man and	the sea
634 . The Owl and	the Pussycat

635 . The power and	the glory
636 . The Prince and	the Pauper
637 . The Prince and	the showgirl
638 . The Princess and	the pea
639 . The professor and	Mary Anne
640 . The rich get richer and	the poor get poorer
641 . The straight and	narrow path
642 . The tall and	short of it
643 . The tortoise and	hare
644 . The whys and	wherefores
645 . The yin and	the yang
646 . The young and	the restless
647 . Thelma and	Louise
648 . There is a time and	a place (for everything)
649 . Thomson and	Thomson
650 . Three men and	a baby
651 . Three strikes and	you're out
652 . Through thick and	thin
653 . Time and	time again
654 . Time and	tide (wait no man)
655 . Timon and	Pumbaa
656 . Tippecanoe and	Tyler too
657 . To and	fro
658 . To have and	to hold
659 . To Hell and	back
660 . Toast and	jelly / jam
661 . Tom and	Jerry
662 . Tony Orlando &	Dawn
663 . Too few and	far between
664 . Toobers and	Zots
665 . Tooth and	nail
666 . Top and	bottom
667 . Toss and	turn
668 . Touch and	go
669 . Town and	country
670 . Town and	gown
671 . Track and	field
672 . Trial and	error
673 . Trials and	tribulations
674 . Tried and	true

675 . Trinidad and	Tobago
676 . Troilus and	Cressida
677 . Tweedle Dee and	Tweedle Dum
678 . Twist and	shout
679 . Two turtle doves and	a partridge in a pear tree
680 . Tyne and	wear
681 . Up and	at 'em
682 . Up and	coming
683 . Up and	down
684 . Up close and	personal
685 . US News and	World report
686 . Venus and	Mars
687 . Vim and	vigor
688 . Vinegar and	oil
689 . Vitamins and	minerals
690 . Wait and	see
691 . Waited on hand and	foot
692 . Wake up and	smell the coffee
693 . War and	Peace
694 . Warp and	woof
695 . Waste not and	want not
696 . Wash and	dry
697 . Wax and	wane
698 . Ways and	means
699 . Wear and	tear
700 . We looked high and	low
701 . Weep and	you weep alone
702 . Wet and	dry (wild)
703 . Wheel and	deal
704 . When all is said and	done
705 . Whimpering and	whining
706 . Why keep a dog and	bark yourself
707 . Wide is the gate and	narrow is the path
708 . Wilbur and	Orville
709 . Wild and	woolly
710 . William and	Mary
711 . Willy Wonka and	the Chocolate Factory
712 . Wine and	cheese
713 . Wine and	dine
714 . Winners and	losers

715 · With liberty and	justice for all
716 · With might and	mane
717 · Wreck and	ruin
718 · Yogi and	Boo Boo
719 · You cannot serve God and	mammon
720 · You win some and	you lose some

THREEsomes

1 · A, B and	C
2 · Angles, Saxons and	Jutes
3 · Animal, vegetable,	mineral
4 · Athos, Porthos, and	Aramis
5 · Bacon , lettuce and	tomato
6 · Bad, worse,	worst
7 · Baseball, apple pie and	Cheverolet
8 · Baubles, gangles and	beads
9 · Beg, borrow or	steal
10 · Bell, book and	candle
11 · Between you and me and	the bedpost (or wall)
12 · Black and white and	read all over
13 · Blood, sweat and	tears
14 · Body, mind and	soul
15 · Calm, cool and	collect
16 · Cirrus, cumulus, and	stratus
17 · Coffee, tea, or	milk (me)
18 · Corinthian, Doric and	Ionic
19 · Crick, Francise and	Watson
20 · Doctor, lawyer and	Indian chief
21 · Earth, Wind and	Fire
22 · East is east and west is west and	never the twain shall meet
23 · Eat, drink and	be merry
24 · Emerson, Lake and	Palmer
25 · Executive, legislative and	judicial
26 · Fair, fat, and	forty
27 · Faith, hope and	charity
28 · Family, friends and	neighbors
29 · Fat, dumb and	happy
30 · Father, son and	Holy Ghost (Spirit)

31 · First in war, first in peace and	first in the hearts of his country men
32 · Flopsy, Mopsy, and	Cottontail
33 · Fold, spindle or	mutilate
34 · Food, shelter and	clothing
35 · Frankincense, gold and	myrrh
36 · Friends, Romans and	countrymen (lend me your ear)
37 · Gasper, Melchoir and	Balthasar
38 · God, motherhood and	apple pie
39 · Going, going	gone
40 · Gold, glory and	God
41 · Good, bad or	indifferent
42 · Good, better,	best
43 · Hail, fire and	brimstone
44 · Hamilton, Frank and	Reynolds
45 · Healthy, wealthy and	wise
46 · Hear no evil, see no evil	speak no evil
47 · Hello, good evening, and	welcome
48 · Here, there and	everywhere
49 · Hickory, Dickory	Dock
50 · High, wide and	handsome
51 · Hither, thither and	yon
52 · Hook, line and	sinker
53 · Hop, skip and	jump
54 · Huey, Dewey and	Louie
55 · Huff and Puff and	blow the house down
56 · I came, I saw,	I conquered
57 · Igneous, metamorphic, and	sedimentary
58 · It's a bird, it's a plane,	it's superman
59 · Knife, fork and	spoon
60 · Kukla, Fran and	Ollie
61 · Larry, Darryl and	Darryl
62 · Larry, Moe and	Curly Joe
63 · Liberty, equality and	fraternity
64 · Life, Liberty and	the pursuit of happiness
65 · Lights, camera,	action
66 · Lions, tigers and	bears
67 · Lock, stock and	barrel
68 · Love, honor and	obey
69 · Man, women and	child
70 · Manny, Moe and	Jack

71 . Masculine, feminine and   neuter

72 . Me, myself and   I

73 . Men, women and   children

74 . Morning, noon and   night

75 . Name, rank and   serial number

76 . Neither fish, flesh nor   fowl

77 . Nina, Pinta and   the Santa Maria

78 . No if's and's or   but's

79 . Of the people, for the people and   by the people

80 . One, two,   buckle my shoe

81 . On land, on sea and   in the air

82 . On your mark, get set,   GO!

83 . Papa bear, mama bear, and   baby bear

84 . Past, present,   future

85 . Person, place or   thing

86 . Peter, Paul and   Mary

87 . Planes, trains and   automobiles

88 . Princes, powers and   potentates

89 . Protons, neutrons and   electrons

90 . Rain, sleet or   snow

91 . Rank, file and   serial number

92 . Reading, writing and   arithmetic

93 . Ready, aim,   fire

94 . Ready, set,   go

95 . Ready, willing and   able

96 . Red, white and   blue

97 . Ringling Bros., Barnum   and Bailey

98 . Rock, paper,   scissors

99 . Scalene, isosceles and   equilateral

100 . Screwed, blued and   tattooed

101 . Shadrach, Meshach and   Abednego

102 . Shake, rattle and   roll

103 . Signed, sealed,   delivered

104 . Snakes, snails and   puppy dog tails

105 . Snap, crackle and   pop

106 . Snips, snails and   puppy dog tails

107 . Solid, liquid and   gas

108 . Stop, drop and   roll

109 . Stop, look and   listen

110 . Sugar and spice and   everything nice

111 · Sun, moon and	stars
112 · Surf, sand and	sun
113 · Swifter, higher,	faster
114 · Tall, dark and	handsome
115 · The Atchison, Topeka and	Santa Fe
116 · The Butcher, the Baker and	the Candlestick maker
117 · The fox, the goose and	the corn
118 · The Good, the Bad and	the Ugly
119 · The hammer, the anvil and	the stirrup
120 · The Lion, the Witch and	the Wardrobe
121 · The right way, the wrong way and	the army way
122 · The truth, the whole truth and	nothing but the truth
123 · Theodore, Simon and	Alvin
124 · Tic, Tac,	Toe
125 · Tinkers to Evers to	Chance
126 · Tired, poor and	hungry
127 · Tom, Dick and	Harry
128 · Up, up and	away
129 · Upstairs, downstairs and	in my lady's chamber
130 · Veni, vidi,	vici
131 · Vim, vigor and	vitality
132 · Was, is and	evermore shall be
133 · Way, shape and	form
134 · Wham, bam	thank you mam
135 · Wood, hay and	stubble
136 · Win, lose or	draw
137 · Win, place or	show
138 · Wine, women and	song
139 · Wynken, Blynken and	Nod
140 · Yakko, Wakko and	Dot

FOURsomes

1 · Add, subtract, multiply and	divide
2 · Blood, toil, tears and	sweat
3 · Crosby, Stills, Nash and	Young
4 · Donetello, Leonardo, Michaelangelo and	Raphael
5 · Ears, eyes, nose	throat (mouth)

6 .	Earth, Moon, Sun and	Stars
7 .	Eeny, meenie, miney,	mo
8 .	Fee, fi, fo,	fum
9 .	Fire, water, earth and	air
10 .	Fred, Wilma, Barney and	Betty
11 .	Head and shoulders, knees and	toes
12 .	Hearts, diamonds, clubs and	spades
13 .	John, Paul, Ringo and	George
14 .	Ladies and gentlmen, boys and	girls
15 .	Lucy, Ricki, Fred and	Ethel
16 .	Mattew, Mark, Luke and	John
17 .	North, East, South,	West
18 .	Nouns, verbs, adjectives and	adverbs
19 .	1 for the money, 2 for the show... 3 to get ready and	4 to go!
20 .	Parsley, sage, rosemary, and	thyme
21 .	Pennies, nickles, dimes and	quarters
22 .	Rain, hail, sleet or	snow
23 .	Rich man, poor man, beggar man,	thief
24 .	Tinker, tailor, soldier,	spy
25 .	Winter, Spring, Summer,	Fall

Fives

1 .	Who, what, when, where and	why

Sevens

1 .	Bashful, Doc, Dopey, Grumpey, Happy, Sleepy and	Sneezy

Nines

1 . Dasher, Dancer, Prancer, Blitzen,
Comet, Cupid, Donner, Vixon and Rudolph

COMMONYMS

As the name implies, in these riddles you must find the *common* thread or trait in the three listed items. In many cases there are more than one characteristic in common. For instance: A bell, a mouth, and a shoe all *could* contain metal. (Braces or fillings in the mouth, eyelet's or spikes for the shoes.) They all could be red but the answer is they all have TONGUES! Now, some people won't know that the inside of a bell is called a tongue so, it would be hard to match the answer. Any thinking is good so, if you discover some other commonalties other than the one that I list, that's OK! The point is...let people think. Encourage thinking. When the answer is given, they'll learn. Making up your own, or having students make some up, is a great extension. Have FUN!

COMMONYMS

1. BIRD * POWDER * BERRY ⟹ All can be described with black.

2. "OLD MAN RIVER" * "OLD MUDDY" * "OLD AL" ⟹ Nicknames for the Mississippi.

3. 16 * SEVENTEEN * REDBOOK ⟹ Magazines.

4. 4 * 9 * 16 ⟹ Perfect square numbers.

5. 4-COLOR * BENCH * CIDER ⟹ Presses.

6. 60 MINUTES * SOUTH AMERICA * RAGGEDY ANN ⟹ They have Andies (Andys).

7. A BAD CHILD * AN ICY PLANE * AN ELECTRICAL WIRE ⟹ They are grounded.

8. A BALL * A FISH * A COLD ⟹ They are caught.

9. A BALL * A SALAD * A COIN ⟹ They are tossed.

10. A BALLOON * A CORK * A QUESTION ⟹ They are popped.

11. A BANANA * A LEMON * A COWARD ⟹ They are yellow.

12. A BANK * A RESTAURANT *A HOCKEY GAME ⟹ They have checks.

13. A BARBER * A PAINTER * A GROOM ⟹ They have brushes.

14. A BASEBALL GLOVE * A POOL TABLE * PITA BREAD ⟹ They have pockets.

15. A BASEBALL PLAYER * A BOTTLE * A MUSHROOM ⟹ They have caps.

16. A BASKETBALL PLAYER * A SOCCER PLAYER * A BABY ⟹ They dribble.

17. A BATTERY * A PHONE COMPANY * POLAND ⟹ They have Poles.

18. A BEETLE * A FOX * A RABBIT ⟹ Cars by Volkswagon.

19. A BELL * MOUTH * A SHOE ⟹ They have tongues.

20. A BILLY GOAT * SANTA CLAUS * RIP VAN WINKLE ⟹ They have beards.

21. A BOAT * A CRADLE * VAN HALEN ⟹ They rock.

22. A BOAT * A LEMON * A JALOPY ⟹ Slang terms for cars

23. A BOAT * THE NIGHTLY NEWS * A TUG OF WAR ⟹ They have anchors.

24. A BODY BUILDER * A JACK * FOG ⟹ They lift.

25. A BOOK * A STOP SIGN * A RIPE STRAWBERRY ⟹ They are red or read.

26. A BOWLING ALLEY * A BASKETBALL COURT * A HIGHWAY ⟹ They have lanes.

27. A BRAIN * HAIR * AN OCEAN ⟹ They have waves.

28. A BRIDAL * A VAUDEVILLIAN * A DRILL ⟹ They have bits.

29. A BRIDE AND GROOM * A BOAT AND TRAILER * A HORSE AND BUGGY ⇒ They are hitched.

30. A BROADWAY MUSICAL * A MOTION PICTURE * A SPORTS PAGE ⇒ They have scores

31. A BULL * A CAR * A SHOE SALESMAN ⇒ They have horns.

32. A BULL DOG * KARATE * A BUTCHER ⇒ They have chops.

33. A BUTCHER SHOP * A HORSE RACE * A HORSEHOE PIT ⇒ All have steaks (stakes)

34. A CAFETERIA * A SMOKING LOUNGE * A REFRIGERATOR ⇒ They have trays.

35. A CAMERA * A GUN * A DISHWASHER ⇒ They are loaded.

36. A CAP * A BOND * A BRIDGE ⇒ Dental work.

37. A CAR * A TREE * AN ELEPHANT ⇒ They have trunks.

38. A CAR * AN AQUARIUM * AN ARMY ⇒ They have tanks.

39. A CAR * THE GRIM REAPER * A KING COBRA ⇒ They have hoods.

40. A CAR DEALERSHIP * A FASHION SHOW * A HOBBY STORE ⇒ They have models.

41. A CAVITY * A DOUGHNUT * A PRESCRIPTION ⇒ They are filled.

42. A CELL * A COMET * AN ATOM ⇒ They have a nucleus.

43. A CHAIN SAW * A PARACHUTE * A NEWBORN ⇒ They all have cords.

44. A CHECKBOOK * A TIRE * A SCALE ⇒ They are balanced.

45. A CHEMIST * A NEW MOTHER * A GRAN PRIX RACE ⇒ They have formulas.

46. A CHERRY * A ROSE * A WINE GLASS ⇒ They have stems.

47. A CHRISTMAS TREE * FOOT * THE STORY OF CINDERELLA ⇒ They have balls.

48. A CITY * A SPRINTER * AN ICE HOUSE ⇒ They have blocks.

49. A CLOSET * AN AIRPORT * A CARPENTER ⇒ They have hangers/hangars.

50. A COIN * A MUG OF BEER * AN ARROW ⇒ They have heads.

51. A COOK * COLLEGE FOOTBALL * TOILET ⇒ They have bowls.

52. A COPY MACHINE * A ROCK BAND * TRAFFIC ⇒ They jam.

53. A COURT ROOM * A DUGOUT * A PARK ⇒ They have benches.

54. A DART * A STAIRWELL * AN AIRLINE ⇒ They have flights.

55. A DELI * THE NAVY * AN ABSENT TEACHER ⇒ They have subs.

56. A DENTED CAR * THE 1930'S * A GRIEVING PERSON ⇒ They have depressions.

57. A DENTIST * A CARPENTER * AN OIL BARON ⇒ They drill.

58. A DENTIST * A COAL MINER * A GUITAR PLAYER ⇒ They have picks.

59. A DIME * THE PLANET MERCURY * RHODE ISLAND ⇒ Smallest of their kind

60. A DOCTOR * A COMPASS * AN EVERGREEN ⇒ They have needles.

61. A DOCTOR * A MAILMAN * DOMINO'S ⇒ They deliver.

62. A DOLLAR * A MALE RABBIT * A MALE GOAT ⇒ They are all bucks.

63 .	A FENCE * A FOOTBALL FIELD * A CANOPY BED	⇒ They all have posts.
64 .	A FIANCEE * A BASEBALL FIELD * A DECK OF CARDS	⇒ They have diamonds.
65 .	A FIELD GOAL * A 25 FOOT JUMP SHOT * A RINGER	⇒ All worth three points.
66 .	A FILM STRIP * A GAME OF BOWLING * A WINDOW	⇒ They have frames.
67 .	A FISH * A MOUNTAIN * A LADDER	⇒ They are scaled.
68 .	A FISHERMAN * A DOG CATCHER * A TRAPEZE ARTIST	⇒ They use nets.
69 .	A FLAG * A KITE * TIME	⇒ They fly.
70 .	A GAME OF HORSESHOES * A BAR * BASEBALL TEAM	⇒ They have pitchers.
71 .	A GLASS * A BASKETBALL COURT * CAR TIRES	⇒ They have rims.
72 .	A GOLF BALL * A CABBAGE PATCH DOLL * SHIRLEY TEMPLE	⇒ They all have dimples.
73 .	A GOLF COURSE * A BOWLING ALLEY * A WRESTLING STAR	⇒ They have pins.
74 .	A GOSLING * A KIT * A JOEY	⇒ Young animals.
75 .	A GRAVEL COMPANY * THE HERSHEY COMPANY * A BASEBALL FIELD	⇒ They have mounds.
76 .	A GUITAR * A RIVER * A BOTTLE	⇒ They have necks.
77 .	A GUITAR SHOP * A BASEBALL FIELD * THE MILITARY	⇒ They have bases.
78 .	A GUN SHOP * A BUTCHER SHOP * A BOXING MATCH	⇒ They have rounds.
79 .	A HAMMER * A LOBSTER * A BEAR	⇒ They have claws.
80 .	A HAND GRENADE * A BOWLING ALLEY * A TAILOR	⇒ They have pins.
81 .	A HAPPY CHILD * A SCRATCHED RECORD * A FLAT STONE	⇒ They skip.
82 .	A HARDWARE STORE * THE PANAMA CANAL * A JEWISH DELI	⇒ They have locks (or lox).
83 .	A HEAT * A FOOTBALL * A SPRINKLER SYSTEM	⇒ They have valves.
84 .	A HORSE * A CAR * A BEAN	⇒ All "Pintos".
85 .	A HORSE * AN ATTACK * A TROPHY FISH	⇒ They are mounted.
86 .	A HORSE STABLE * AN ENGLISH ROYAL HOUSEHOLD * A WEDDING	⇒ They have grooms.
87 .	A HUNTING STORE * A DRAIN PIPE * A GOLF COURSE	⇒ They have traps.
88 .	A JOKE * A SAFE * A WHIP	⇒ They are cracked.
89 .	A JUDGE * A DOCTOR * A GRADUATE	⇒ They wear gowns.
90 .	A KISS * A FLOWER * A BOMB	⇒ They are planted.
91 .	A KISS * MULTIPLICATION * A TREASURE	⇒ Represented with an "X"
92 .	A KITCHEN * THE US PRESIDENT * THE PRIME MINISTER OF GREAT BRITAIN	⇒ They have cabinets.
93 .	A KITE * A DOG * A STORYTELLER	⇒ They have tails.

94 . A LAMP STORE * A BEACH SHOP * S PINT STORE	⇒	They have shades.
95 . A LEG * A LEAF * AN ARROW	⇒	They have vanes (veins).
96 . A LIGHT BULB * A HIP JOINT * AN EYEBALL	⇒	They have sockets.
97 . A LIQUOR STORE * A LUGGAGE STORE * A LAWYER	⇒	They have cases.
98 . A LOAF OF BREAD * A GOLF BALL * A PIE	⇒	They are sliced.
99 . A MAP * A FISH * A WEIGHT-LOSS CLINIC	⇒	They have scales.
100 . A MATADOR * LITTLE RED RIDING HOOD * AFRICA	⇒	They have capes.
101 . A MICROSCOPE * A PLAY GROUND * A TROMBONE	⇒	They have slides..
102 . A NAIL * A CAR * A GOLF BALL	⇒	They are driven.
103 . A NEWSPAPER * A MILEAGE CHART * GREEK ARCHITECTURE	⇒	They have columns.
104 . A PAPER AIRPLANE * AN ORIGAMI ANIMAL * A SHEPHERD	⇒	They fold.
105 . A PARADE * A TOILET TANK * AN ICE CREAM PARLOR	⇒	They have floats.
106 . A PARADE * NEWLYWEDS * A WATCH	⇒	They have bands.
107 . A PARTY * A BULL RIDER * A BALL	⇒	They are thrown.
108 . A PARTY * A TAPEWORM * A TALK SHOW	⇒	They all have hosts.
109 . A PEACH * A POLE VAULT * A LONG JUMP	⇒	They have pits.
110 . A PERSON * A SHOE * SOUTH KOREA	⇒	They have soul, sole or Seoul.
111 . A PERSON * A WATCH * A MOUNTAIN	⇒	They have faces.
112 . A PERSON * AN ARTICHOKE * A DECK OF CARDS	⇒	They all have hearts.
113 . A PHONE * A FOOTBALL TEAM * A STEREO	⇒	They have receivers.
114 . A PIANO STORE * A HUMAN BEING * A CHURCH	⇒	They have organs.
115 . A PILLOW * A LINGERIE STORE * A HARBOR FOR SAILBOATS	⇒	They have slips.
116 . A PINE TREE * AN ICE CREAM PARLOR * BELDAR & PRYMAAT	⇒	They have cones.
117 . A PIRATE SHIP * A SCHOOL * A MAIL BOX	⇒	They have flags.
118 . A POOL PARLOR * AN OVEN * A TEN POINT BUCK	⇒	They have racks.
119 . A POOL PLAYER * A GYMNAST * A TEACHER	⇒	They use chalk.
120 . A PRISON * A TAVERN * A CANDY STORE	⇒	They have bars.
121 . A PROMOTION * A SPACE SHUTTLE * A NEW BOAT	⇒	They are launched.
122 . A RABBIT * A MAN * A CORN PLANT	⇒	They have ears.
123 . A RIFLE * A WINERY * A BASEBALL BAT	⇒	They have barrels.
124 . A RIVER * A PICKUP TRUCK * A HOSPITAL	⇒	They have beds.
125 . A ROCK GROUP * A SPORTS TEAM * A CAR ENGINE	⇒	They have fans.
126 . A RODEO * A CIRCUS * MCDONALD'S	⇒	They have clowns.
127 . A ROOF * A BOWLING ALLEY * A STREET	⇒	They have gutters.

128 . A ROOSTER * A BARBER SHOP * A BEEHIVE	⇒ They have combs.
129 . A SAFE * A SEAFOOD RESTAURANT * A BOXER	⇒ They have combinations.
130 . A SAILBOAT * AN OFFICE SUPPLY STORE * A BED	⇒ They have sheets.
131 . A SATELLITE * A MIRROR * A REMINISCENT PERSON	⇒ They reflect.
132 . A SAW * A COMB * HUMANS	⇒ They have teeth.
133 . A SCUBA DIVER * A PINBALL MACHINE * A SEAL	⇒ They have flippers.
134 . A SCULPTOR * A PLASTIC SURGEON * AN ACCOUNTANT	⇒ They work with figures.
135 . A SENTENCE * THE GEOLOGICAL TIME SCALE * A HOCKEY GAME	⇒ They have periods.
136 . A SHIPS CREW * A NIGHT GUARD * A JEWELRY STORE	⇒ They have watches.
137 . A SHOULDER * A FAN * AN ICE SKATE	⇒ They have blades.
138 . A SMALL DRINK * A HEAVY BALL * AN INJECTION	⇒ Shots.
139 . A SMOKER * A GAMBLER * A NUN	⇒ They have habits.
140 . A SNEAKER * A FOOTBALL * SPIKED PUNCH	⇒ They are laced.
141 . A SOLDIER * A TENNIS PLAYER * A WAITRESS	⇒ They serve.
142 . A SONG * A HEART * A POLICEMAN	⇒ They have a beat..
143 . A SPINE * A SONG * A VACUUM CLEANER	⇒ They have chords (cords).
144 . A STEAK * A STEEP ROAD * A STUDENT	⇒ They have grades.
145 . A STORM * A NEEDLE * A POTATO	⇒ They have eyes.
146 . A SURF SHOP * A LAWYER * A DECK OF CARDS	⇒ They have suits.
147 . A SWIMMING POOL * A FIRE ENGINE * A HOUSE PAINTER	⇒ They have ladders.
148 . A T.V. * A C.B. RADIO * ENGLAND	⇒ They have channels.
149 . A TELEGRAM * A VCR * A HYPER ACTIVE CHILD	⇒ They are wired.
150 . A TELETHON * A FRATERNITY * A BOY SCOUT	⇒ They take (have) pledges.
151 . A TENNIS MATCH * A TV SHOW * A CHINA CABINET	⇒ They have sets.
152 . A TENT * A BASEBALL * A HORSESHOE	⇒ They are pitched.
153 . A TENT * A MOVIE SET * A MOTOR BOAT	⇒ They have props.
154 . A TIE * A NERVOUS STOMACH * A PIECE OF LUMBER	⇒ They have knots.
155 . A TOBACCO SHOP * A TWIN * A TENNIS TOURNAMENT	⇒ They have matches.
156 . A TOE * A CARPENTER * A FINGER	⇒ They have nails.
157 . A TOOTH * A KING * A GEMSTONE	⇒ They have crowns.
158 . A TOY STORE * A LINGERIE STORE * THE KENNEDY FAMILY	⇒ They have Teddies.
159 . A TRAIN * AN ORCHESTRA * A BATTERY	⇒ They have conductors.
160 . A TREE * A BANK * THE MILITARY	⇒ They have branches.
161 . A TRUCKER * A MUG * A FRYING PAN	⇒ They have handles.
162 . A TURKEY * A BASKETBALL * A CHRISTMAS STOCKING	⇒ They are stuffed.

163 . A TURKEY * A CHICKEN * BUDDY RICH ⇒ They have drumsticks.

164 . A VACUUM * A DAM * A PRESIDENT ⇒ They have Hoovers

165 . A VCR * A TENNIS RACKET * A PIN ⇒ They have heads.

166 . A VIOLINIST * AN ARCHER * A GIFT WRAPPER ⇒ They have or use bows.

167 . A WAGON * A WEED * A PRACTICAL JOKE ⇒ They are pulled.

168 . A WHOPPER * A FIB * A TALE ⇒ Lies

169 . A WRINKLED SHIRT * A BUTTON * A BARBELL ⇒ They are pressed.

170 . A YEAR * A MATTRESS * A CAR ⇒ They have springs.

171 . A ZOO * A ZIPLOCK BAG * THE NAVY ⇒ They have seals.

172 . ACE * EAGLE * BOGEY ⇒ Golf terms.

173 . ACORN * BUTTERNUT * SUMMER ⇒ Squash.

174 . ACTORS * HAIRDOS * AUTOMOTIVE STORES ⇒ They have parts.

175 . ALARM * GRANDFATHER * CUCKOO ⇒ Clocks.

176 . ALBERT EINSTEIN * RABBITS * CALCULATORS ⇒ Great multipliers.

177 . ALL STATE INSURANCE COMPANY * STEVE LARGENT * JERRY RICE ⇒ They have good hands.

178 . AMERICAN AIRLINES * GEOMETRY * NEBRASKA ⇒ They have planes (plains).

179 . AN ABBREVIATED ALPHABET * A PEACOCK * AN EYEBALL ⇒ TV network logos.

180 . AN ACTOR * A CROWDED AMUSEMENT PARK * A FOOTBALL FIELD ⇒ They have lines.

181 . AN AIRLINE * NEW YORK * A JACUZZI ⇒ They have jets.

182 . AN ANGRY PERSON * A FOOTBALL * A GOLF BALL ⇒ They are teed.

183 . AN ANT * A LOBSTER * A TELEVISION ⇒ They have antennas.

184 . AN AREA CODE * A HAND * A ZIP CODE ⇒ They have digits.

185 . AN ARROW * A GOLD MINE * AN ELEVATOR ⇒ They have shafts.

186 . AN ART GALLERY * A TRAMPOLINE * A KITE ⇒ They have frames.

187 . AN ELEPHANT * A WALRUS * A WILD BOAR ⇒ They have tusks.

188 . AN EYE * A TELESCOPE * A MAGNIFYING GLASS ⇒ They have lenses.

189 . AN ICEBERG * A TONGUE * A WAITRESS ⇒ They have tips.

190 . AN IGLOO * THE CAPITOL BUILDING * THE ASTROS ⇒ They have domes

191 . AN OCTOPUS * A TRAFFIC LIGHT * A CHAMELEON ⇒ They can change color.

192 . AN OLD FAUCET * A FLAT TIRE * THE ONION FAMILY ⇒ They have leaks (leeks).

193 . AN OLIVE * A RACE TRACK * AN ARM ⇒ They have pits.

194 . AN OLIVE BRANCH * A BUNCH OF ARROWS * A RIBBON ⇒ Items held by the eagle on the Great seal of the U.S.

195 . AN OLYMPIC DECATHLETE * A BANK * AN OLYMPIC GYMNAST ⇒ They have vaults.

196 .	AN OPENED SODA * A PUNCTURED TIRE * AN OFF-KEY SINGER	⇒ They are flat.
197 .	AN ORCHESTRA * A TENNIS RACKET * A MARIONETTE	⇒ All have strings
198 .	AN UMPIRE * A TELEMARKETER * A QUARTER BACK	⇒ They make calls.
199 .	ANGLES * BURNS * TEMPERATURES	⇒ Measured in degrees.
200 .	ARCADES * FOOTBALL GAMES * ARMY BARRACKS	⇒ They have quarters.
201 .	ARMADILLO * IRON MAN * A KNIGHT	⇒ They all have armor.
202 .	ARTHUR * KONG * TUT	⇒ Kings.
203 .	ASTRO * PLUTO * LASSIE	⇒ Dogs.
204 .	ATLAS * GOLIATH * PAUL BUNYAN	⇒ Giants.
205 .	B & O * READING * SHORT LINE	⇒ Railroads in Monopoly.
206 .	B * O * A POSITIVE	⇒ Blood types.
207 .	BABE RUTH * MARGE SIMPSON * HANK AARON	⇒ They have Homers.
208 .	BAGS * SLACKS * TROUSERS	⇒ Pants.
209 .	BALD * SNOW * WHITEWALL	⇒ Tires.
210 .	BAR * PIE * LINE	⇒ Graphs.
211 .	BASEBALL * FRUIT * BROWN	⇒ Bats.
212 .	BASEBALL GAMES * TRASH DUMPS * BLUE JEANS	⇒ They have flies.
213 .	BASH * HOEDOWN * SHINDIG	⇒ Parties.
214 .	BASKET- * FOOT- * VOLLEY-	⇒ Balls.
215 .	BASKETBALL * EMBROIDERY * HULA	⇒ Hoops.
216 .	BAWL * BLUBBER * WEEP	⇒ Slang for cry.
217 .	BAY * ROSE * STAINED GLASS	⇒ Windows.
218 .	BEACH * BASE * BILLIARD	⇒ Balls.
219 .	BELLY * BREAK * WAR	⇒ Dances.
220 .	BEN FRANKLIN * BROOKLYN * GOLDEN GATE	⇒ Bridges.
221 .	BENCH * CARSON * CASH	⇒ Johnnys.
222 .	BERMUDA * LOVE * RIGHT	⇒ Triangles.
223 .	BICYCLE * COAT * SPICE	⇒ Have racks
224 .	BIDDY * HEN * ROOSTER	⇒ Chickens.
225 .	BIRCH * DRAFT * ROOT	⇒ Beers.
226 .	BIRD * STEAM * BUBBLE	⇒ Baths.
227 .	BIRD * MAGIC * JORDAN	⇒ Basketball players.
228 .	BIRDS * HOCKEY TEAMS * HOSPITALS	⇒ They have wings.
229 .	BIRTHDAY * THANK YOU * GET WELL	⇒ Cards.
230 .	BLACK * GREEN * ICED	⇒ Teas.
231 .	BLACK * RAIN * ENCHANTED	⇒ Forests.
232 .	BLACKSTONE * HOUDINI * COPPERFIELD	⇒ Magicians.

233 .	BLOOD * FOX * BASSET	⇒ Hounds.
234 .	BLOOD * INK BLOT * MULTIPLE CHOICE	⇒ Tests.
235 .	BLOOD * SPERM * PIGGY	⇒ Banks.
236 .	BLUE * BRICK * SWISS	⇒ Cheese.
237 .	BLUE * HORSHOE * KING	⇒ Crabs.
238 .	BLUE RIDGE * THE CASCADES * THE ALETIANS	⇒ Mountain ranges.
239 .	BLUEBERRY * BEVERLY * BUNKER	⇒ Hills.
240 .	BOB * TOM * ALLEY	⇒ Cats.
241 .	BOBBY * SAFETY * KING	⇒ Pins.
242 .	BOOTLEGGERS * FLAGPOLE SITTERS * FLAPPERS	⇒ Associated with the 1920's.
243 .	BOSTON * ROMAINE * ICEBERG	⇒ Lettuce.
244 .	BOX * MONKEY * CRESCENT	⇒ Wrenches.
245 .	BRAZIL * HAZEL * CORN	⇒ Nuts.
246 .	BRIDAL * APRIL * BABY	⇒ Showers.
247 .	BRONZE * IRON * STONE	⇒ Ages in the history of man.
248 .	BROWN * BLACK * POLAR	⇒ Bears.
249 .	BROWN * CANE * POWDERED	⇒ Sugar.
250 .	BROWN * WILD * WHITE	⇒ Rice.
251 .	BUCK * BABY * WISDOM	⇒ Teeth.
252 .	BUCKINGHAM PALACE * A BASKETBALL TEAM * A PRISON	⇒ They have guards.
253 .	BULL * HOUND * SHEEP	⇒ Dogs.
254 .	BUS * SHORT * REST	⇒ Stops
255 .	BUTTER * STEAK * SWISS ARMY	⇒ Knives.
256 .	BUTTERFLY * BOX * CROSSFRAME	⇒ Kites.
257 .	CALIFORNIA * A PERSON WITH MANY VICES * A POOR SERVE IN TENNIS	⇒ All have faults.
258 .	CALIFORNIA * HEAVEN * CHARLIE	⇒ They have angels.
259 .	CANDIDATES * TRACK STARS * PANTYHOSE	⇒ They run.
260 .	CANTEENS * DAMS * CAMELS	⇒ They hold water.
261 .	CAR * PAY * TOUCH-TONE	⇒ Phones.
262 .	CAR COMPANIES * CASINOS * COMPUTER COMPANIES	⇒ They have dealers.
263 .	CAR STEREO DEALERS * BLACKJACK DEALERS * CRUISE SHIPS	⇒ They have decks.
264 .	CAR TIRES * CROPS * ROASTING PIGS	⇒ They are rotated.
265 .	CARD * BOARD * VIDEO	⇒ Types of games.
266 .	CARDS * CHESS * PROMS	⇒ They have queens.
267 .	CARROT * POUND * DEVIL'S FOOD	⇒ Cakes.

268 . CART * WAGON * FERRIS	⇒ Wheels
269 . CATWOMAN * INDIANA JONES * ZORRO	⇒ They use whips.
270 . CHAIN * LOVE * DEAR JOHN	⇒ Letters.
271 . CHARGING * BLOCKING * TRAVELING	⇒ Not legal in basketball.
272 . CHICAGO * SMOKEY * YOGI	⇒ Bears.
273 . CHICKENS * GUITARS * EYEBROW	⇒ They are plucked.
274 . CHILI * HOT * CORN	⇒ Types of dogs.
275 . CHINESE * JIGSAW * CROSSWORD	⇒ Puzzles.
276 . CHOCOLATE * RICE * TAPIOCA	⇒ Pudding.
277 . CHOCOLATE * WHOLE * SKIM	⇒ Milk.
278 . CHOW * GRUB * FARE	⇒ Slang for food.
279 . CHRISTMAS * EASTER * VIRGIN	⇒ Islands.
280 . CHRISTMAS * FORTUNE * CHOCOLATE CHIP	⇒ Cookies.
281 . CHRISTMAS PAST * SLIMER * CASPER	⇒ Ghosts.
282 . CHURCHES * SANTA'S SLEIGH * SCHOOLS	⇒ They have bells.
283 . CIGARETTES * COFFEEMAKERS * CARS	⇒ They have filters.
284 . CITIES * SONGS * NOSES	⇒ They have bridges.
285 . CLAW * BALL-PEEN * SLEDGE	⇒ Hammers.
286 . CLEVELAND * WASHINGTON * MADISON	⇒ Presidents.
287 . CLIPPER * CUTTER * SPEED	⇒ Boats.
288 . COBAL * FRENCH * SIGN	⇒ Languages.
289 . COFFEE * LAYER * SPICE	⇒ Cakes.
290 . COLONEL KLINK * THE PENGUIN * MR. PEANUT	⇒ They wore monocles.
291 . COLUMBUS * LABOR * GROUND-HOG	⇒ Days.
292 . COMPUTERS * FOOTBALL TEAMS * PORCH DOORS	⇒ They have screens.
293 . CONGRESS * HILLARY CLINTON * A PLATYPUS	⇒ They have Bills.
294 . COPPERTONE * CRACKERJACKS * BUSTER BROWN	⇒ Products with a child and a dog in their logo.
295 . CORK * RUBBER * GUM	⇒ Trees.
296 . CORN * OLIVE * BABY	⇒ Oils.
297 . COW * SCHOOL * WEDDING	⇒ Bells.
298 . CRAB * CANDY * CARAMEL	⇒ Apples.
299 . CRAFT * VESSEL * SHIP	⇒ All boats.
300 . CREAM * SHARP * COTTAGE	⇒ Cheese.
301 . CRICKET * ZIPPO * BIC	⇒ Lighters.
302 . CRUNCH * AMERICA * KANGAROO	⇒ Captains.
303 . CRUSH * SQUIRT * TAB	⇒ Sodas or pops.
304 . CUB * BOY * GIRL	⇒ Scouts.

305 . DATE * COCONUT * SABAL	⇒	Palm trees.
306 . DAY * NIGHT * SUN	⇒	Lights.
307 . DAYS * CONTINENTS * SEAS	⇒	There are seven of them.
308 . DEAD * RED * NORTH	⇒	Seas.
309 . DENVER * THE FORD MOTOR COMPANY * RODEOS	⇒	They have Broncos.
310 . DEWEY * LOUIE * HUEY	⇒	Donald Duck's nephews.
311 . DIAMOND RING * A STORY * A TOASTER	⇒	They have settings.
312 . DIAMONDS * CLUBS * SPADES	⇒	Card suits.
313 . DIESEL ENGINE * EIFFEL TOWER * FERRIS WHEEL	⇒	Named after their designer.
314 . DINER * HOME * LICENSE	⇒	Plates.
315 . DINNER * LEATHER * STRAIGHT	⇒	Jackets.
316 . DIRT * PRIVATE * YELLOW BRICK	⇒	Roads.
317 . DNA * MCDONALDS * A POCKET WATCH	⇒	They have chains.
318 . DODO * CUCKOO * TWEETY	⇒	Birds.
319 . DOG * PILLOW * FIST	⇒	Flights.
320 . DOLLY * JACKIE * ELEANOR	⇒	First Ladies.
321 . DOOR * GRAND * NOBEL	⇒	Prizes.
322 . DOTS * KISSES * GUMMIBEARS	⇒	Candy.
323 . DOUBLE * KING * BUNK	⇒	Beds.
324 . DOUBLE * SECRET * REAL ESTATE	⇒	Agents.
325 . DOUBLE * TUNNEL * 20/20	⇒	Vision.
326 . DOUGHNUT * POT * BLACK	⇒	Holes.
327 . DOVE * TONE * ZEST	⇒	Soap brand names.
328 . DRAW * FADE * SLICE	⇒	Golf terms.
329 . DRUG * LIQUOR * HARDWARE	⇒	Stores.
330 . DUCK * MINI * VENETIAN	⇒	Blinds.
331 . DUCKS * DEBTORS * CONGRESS	⇒	They have bills.
332 . EAR * CANDLE * BEE'S	⇒	Wax.
333 . EAR * KETTLE * STEEL	⇒	Drums.
334 . EARLY GIRL * BIG BOY * CHERRY	⇒	Tomatoes.
335 . EASTER * PICNIC * WASTEPAPER	⇒	Baskets.
336 . EGGS * BRICKS * CARPETS	⇒	They are laid.
337 . ELECTRIC * FREIGHT * CHOO-CHOO	⇒	Trains.
338 . ELVIS * BUDWEISER * A LION	⇒	They are kings.
339 . EM * BEA * JEMIMA	⇒	Ants.
340 . END * TWILIGHT * NO PARKING	⇒	Zones.
341 . ENGLAND * CHESS SETS * BEEHIVES	⇒	They have queens.
342 . ERNEST HEMINWAY * A SKYSCRAPER * MARK TWAIN	⇒	They have stories.

343 . FAMILIES * TREES * HAIR ⇒ They have roots.

344 . FAN * JUNK * EXPRESS ⇒ Mail

345 . FARMS * CLOCKS * POKER PLAYER ⇒ They have hands.

346 . FERTILE SOIL * A DOUBLE CHOCOLATE CHEESECAKE * A ⇒ They are rich.
MILLIONAIRE

347 . FIGHTER * GLIDER * 747 ⇒ Planes.

348 . FINGER * OIL * LATEX ⇒ Paints

349 . FIRE * AREA * ZIP ⇒ Codes.

350 . FIRE * FRUIT * TSETSE ⇒ Flys

351 . FISHING * FINISH * DOTTED ⇒ Lines

352 . FLAKES * HAIR * A MUG ⇒ They are frosted.

353 . FLASH * PILOT * FLOOD ⇒ Lights.

354 . FLAT * GLOSS * SEMI-GLOSS ⇒ Paint finishes.

355 . FLORIDA * A PIANO * A JAILOR ⇒ They all have keys.

356 . FLY * TOILET * WRAPPING ⇒ Paper.

357 . FOOT * TOAD * BAR ⇒ Stools.

358 . FOREST * HUNTER * LIME ⇒ Greens.

359 . FORTUNE * BANK * STORY ⇒ Tellers.

360 . FOX * TREASURE * SCAVENGER ⇒ Hunts.

361 . FRANKINCENSE * GOLD * MYRRH ⇒ Gifts to baby Jesus.

362 . FRENCH * CAR * UNICORN ⇒ Horns.

363 . FRENCH * ESKIMO * HERSHEY'S ⇒ Kisses.

364 . FRENCH * RUSSIAN * THOUSAND ISLAND ⇒ Salad dressings.

365 . FRENCH * STRING * 1-PIECE ⇒ Bathing suits.

366 . FRINGE * CURTAIN * ROUGH ⇒ Parts of a golf course.

367 . FRUIT * CHEESE * UP-SIDE DOWN ⇒ Cakes.

368 . FURNITURE * MUSTACHES * SKIS ⇒ They are waxed.

369 . GEORGE * PAUL * RINGO ⇒ Beatles.

370 . GIG * ARK * YACHT ⇒ Boats.

371 . GOATS * COCONUTS * COWS ⇒ They produce milk.

372 . GOLD * CAT * DOG ⇒ Fish.

373 . GOLF * TIME * GAMES ⇒ Magazines.

374 . GOLF COURSE * A COFFEE SHOP * A QUART ⇒ They have cups.

375 . GOLFERS * CHARITIES * COMPUTERS ⇒ They have drives.

376 . GOOSE * TERESA * HUBBARD ⇒ Mothers.

377 . GRADUATIONS * SOUND SYSTEMS * THE HOUSE OF ⇒ They have speakers.
REPRESENTATIVES

378 . GRAY * RED * TIMBER ⇒ Wolves.

379 .	GREAT * TROPICAL * CLINICAL	⇒ Depressions.
380 .	GREEN * DOUGH * MOOLAH	⇒ Slang for money.
381 .	GREEN * NAVY * WAX	⇒ Beans.
382 .	GREEN * RED * BELL	⇒ Peppers.
383 .	GREEN * ROCKY * EVEREST	⇒ Mountains.
384 .	GREEN * YELLOW * CHECKERED	⇒ Flags in racing.
385 .	GREENHOUSES * CAR COMPANIES * BOTANIST	⇒ They have plants.
386 .	GREETING * PLAYING * TIME	⇒ Types of cards.
387 .	GUITAR * ICE * TOOTH	⇒ Picks.
388 .	GULF * KOREAN * CIVIL	⇒ Wars.
389 .	GUN * BABY * TALCUM	⇒ Powders.
390 .	HAIR * PUNCH * A VOLLEYBALL	⇒ They can be spiked.
391 .	HAIR * TOOTH * PAINT	⇒ Types of brushes.
392 .	HALLOWEEN * THE WORLD SERIES * END OF DAYLIGHT SAVINGS	⇒ October events.
393 .	HAND * BABY * CALAMINE	⇒ Lotions.
394 .	HAND -HELD * TWO-WAY * REAR-VIEW	⇒ Mirrors.
395 .	HARD * CLAY * GRASS	⇒ Tennis court surfaces.
396 .	HARE * COTTONTAIL * BUNNY	⇒ Rabbits.
397 .	HE * SHE * THEY	⇒ Pronouns.
398 .	HEAD * GOAT * STRING	⇒ Cheese.
399 .	HEAD * TAIL * CROSS	⇒ Winds.
400 .	HEART * SUN * THIRD DEGREE	⇒ Burns.
401 .	HEARTS * MOONS * CLOVERS	⇒ Pieces in Lucky Charms.
402 .	HEAT * DOUGH * TAXES	⇒ They all rise.
403 .	HEAT * FUZZ * COPS	⇒ Slang for police.
404 .	HEATHER * LILY * TULIP	⇒ Flower.
405 .	HEAVEN * GRACELAND * AIRPORTS	⇒ They have gates.
406 .	HELP * YESTERDAY * REVOLUTION	⇒ Songs by the Beatles.
407 .	HIGH * LASER * BALANCE	⇒ Beams.
408 .	HIGH * UNEVEN * PARALLEL	⇒ Bars in gymnastics.
409 .	HOOK * SET * BANK	⇒ Shots in basketball.
410 .	HOUSE * HORSE * DRAGON	⇒ Types of flys.
411 .	HOUSE * WAR * FINGER	⇒ Paints.
412 .	HOUSTON * PANAMA * SUEZ	⇒ Canals.
413 .	HOWARD * DONALD * DAFFY	⇒ Ducks.
414 .	HUMAN * RAT * RELAY	⇒ Races.
415 .	HUMANS * PORCUPINES * BOOKS	⇒ They have spines.

416 .	HUMPTY DUMPTY * A WRESTLING MATCH * A YEAR	⇒ They have falls.
417 .	I * V * X	⇒ Roman numerals.
418 .	IBM * NALLEY'S * WOOD PRODUCTS COMPANY	⇒ They have chips.
419 .	ICE * FIGURE * ROLLER	⇒ Types of skating.
420 .	IMPROPER * UNIT * MIXED	⇒ Fractions.
421 .	JACK * PETER * ROGER	⇒ Rabbits.
422 .	JACK * SHARP * COLBY	⇒ Cheese.
423 .	JAPAN * CUBA * IRELAND	⇒ Island nations.
424 .	JAZZ * MARCHING * BIG	⇒ Bands.
425 .	JELLY * SWORD * SAIL	⇒ Fish.
426 .	JOE * BATTERY ACID * PAINT REMOVER	⇒ All slang for coffee.
427 .	JOE * MUD * JAVA	⇒ Slang for coffee.
428 .	JOHN * THOMAS * JUDAS	⇒ Disciples.
429 .	JULIUS CAESAR * ROBERT KENNEDY * JOHN LENNON	⇒ All assassinated.
430 .	JUMP * SWIM * THREE-PIECE	⇒ Suits.
431 .	JUNK * FIRST CLASS * BLACK	⇒ Mail.
432 .	JUPITER * ALASKA * THE BLUE WHALE	⇒ Largest of their kind.
433 .	KANGAROO * WOMBAT * OPOSSUM	⇒ Marsupials (Animals with pouches.)
434 .	KENTUCKY FRIED CHICKEN * CORN * THE U.S. ARMY	⇒ They have colonels (Kernels).
435 .	KID * NANNY * BILLY	⇒ Goats.
436 .	KILLER * HONEY * BUMBLE	⇒ Bees.
437 .	KILLER WHALES * OLD T.V.'S * REFEREES	⇒ They're black and white.
438 .	KING * QUEEN * BISHOP	⇒ Chess pieces.
439 .	KINGS * JUDGES * NUMBERS	⇒ Books of the Bible.
440 .	L'EGGS * SILLY PUDDY * CHICKENS	⇒ Come in eggs.
441 .	LAMB * PORK * KARATE	⇒ Chops.
442 .	LAUGHTER * INFLUENZA * YAWNING	⇒ They are contagious.
443 .	LAZY * BLACK * BLOODSHOT	⇒ Eyes.
444 .	LEECH * WOOD TICK * MOSQUITO	⇒ Blood suckers.
445 .	LEMON * TIGER * HAMMERHEAD	⇒ Sharks.
446 .	LET * SLICE * SMASH	⇒ All terms in tennis.
447 .	LIFE * BODY * CROSSING	⇒ Guards.
448 .	LIFE * CAR * HOME	⇒ Insurance.
449 .	LIFE * SUIT * BULLET PROOF	⇒ Vests.
450 .	LINCOLN * COLUMBUS * CHICAGO	⇒ Cities.
451 .	LITTLE * MINOR * MAJOR	⇒ Leagues in baseball.
452 .	LITTLE * SLOPPY * G.I.	⇒ Joes.

453 .	LITTLE RED RIDING HOOD * A HOT-AIR BALLOON A HIGH SCHOOL GYM	⇒ They have baskets.
454 .	LONG * HIGH * TRIPLE	⇒ Jumping events in track.
455 .	LOS ANGELES * LOUISIANA * LOUIS ARMSTRONG	⇒ All L.A.'s
456 .	LOUNGE * EASY * HIGH	⇒ Chairs.
457 .	LOVERS * SAILORS * HITCH	⇒ Types of knots.
458 .	MAGAZINES * BEDS * MATCHBOOKS	⇒ They have covers.
459 .	MALIBU * BELAIR * SALEM	⇒ Cigarette brands.
460 .	MALLS * COMIC * BACON	⇒ They come in strips.
461 .	MANHATTAN * RHODE ISLAND * NEW ENGLAND	⇒ Chowders (Usually clam).
462 .	MANUAL * 3 ON THE TREE * 4 ON THE FLOOR	⇒ Transmissions.
463 .	MARBLE * SPONGE * ANGEL FOOD	⇒ Cakes.
464 .	MARBLES * JACKS * CHECKERS	⇒ Games.
465 .	MARE * MUSTANG * BRONCO	⇒ Horses.
466 .	MARIGOLD * MUSTARD * CANARY	⇒ Shades of yellow.
467 .	MAUI * JAVA * GILLIGAN'S	⇒ Islands.
468 .	MAY * FLAG * BEAN	⇒ Poles.
469 .	MCDONALDS * ST LOUIS * A FOOT	⇒ They have arches.
470 .	MEMORY * BRIDGE * GO FISH	⇒ Card games.
471 .	MENS GYMNASTICS * BULLFIGHTING * PROFESSIONAL WRESTLING	⇒ They have rings.
472 .	METAL * RADAR * LIE	⇒ Detectors.
473 .	MINNESOTA * IDENTICAL * SIAMESE	⇒ Twins.
474 .	MOBS * GAGGLES * PODS	⇒ Groups of animals.
475 .	MOM * TOOT * ROTOR	⇒ Palindromes.
476 .	MONEY * LIFE * SUNSET	⇒ Magazines.
477 .	MORRIS * FELIX * GARFIELD	⇒ Cats.
478 .	MOTH * MEAT * MEDICINE	⇒ Balls.
479 .	MOUSE * BOOBY * LIVE	⇒ Traps.
480 .	MOVIE * PARKING * RAFFLE	⇒ Tickets.
481 .	MUD * POT * COCONUT	⇒ Pies.
482 .	MULE * LOAFER * PUMP	⇒ Shoes.
483 .	MULTIPLE * DAILY * CHEWABLE	⇒ Vitamins.
484 .	MUSIC * MAIL * SAFE DEPOSIT	⇒ Boxes.
485 .	NAPOLEON * SOLITAIRE * 21	⇒ Card games.
486 .	NAVY * ROYAL * SKY	⇒ Blues.
487 .	NEBRASKA * A PENNY * FORD MOTOR COMPANY	⇒ They all have Lincolns.
488 .	NECK * CROWN * ROOT	⇒ Parts of tooth.

489 .	NEW * FULL * CRESENT	⇒ Moons.
490 .	NEW YORK * T-BONE * SIRLOIN	⇒ Steaks.
491 .	NEWLYWEDS * SATURN * DIRTY SHIRT COLLARS	⇒ They have **rings**.
492 .	NIAGARA * DOWN * RAIN	⇒ Falls.
493 .	NICKEL * SILVER * TIN	⇒ Metals.
494 .	NOAH'S ARK * A FRUIT STAND * A SOCK DRAWER	⇒ They have pairs / **pears**.
495 .	ODD * IRRATIONAL * EVEN	⇒ Numbers.
496 .	OIL * COFFEE * AIR	⇒ Filters.
497 .	OLIVE * KELLY * EMERALD	⇒ Greens.
498 .	ONION * TULIP * LAMP	⇒ They have **bulbs**.
499 .	ONTARIO * ERIE * MICHIGAN	⇒ Great Lakes.
500 .	ORANGE * OLIVE * FIG	⇒ Trees.
501 .	ORBS * BABY BLUES * KEEPERS	⇒ Slang for eyes.
502 .	ORCHESTRAS * EARS * BRAKES	⇒ They have **drums**.
503 .	PACIFIC * CENTRAL * MOUNTAIN	⇒ Time zones.
504 .	PAINTINGS * DOORS * EYE GLASSES	⇒ They have **frames**.
505 .	PALM * EASTER * HOT FUDGE	⇒ Sundays / Sundaes.
506 .	PALM * PINE * CHRISTMAS	⇒ Trees.
507 .	PEACE * OK * HANG LOOSE	⇒ Hand expressions.
508 .	PEN * JOINT * SLAMMER	⇒ Slang for jail or **prison**.
509 .	PENGUIN * KIWI * OSTRICH	⇒ Flightless birds..
510 .	PEPPER * CHESS * SQUASH	⇒ Games
511 .	PEPPER * SPOCK * SEUSS	⇒ Doctors.
512 .	PERIWINKLE * AZURE * CERULEAN	⇒ Shades of blue.
513 .	PHONE * DATE * COOK	⇒ Books.
514 .	PHOTOGRAPHER * SKYDIVER * BAMBOO	⇒ They have **shoots** (chutes).
515 .	PICK-UP * FIRE * 4X4	⇒ Trucks.
516 .	PIG * BULL * BALL-POINT	⇒ Pens.
517 .	PIN * SEAT * WHOOPEE	⇒ Cushions.
518 .	PINOCCHIO * GEPPETTO * JONAH	⇒ Swallowed by whales.
519 .	PIPERS * DRUMMERS * LORDS	⇒ Gifts in the Twelve **days** of Christmas.
520 .	PIPPIN * STAR * KIWI	⇒ Fruits.
521 .	PLATFORM * SPRINGBOARD * CLIFF	⇒ Dives.
522 .	PLAYER * CONCERT * BABY GRAND	⇒ Pianos.
523 .	POEMS * POST OFFICES * KILOMETERS	⇒ They have **meters**.
524 .	POLARIS * SIRIUS * THE SUN	⇒ Stars.
525 .	POLK * FORD * BUSH	⇒ Presidents.

526. POOL * LOAN * GREAT WHITE ⇒ Sharks.
527. POOL * PICNIC * COFFEE ⇒ Tables.
528. POPEYE THE SAILOR * A MARTINI * A GREEK SALAD ⇒ They have olives.
529. PORKY * SPANKY * ALFALFA ⇒ Little Rascal characters.
530. POTATO * ROSE * TASTE ⇒ Buds.
531. POTTERY * A GUN * A BAD EMPLOYEE ⇒ They are fired.
532. PRAYER * PAPERBACK * PICTURE ⇒ Books.
533. PRESIDENTIAL ELECTION * LEAP YEAR * THE OLYMPICS ⇒ Happen every four years.
534. PROCTER & GAMBLE * EDMOND HALLEY * SANTA CLAUS ⇒ They have Comets.
535. PUG * BOXER * BEAGLE ⇒ Dogs.
536. PUMP * FLAT * CLOG ⇒ Shoes.
537. QUACK * SAWBONES * DOLITTLE ⇒ Doctors.
538. QUEEN * KING * PAWN ⇒ Chess pieces.
539. QUEEN * WORKER * DRONE ⇒ Bees.
540. RACE * COMPACT * CONVERTIBLE ⇒ Cars.
541. RADAR * AIDS * SCUBA ⇒ Acronyms.
542. RADIO * BRAIN * TIDAL ⇒ Waves.
543. RAIL * CHAIN * PICKET ⇒ Fences.
544. RAILROAD TRACKS * MEN'S CLOTHING STORES * TRASH BAGS ⇒ They have ties.
545. RAIN * WATUSI * WALTZ ⇒ Dances.
546. RAIN * TRENCH * FUR ⇒ Coats.
547. RALLY * STOCK * DRAG ⇒ Car races.
548. RED * DUCT * MASKING ⇒ Tape.
549. RED * MAGIC * SHAG ⇒ Carpets.
550. RED DWARF * BLUE DWARF * SUPER GIANT ⇒ Stars.
551. RING * INDEX * PINKY ⇒ Fingers.
552. RINGO STARR * A DEAD JUNE BUG * A DEAD LADY BUG ⇒ Former Beatle (beetles).
553. RIP * HACK * BUZZ ⇒ Saws.
554. ROAD * WEATHER * TREASURE ⇒ Maps.
555. ROCK * TABLE * EPSOM ⇒ Salt.
556. ROLLER * DEMOLITION* KENTUCKY ⇒ Derbys.
557. ROSES * DOUGHNUTS * JURORS ⇒ They come in dozens.
558. RUBBER * HEAD * WEDDING ⇒ Bands.
559. RUBIK'S * ICE * SUGAR ⇒ Cubes.
560. SAFE * FIRE * SODA ⇒ Crackers.
561. SCOTLAND * RAPUNZEL * THE PANAMA CANAL ⇒ They have lochs or locks.

562 . SCREEN * DUMP * HAIL MARY	⇒	Passes in football.
563 . SEA SHELLS * WAGON WHEELS * BOWTIES	⇒	Shapes of pasta.
564 . SEATTLE * A KNITTER * A SPEEDOMETER	⇒	They have needles.
565 . SEVEN -UP * GIN * POKER	⇒	Card games.
566 . SHEETS * BOOKS * ROLLS	⇒	Way stamps are sold.
567 . SHERLOCK HOLMES * AN ORGAN * FROSTY THE SNOWMAN	⇒	They have pipes.
568 . SHIELD * COAST * LAVA	⇒	Soap brand names.
569 . SHOOTERS * CAT'S EYE * PUREE	⇒	Marbles.
570 . SHOW * ROW * TOW	⇒	Boats.
571 . SIDE * BACK * BUTTERFLY	⇒	Swimming strokes.
572 . SIGHT * SMELL * TASTE	⇒	Senses.
573 . SILVER * BLACK * LOCK	⇒	Smiths.
574 . SILVER * TRIGGER * MR. ED	⇒	Horses.
575 . SILVER QUEEN * COUNTRY GENTLEMAN * GOLDEN BANTAM	⇒	Types of corn.
576 . SIX FEET * TWO YARDS * ONE FATHOM	⇒	All the same length.
577 . SKY * CLIFF * SCUBA	⇒	Divers or divin.
578 . SLIDE * SLIP * SQUARE	⇒	Knots.
579 . SNAIL * OYSTER * EGG	⇒	They have shells.
580 . SNAKE * CAVITY * BOTTOMLESS	⇒	Pits.
581 . SNOW * CORN * DANDRUFF	⇒	Flakes.
582 . SNOW * GUM * MOTH	⇒	Balls.
583 . SNOW * WINGTIP * LEATHER	⇒	Shoes.
584 . SOFT * SUPER * WHIFFLE	⇒	Balls.
585 . SPEARS * CHIPS * SWEET	⇒	Pickles.
586 . SPIDER * FIDDLER * HERMIT	⇒	Crabs.
587 . SPIDER WEB * A BOBBIN * A SCREW	⇒	They have threads.
588 . SPIKE * DIG * SET	⇒	Volleyball terms.
589 . SPINES * COMPUTER STORES * MUSIC STORES	⇒	They have disks.
590 . SPIRAL * COMPOUND * GREENSTICK	⇒	Fractures.
591 . SPLITTING * SINUS * MIGRAINE	⇒	Headaches.
592 . SPOONS * SPADES * PAIRS	⇒	Card games.
593 . SPRING * RUBBER * KENTUCKY FRIED	⇒	Chickens.
594 . SPRING * SALT * MINERAL	⇒	Water.
595 . SQUARE * WING * LUG	⇒	Nuts.
596 . SQUEEZE * KISS * CREAM	⇒	Musical groups.
597 . STAMPS * CHECKS * BAD T.V. SHOWS	⇒	They get cancelled.

598.	STAR * WORLD * REVOLUTIONARY	⇒ Wars.
599.	STATE * SALES * INCOME	⇒ Taxes.
600.	STEAK * SPAGHETTI * TARTAR	⇒ Sauces.
601.	STEAM SHOVEL * POWERLINE TRUCKS * KFC	⇒ All have buckets.
602.	STEVEN SPIELBERG * CLAMPS * PLIERS	⇒ All have jaws (Jaws).
603.	STICK * HIP * BODY	⇒ Checks in hockey.
604.	STICK * PUMP * ROLL-ON	⇒ Deodorants.
605.	STOCK CAR * CROSS COUNTRY * THREE LEGGED	⇒ Races.
606.	STONE * VINE * CITRUS	⇒ Fruits.
607.	STOP * CANCER * EXIT	⇒ Signs.
608.	STOP * POCKET * WRIST	⇒ Watches.
609.	STOP * SPOT * STROBE	⇒ Lights.
610.	STRAW * STICKS * BRICKS	⇒ Little pigs building materials.
611.	STRING * BLACK * KIDNEY	⇒ Beans.
612.	SUPERMAN * BATMAN * MASSACHUSETTS	⇒ They have capes.
613.	SUPERMAN * ELVIS * LITTLE RED RIDING HOOD	⇒ They wore capes.
614.	SURPRISE * SEARCH * SLUMBER	⇒ Parties.
615.	SWEET * CHICK * BLACK-EYED	⇒ Peas.
616.	SWISS CHEESE * OLD SOCKS * THE POPE	⇒ They are holey or holy.
617.	T'S * HEARTS * FINGERS	⇒ They are crossed.
618.	TEA * DOGGY * DUFFEL	⇒ Bags.
619.	TEAM * ALL AROUND * VAULT	⇒ Gymnastic events.
620.	TELEPHONE * COPPER * BARBED	⇒ Wire.
621.	TELEPHONE * NORTH * TOTEM	⇒ Poles.
622.	TENNIS * SUPREME * SMALL CLAIMS	⇒ Courts.
623.	THE ANTARCTIC CIRCLE * THE ARCTIC CIRCLE * A BARBER SHOP	⇒ They all have poles.
624.	THE BRAIN * THE EAR * THE LUNG	⇒ They have lobes.
625.	THE EARTH * AN APPLE * A NUCLEAR REACTOR	⇒ They have cores.
626.	THE EARTH * A PIZZA * A PIE	⇒ They have crusts.
627.	THE EARTH * THE 1956 NEW YORK YANKEES * A FIREPLACE	⇒ They have Mantles.
628.	THE EARTH'S CRUST * A BASEBALL DIAMOND * A CHINA CABINET	⇒ They have plates.
629.	THE FIRST DAY OF SUMMER * FLAG DAY * FATHER'S DAY	⇒ Events in June..
630.	THE FIRST MAN IN SPACE * RIN TIN TIN * JESUS	⇒ They were Shepherds.
631.	THE GAP * THE LIMITED * CHROMOSOMES	⇒ They have jeans or genes.

632 .	THE HAMMER * THE ANVIL * THE STIRRUP	⇒ Bones of the upper ear
633 .	THE JERK * THE PONY * THE TWIST	⇒ Dances.
634 .	THE KEY * THE SCALE * THE LEGEND	⇒ Parts of map.
635 .	THE MUSIC INDUSTRY * THE ROYAL FAMILY * A TENNIS SHOP	⇒ They have Princes.
636 .	THE STATUE OF LIBERTY * DIAMOND HEAD * ALCATRAZ	⇒ On islands.
637 .	THE SUN * THE GLOBE * THE TRIBUNE	⇒ Newspapers.
638 .	THE WHITE HOUSE * A SHEPHERD * SHEET MUSIC	⇒ They have staffs.
639 .	THOMAS JEFFERSON * NEW JERSEY * EARTH	⇒ All thirds.
640 .	THROW * ORIENTAL * BEARSKIN	⇒ Rugs.
641 .	TIME * STINK * ATOMIC	⇒ Bombs.
642 .	TOILET PAPER * FILM * LIFESAVERS	⇒ They come in rolls.
643 .	TOILETS * EYES * TRASH CANS	⇒ They have lids.
644 .	TOMATO * NUCLEAR POWER * SPIDER	⇒ Plants.
645 .	TOMBSTONES * A POPULAR GIRL * A DRIED FRUIT VENDOR	⇒ They all have dates.
646 .	TONY * DETROIT * TIGER	⇒ Tigers.
647 .	TOOTHPASTE * TV'S * SURFING WAVES	⇒ They have tubes.
648 .	TOSSED * POTATO * BEAN	⇒ Salads.
649 .	TOTAL * TEAM * LIFE	⇒ Cereals.
650 .	TOY * SAND * JUKE	⇒ Boxes.
651 .	TRACK MEETS * SLEDS * BASEBALL GAMES	⇒ They have runners.
652 .	TRAINS * REFEREES * TEAPOTS	⇒ They have whistles.
653 .	TRAP * FRENCH * GLASS	⇒ Doors.
654 .	TUG * STEAM * SAIL	⇒ Boats.
655 .	TURKEY * CHRISTMAS STOCKING * TEDDY BEAR	⇒ They are stuffed.
656 .	TURKEYS * STATUES * INITIALS	⇒ They're carved.
657 .	TURTLE * SEA * TACO	⇒ Shells.
658 .	TWENTY FIVE CENTS * FIFTEEN MINUTES * THREE MONTHS	⇒ They are quarters.
659 .	TWIST * CHA-CHA * REEL	⇒ Dances.
660 .	VEGETABLE * MINERAL * MOTOR	⇒ Oils.
661 .	VIOLET * LILAC * PLUM	⇒ Purples.
662 .	VOCALISTS * GOLF COURSE * APPLIANCE STORES	⇒ They have ranges.
663 .	VOLLEYBALL * COMPANIES WITH COMPUTERS * FISHERMAN	⇒ They have nets.
664 .	WALT DISNEY * A COMPUTER STORE * HANNA BARBERA	⇒ They have mouses (or mice).

665 . WASHINGTON * WILSON * RAINIER	⇒	Mountains in North America.
666 . WATCH * SHEEP * SEEING-EYE	⇒	Dogs.
667 . WATER * EYE * MAGNIFYING	⇒	Glasses.
668 . WATER * FLOWER * BUNK	⇒	Bed sizes.
669 . WATER * HELIUM * HOT AIR	⇒	Balloons.
670 . WATER * METAL * LEONARD BERNSTEIN	⇒	Conductors-electricity & music.
671 . WATER * WATCH * EIFFEL	⇒	Towers.
672 . WAYNE * FIG * SIR ISAAC *	⇒	Newtons.
673 . WHEEL * LAWN * ROCKING	⇒	Chairs.
674 . WHITE * DARK * MILK	⇒	Chocolates.
675 . WHITE * KILLER * SPERM	⇒	Whales.
676 . WHITE * RAISIN * RYE	⇒	Bread.
677 . WHITE * SWEET * IDAHO	⇒	Potatoes.
678 . WILBER * ARNOLD * PORKY	⇒	Pigs.
679 . WINDOW * CENTER * AISLE	⇒	Seats.
680 . WINDOW PANES * BIRTHDAY CAKES * CORN FLAKES	⇒	They can be frosted.
681 . WOOD * CANVASBACK * TEAL	⇒	Ducks.
682 . YARD * CHOP * POGO	⇒	Sticks.
683 . YEAR * ADDRESS * SCRAP	⇒	Books.
684 . YELLOW * BLACK * BALTIC	⇒	Seas.
685 . YELLOW * SCARLET * CABIN	⇒	Fevers.
686 . YELLOW * SPICY BROWN * DIJON	⇒	Mustards.
687 . YOUR VOICE * YOUR HAND * YOUR CHILDREN	⇒	Things you raise.
688 . ZOOS * CHURCHES * ART GALLERIES	⇒	They have collections.
689 . APPLE * HOUSE * FAMILY	⇒	All used with TREE.

RHYME TIME

These "riddles" have been around for a long time. I have chosen the name RHYME TIME, though you might have heard them called HINK PINKS, HINKY PINKIES, and HINKETY PINKETIES. They are challenging and fun. The riddle has four subtle clues. They are as follows:

- The answer will always be two words.
- The answer will always mean basically the same as the clue.
- Both words in the answer will always have the same number of syllables. (Determined before hand.)
- Both words in the answer will always RHYME!

EXAMPLE: In the 1 syllable category, the answer to ANGRY FATHER would be MAD DAD. (Two words, meaning is the same, same number of syllables, and they rhyme). The answer to the 2 syllable riddle, HAPPY BOAT CAPTAIN, is CHIPPER SKIPPER!

NOTE: There were, almost, an endless combination of Rhyme Times to be made. For instance the word "WHALE" could be used in these combinations: FRAIL WHALE, WHALE JAIL, MALE WHALE, PALE WHALE, WHALE SALE, WHALE SCALE, STALE WHALE, WHALE TALE, WHALE TAIL, and WHALE TRAIL! I did not include EVERY possible combination. But, with close to 2000 Rhyme Time Riddles, you should be challenged for quite some time!

RHYME TIME - 1 Syllable

CLUE

ANSWER

	CLUE	ANSWER
1 .	"Burn insect!"	FRY FLY
2 .	"Go ahead, oxidize!"	JUST RUST
3 .	"Move" , female deer	GO DOE
4 .	"Sniffer", iced up	NOSE FROZE
5 .	1/2 dozen, clay blocks	SIX BRICKS
6 .	24 hours with toys	PLAY DAY
7 .	4 + 5 could eat	NINE DINE
8 .	48 hours of giving thanks	PRAISE DAYS
9 .	50% giggle	HALF LAUGH
10 .	6th month's satellite	JUNE MOON
11 .	A "totally cool" father	RAD DAD
12 .	A alcoholic beverage "hooray"	BEER CHEER
13 .	A bar that supports the propeller on a log boat	RAFT SHAFT
14 .	A birds foot defect	CLAW FLAW
15 .	A blah side of the face	BLEAK CHEEK
16 .	A blood sucking animal that lives on a fuzzy fruit	PEACH LEECH
17 .	A blue-green moray	TEAL EEL
18 .	A boring Choo-choo	PLAIN TRAIN
19 .	A box for holding worms for fishing	BAIT CRATE
20 .	A boy slug with a shell	MALE SNAIL
21 .	A burnt house lot	CHARD YARD
22 .	A cap that got sat on	FLAT HAT
23 .	A chloroxed sandy area by water	BLEACHED BEACH
24 .	A cloudy 24 hours	GRAY DAY
25 .	A college dorm for vampires	BAT FRAT
26 .	A contest to see who can tie their shoes the fastest	LACE RACE
27 .	A daring removal of hair on the face	BRAVE SHAVE
28 .	A Englishman's catching devices	CHAPS TRAPS

29 .	A fake formal dance	FALSE WALTZ
30 .	A farm house used to store the favorite string	YARN BARN
31 .	A feathered animals droppings	BIRD TURD
32 .	A fragile end of the finger	FRAIL NAIL
33 .	A green mineral made into a cutting device	JADE BLADE
34 .	A happy post High School student	GLAD GRAD
35 .	A house of worship made from a white barked tree	BIRCH CHURCH
36 .	A keen eyed bird's discussion	HAWK TALK
37 .	A large branch	BIG TWIG
38 .	A literary thief	BOOK CROOK
39 .	A literature hiding place	BOOK NOOK
40 .	A little toy baby	SMALL DOLL
41 .	A muddy looking night garment	BROWN GOWN
42 .	A naked sitting device	BARE CHAIR
43 .	A not fully cooked animals foot	RAW PAW
44 .	A person who is wearing orthodontal gear	BRACE FACE
45 .	A pig meat rip off	HAM SCAM
46 .	A place for hobo's to set up camp	TRAMP CAMP
47 .	A prison for Moby	WHALE JAIL
48 .	A promise to grow	GROWTH OATH
49 .	A quick explosion	FAST BLAST
50 .	A rear-end incision	BUTT CUT
51 .	A reasonable request to God	FAIR PRAYER
52 .	A relaxed mother	CALM MOM
53 .	A rotting plant that is related to cabbage	STALE KALE
54 .	A run for the money	CASH DASH
55 .	A sack for holding the Stars & Stripes	FLAG BAG
56 .	A sleeping device made out of toast	BREAD BED
57 .	A slim member of the onion family	SLEEK LEEK
58 .	A split truthful bit of information	CRACKED FACT
59 .	A spoiled feline.	CAT BRAT
60 .	A spoiled flying bug.	GNAT BRAT
61 .	A sport with fire.	FLAME GAME
62 .	A stepped-on flying bug.	FLAT GNAT

63 . A strong feeling about the late breakfast meal.		BRUNCH HUNCH
64 . A sun-darkened male.		TAN MAN
65 . A terrible father.		BAD DAD
66 . A tired nerd.		MEEK GEEK
67 . A tool for chopping blocks of paraffin		WAX AXE
68 . A tool for cutting bales of hay.		STRAW SAW
69 . A twisted penny.		BENT CENT
70 . A visible sign of a previous injury on a car.		CAR SCAR
71 . A walk on the river wall.		DIKE HIKE
72 . A warlock's wife tattletale		WITCH SNITCH
73 . A washed legume		CLEAN BEAN
74 . A weirdo from Athens.		GREEK FREAK
75 . A wild animals diner.		BEAST FEAST
76 . A wise beginning.		SMART START
77 . A yellow fern "leaf"		BLOND FROND
78 . A young cows giggle.		CALF LAUGH
79 . Achoo wind		SNEEZE BREEZE
80 . Acquire a sore.		GAIN PAIN
81 . Admirable gangster		GOOD HOOD
82 . Admire two-wheeler		LIKE BIKE
83 . Adolescent hang-out		TEEN SCENE
84 . Adorable shoe		CUTE BOOT
85 . After nine....		THEN TEN
86 . After winter jewelry		SPRING RING
87 . Agricultural enchantment.		FARM CHARM
88 . Aid the seaweed		HELP KELP
89 . Aircraft, stress		PLANE STRAIN
90 . Airplane collection		JET SET
91 . Alcoholic beverage container (box)		GIN BIN
92 . All individuals grab out.		EACH REACH
93 . Amphibian stump		FROG LOG
94 . An amazed lady.		AWED BROAD
95 . An obese vampire.		FAT BAT
96 . Ancient flu		OLD COLD

97 .	Angora jacket	GOAT COAT
98 .	Angry adolescent	MEAN TEEN
99 .	Angry employer	CROSS BOSS
100 .	Angry father	MAD DAD
101 .	Animal doctor	PET VET
102 .	Apply alcohol	USE BOOZE
103 .	Argumentative feeling.	FEUD MOOD
104 .	Armored mans battle	KNIGHT FIGHT
105 .	Artificial pond	FAKE LAKE
106 .	Artificial pond.	FAKE LAKE
107 .	Athlete stocking	JOCK SOCK
108 .	Athletic cut offs	SPORTS SHORTS
109 .	Athletic playing area	SPORT COURT
110 .	Authentic	TRUE JEW
111 .	Authentic cry	REAL SQUEAL
112 .	Authentic feast	REAL MEAL
113 .	Avenue hail	STREET SLEET
114 .	Azure adhesive	BLUE GLUE
115 .	Azure beer	BLUE BREW
116 .	Baby's attached napkin used in their bed.	CRIB BIB
117 .	Banner label	FLAG TAG
118 .	Bar bush	PUB SHRUB
119 .	Bar food	PUB GRUB
120 .	Base ribbon	LOW BOW
121 .	Bashful plaything	COY TOY
122 .	Basin beverage	SINK DRINK
123 .	Beach front, growl	SHORE ROAR
124 .	Beggar buddy	BUM CHUM
125 .	Below the chin, kiss	NECK PECK
126 .	Bend 14carrot metal	FOLD GOLD
127 .	Big pituitary	GRAND GLAND
128 .	Bird bark	FOWL HOWL
129 .	Black "Jaws"	DARK SHARK
130 .	Black covering around a tree.	DARK BARK

131 .	Black rocks dish	COAL BOWL
132 .	Bleached bed bugs	WHITE MITE
133 .	Boat voyage	SHIP TRIP
134 .	Bobby Fischers anxiety	CHESS STRESS
135 .	Bobwhite appendage	QUAIL TAIL
136 .	Bog frolic	SWAMP ROMP
137 .	Bogus earth movement	FAKE QUAKE
138 .	Boisterous assembly	LOUD CROWD
139 .	Booger place	SNOT SPOT
140 .	Boring property	BLAND LAND
141 .	Boring seabird.	DULL GULL
142 .	Bottom bruise	RUMP BUMP
143 .	Bozo's sad look	CLOWN FROWN
144 .	Brave flu	BOLD COLD
145 .	Brave fungus	BOLD MOLD
146 .	Breath candy, suggestion	MINT HINT
147 .	Brilliant photons	BRIGHT LIGHT
148 .	Brilliant plane trip	BRIGHT FLIGHT
149 .	Broad conceit	WIDE PRIDE
150 .	Broad playground toy	WIDE SLIDE
151 .	Broil, bread	ROAST TOAST
152 .	Bruised hog	SORE BOAR
153 .	Bullwinkles, harness	MOOSE NOOSE
154 .	Bump the magistrate	NUDGE JUDGE
155 .	Burial tunnel or den	GRAVE CAVE
156 .	Burn the front deck	SCORCH PORCH
157 .	Burning bed	HOT COT
158 .	Burning stain	HOT SPOT
159 .	Calm kid	MILD CHILD
160 .	Camping shelter depression.	TENT DENT
161 .	Cantaloupe criminal	MELON FELON
162 .	Cardiac graph	HEART CHART
163 .	Cargo entrance fence.	FREIGHT GATE
164 .	Carpal growth	WRIST CYST

165 . Carpet pull	RUG TUG
166 . Carry fungus	HOLD MOLD
167 . Celebrity automobile	STAR CAR
168 . Cellular bee	PHONE DRONE
169 . Certain bird's cage	WREN PEN
170 . Certain number of pigs	NINE SWINE
171 . Change sewing pattern	SWITCH STITCH
172 . Charming apostle	QUAINT SAINT
173 . Chew, noon meal	MUNCH LUNCH
174 . Chic edge of your mouth	HIP LIP
175 . Chicken coop	HEN PEN
176 . Chicken noodle, club	SOUP GROUP
177 . Chief outflow	MAIN DRAIN
178 . Child tried not to be seen	KID HID
179 . Chocolate arbitrator	FUDGE JUDGE
180 . Chocolate smear	FUDGE SMUDGE
181 . Choice hour	PRIME TIME
182 . Chubby kitty	FAT CAT
183 . Circular English money	ROUND POUND
184 . Circular, hill	ROUND MOUND
185 . City dress	TOWN GOWN
186 . Civilized pheasant	TAME GAME
187 . Clammy hobo	DAMP TRAMP
188 . Clan pursuasion	TRIBE BRIBE
189 . Clan secretary	TRIBE SCRIBE
190 . Clever, gal	SLICK CHICK
191 . Clever, joke	SLICK TRICK
192 . Cliff oath	LEDGE PLEDGE
193 . Close by	NEAR HERE
194 . Close equipment	NEAR GEAR
195 . Cloth rod	TOWEL DOWEL
196 . Cloudless brew	CLEAR BEER
197 . Coiled bullion	ROLLED GOLD
198 . Cola riddle	COKE JOKE

199 .	College apartments application.	DORM FORM
200 .	Colorless man	PALE MALE
201 .	Comfortable, upper 1/2 room	SOFT LOFT
202 .	Communicator mortgage	PHONE LOAN
203 .	Communicator sound	PHONE TONE
204 .	Compensated servant	PAID MAID
205 .	Conflict shop	WAR STORE
206 .	Consume flesh.	EAT MEAT
207 .	Consume indigo.	DRINK INK
208 .	Cool accomplishment	NEAT FEAT
209 .	Cool grain	NEAT WHEAT
210 .	Cool shoe spike	NEAT CLEAT
211 .	Cool the cheddar.	FREEZE CHEESE
212 .	Cool vessel	HIP SHIP
213 .	Copy the femur	CLONE BONE
214 .	Coronated beagle	CROWNED HOUND
215 .	Correct stature	RIGHT HEIGHT
216 .	Could probably chomp	MIGHT BITE
217 .	Courageous captive	BRAVE SLAVE
218 .	Courageous servant	BRAVE SLAVE
219 .	Cover up TV schedule	HIDE GUIDE
220 .	Cow chuckle	CALF LAUGH
221 .	Craft wagon	ART CART
222 .	Crafty cornea	SLY EYE
223 .	Criminal got out of chair	HOOD STOOD
224 .	Crimson top of the neck	RED HEAD
225 .	Cruel chromosome	MEAN GENE
226 .	Cul-de-sac doctor.	BLOCK DOC
227 .	Cultivated copy	GROWN CLONE
228 .	Curtain paper adhesive.	DRAPE TAPE
229 .	Cut facial hair	SHEARED BEARD
230 .	Cut the wetlands grain	SLICE RICE
231 .	Connect two times	SPLICE TWICE
232 .	Cycle climb	BIKE HIKE

233 . Czechoslovakian accident	CZECH WRECK
234 . Darling business wear	CUTE SUIT
235 . Dead grass	GONE LAWN
236 . Deceased head	DEAD HEAD
237 . Decent lumber	GOOD WOOD
238 . Deciduous stealer	LEAF THIEF
239 . Definite period	FIRM TERM
240 . Dehydrated dessert	DRY PIE
241 . Dehydrated grain	DRY RYE
242 . Delicate escargo	FRAIL SNAIL
243 . Delicate nibble	LIGHT BITE
244 . Depressed boy	SAD LAD
245 . Despair chamber	DOOM ROOM
246 . Did sell the bullion	SOLD GOLD
247 . Difficult fat	HARD LARD
248 . Discourteous guy	RUDE DUDE
249 . Discovered dog	FOUND HOUND
250 . Disgusting gag	SICK TRICK
251 . Disinterested King	BORED LORD
252 . Disinterested squash	BORED GOURD
253 . Distant auto	FAR CAR
254 . Distant pulsar	FAR STAR
255 . Distant Russian ruler	FAR CZAR
256 . Divided quick thinking	SPLIT WIT
257 . Dock game	PORT SPORT
258 . Dog kiss	POOCH SMOOCH
259 . Dog mug	PUP CUP
260 . Dog noise	HOUND SOUND
261 . Dollar excitement	BILL THRILL
262 . Dollar fortune	BUCK LUCK
263 . Dominant blood vessel	MAIN VEIN
264 . Donkey, step	MULE STOOL
265 . Double wrongdoing	TWIN SIN
266 . Dr. assistant, bad spell	NURSE CURSE

267 .	Dreary crustacean	DRAB CRAB
268 .	Drenched family animal	WET PET
269 .	Droopy ape	LIMP CHIMP
270 .	Dull football kick	BLUNT PUNT
271 .	Dull orchestra	BLAND BAND
272 .	Dull trick	BLUNT STUNT
273 .	Early morning deep breath.	DAWN YAWN
274 .	Earth noise	GROUND SOUND
275 .	Eating this minute.	CHOW NOW
276 .	Ebony bag	BLACK SACK
277 .	Ebony paying card	BLACK JACK
278 .	Ebony tartar	BLACK PLAQUE
279 .	Edge of toast powder.	CRUST DUST
280 .	Either trench?	WHICH DITCH
281 .	Elaborate kiosk	GRAND STAND
282 .	Elderly bullion	OLD GOLD
283 .	Electric measurement jerk	VOLT JOLT
284 .	Elegant Arabian	CHIC SHEIK
285 .	Elegant backbone	FINE SPINE
286 .	Elf dwelling	GNOME HOME
287 .	Emotion chow	MOOD FOOD
288 .	Emphasize affirmative	STRESS YES
289 .	Endangered grizzly	RARE BEAR
290 .	English mother was in the water	MUM SWUM
291 .	Enormous boat	LARGE BARGE
292 .	Equitable portion	FAIR SHARE
293 .	Esgargot prison	SNAIL JAIL
294 .	European country's ditch	FRENCH TRENCH
295 .	Evening ability to see	NIGHT SIGHT
296 .	Evening airplane trip	NIGHT FLIGHT
297 .	Evening bulbs	NIGHT LIGHT
298 .	Evening scare	NIGHT FRIGHT
299 .	Evergreen fluid	SPRUCE JUICE
300 .	Evergreen tomb	PINE SHRINE

301 . Evergreen, notice	PINE SIGN
302 . Evil organ	MEAN SPLEEN
303 . Exactly, correct	QUITE RIGHT
304 . Excellent games cubes	NICE DICE
305 . Exchange store	SWAP SHOP
306 . Exoskeleton, ringer	SHELL BELL
307 . Expansive history	VAST PAST
308 . Explode Thomas.	BOMB TOM
309 . Exquisite alcoholic drink	FINE WINE
310 . Exquisite beer mug	FINE STEIN
311 . Eye closing trick	SQUINT STINT
312 . Fact detective	TRUTH SLEUTH
313 . Fail the holy man.	FLUNK MONK
314 . Fair biscuit, area	SCONE ZONE
315 . Fake femur	PEG LEG
316 . False dessert	FAKE CAKE
317 . Family fellow	CLAN MAN
318 . Farm animal vessel	GOAT BOAT
319 . Farm animals grain	GOATS OATS
320 . Farming failure.	CROP FLOP
321 . Fart	PASS GAS
322 . Fast feel down	BRISK FRISK
323 . Fast film	QUICK FLICK
324 . Fast punt	QUICK KICK
325 . Fast, floating	SWIFT DRIFT
326 . Fat clay block	THICK BRICK
327 . Fat fresh water fish	STOUT TROUT
328 . Fat lawn	LARD YARD
329 . Fawns crying.	DEER TEAR
330 . Feather weight wind toy	LIGHT KITE
331 . Feline rug	CAT MAT
332 . Female sheep display.	EWE ZOO
333 . Femur trouble	LEG PLAGUE
334 . Fermented grape juice's large mug	WINE STEIN

335 . Final actors	LAST CAST
336 . Final explosion	LAST BLAST
337 . Final sail pole	LAST MAST
338 . Finest bird home	BEST NEST
339 . Finest piece of clothing	BEST VEST
340 . Finnish smile.	FINN. GRIN
341 . First lithograph	MINT PRINT
342 . Fish hunt	PERCH SEARCH
343 . Floating idea	SWIM WHIM
344 . Floating walkway time piece.	DOCK CLOCK
345 . Flying fear.	FLIGHT FRIGHT
346 . Following text	NEXT TEXT
347 . Food sale	MEAL DEAL
348 . Foot wear cube.	SOCKS BOX
349 . Footwear adhesive	SHOE GLUE
350 . Forearm (carpal) turn	WRIST TWIST
351 . Fowl lyric	BIRD WORD
352 . Free Canadian bird	LOOSE GOOSE
353 . Fresh adhesive	NEW GLUE
354 . Fried potato sauce.	CHIP DIP
355 . Friend fright	PEER FEAR
356 . Friendly brain	KIND MIND
357 . Frog signal	TOAD CODE
358 . Frozen fungus	COLD MOLD
359 . Fry literature	COOK BOOK
360 . Fuel money hunger.	FEED GREED
361 . Fur den	HAIR LAIR
362 . Fur maintenance	HAIR CARE
363 . Fuzzy fruit lecture	PEACH SPEECH
364 . Gadget idiot	TOOL FOOL
365 . Galaxy relay	SPACE RACE
366 . Games, cunning maneuver	TOY PLOY
367 . Gangster, pig	MOB SLOB
368 . Garbage drowned	JUNK SUNK

369 . Garment worn on a ship.	BOAT COAT
370 . Gasoline law.	FUEL RULE
371 . Geek group	NERD HERD
372 . Get rid of purple sore	LOSE BRUISE
373 . Get your embarrassment under control.	TAME SHAME
374 . Giddy flower	SILLY LILY
375 . Girl friend	GAL PAL
376 . Girl from Switzerland	SWISS MISS
377 . Give a baby a cup of milk and they..	WILL SPILL
378 . Gloomy fruit	GLUM PLUM
379 . Gloomy playground	DARK PARK
380 . Gloomy stream	BLEAK CREEK
381 . Gnome ambition	TROLL GOAL
382 . Gold colored fish.	BRASS BASS
383 . Good cost	NICE PRICE
384 . Gorilla adhesive	APE TAPE
385 . Grab a quick look at.	SNEAK PEEK
386 . Grave sweeper	TOMB BROOM
387 . Great clam house	SWELL SHELL
388 . Greatest visitor	BEST GUEST
389 . Greenish blue king of the beasts	CYAN LION
390 . Grim pinnacle	BLEAK PEAK
391 . Grizzly carnival	BEAR FAIR
392 . Grizzly home	BEAR LAIR
393 . Grizzly trap	BEAR SNARE
394 . Groovy fastener	HIP CLIP
395 . Groovy team	MOD SQUAD
396 . Groups goof	CLUB FLUB
397 . Guaranteed remedy	SURE CURE
398 . Hammer college	TOOL SCHOOL
399 . Hand lotion.	PALM BALM
400 . Hand thrown missile store.	DART MART
401 . Happy father	GLAD DAD
402 . Harbor athletics	PORT SPORT

403 .	Hard fake-out	TOUGH BLUFF
404 .	Hasty run	RASH DASH
405 .	Have written the short letter	WROTE NOTE
406 .	Have written the estimation	WROTE QUOTE
407 .	Head policeman	TOP COP
408 .	Heated boat	HOT YACHT
409 .	Heavy metal sleigh	LEAD SLED
410 .	Hide the burp	SQUELCH BELCH
411 .	Hide the cola	CLOAK COKE
412 .	Hiding your riches	WEALTH STEALTH
413 .	Hog dance	PIG JIG
414 .	Holland's knack.	DUTCH TOUCH
415 .	Holsteins forehead	COW BROW
416 .	Home mate	HOUSE SPOUSE
417 .	Honest depository	FRANK BANK
418 .	Hop over the cut down tree	JUMP STUMP
419 .	Horse gaze	MARE STARE
420 .	Hosiery stock	SOCK STOCK
421 .	Hot drink charge	TEA FEE
422 .	Hot pools rule	SPA LAW
423 .	Household hair tool	HOME COMB
424 .	Housetop, deception	ROOF SPOOF
425 .	How come tears	WHY CRY
426 .	Hueless escargot	PALE SNAIL
427 .	Hypnotic ballet	TRANCE DANCE
428 .	I didn't know but	YOU KNEW
429 .	Ice demand payment	FROST COST
430 .	Icing inferno	GLAZE BLAZE
431 .	Identical title	SAME NAME
432 .	If you would kindly hug	PLEASE SQUEEZE
433 .	Imitate the horse racer	MOCK JOCK
434 .	Imitation hoe	FAKE RAKE
435 .	Impolite naked person	RUDE NUDE
436 .	Impoverished shop	POOR STORE

437 . In want of farm food	NEED FEED
438 . In-line fence door	STRAIGHT GATE
439 . Incorrect large cymbal	WRONG GONG
440 . Indigo church seat	BLUE PEW
441 . Inexpensive 4-wheeler	CHEAP JEEP
442 . Inexpensive pile.	CHEAP HEAP
443 . Influenza indicator.	FLU CLUE
444 . Initial pop.	FIRST BURST
445 . Injure Mr. Douglas (Actor)	HURT KURT
446 . Insect carpet	BUG RUG
447 . Insect carriage	ROACH COACH
448 . Insect embrace	BUG HUG
449 . Insect narcotic.	BUG DRUG
450 . Intelligent adolescent	KEEN TEEN
451 . Intelligent body organ	SMART HEART
452 . Intelligent dessert	SMART TART
453 . Intense photons	BRIGHT LIGHT
454 . Intoxicated body builder.	DRUNK HUNK
455 . Iron the skirt	PRESS DRESS
456 . Ironed waistcoat	PRESSED VEST
457 . It's not your round dessert it's...	MY PIE
458 . Ivory horn oil	TUSK MUSK
459 . Jail odor	CELL SMELL
460 . Japanese cooking pan jolt	WOK SHOCK
461 . Jar cover chart	LID GRID
462 . Javelin fright	SPEAR FEAR
463 . Jelly made from a shell fish.	CLAM JAM
464 . Just purchased church seat	NEW PEW
465 . Just purchased loafer	NEW SHOE
466 . Just rain...	NO SNOW
467 . Keen angels instrument	SHARP HARP
468 . Keep the lumber	HORDE BOARD
469 . Kind rodents	NICE MICE
470 . King Bozo'z head gear	CLOWN CROWN

471 .	Kitten quarrel	CAT SPAT
472 .	Lard pot	FAT VAT
473 .	Lareat end	WHIP TIP
474 .	Large palm	GRAND HAND
475 .	Large person who doesn't like Christmas	HUGE SCROOGE
476 .	Large swine	BIG PIG
477 .	Large toupee	BIG WIG
478 .	Large type of palm	BIG FIG
479 .	Lattice danger	NET THREAT
480 .	Lawn protector	YARD GUARD
481 .	Lazy levy	LAX TAX
482 .	Leading choo choo	MAIN TRAIN
483 .	Lengthy aria	LONG SONG
484 .	Level rodent	FLAT RAT
485 .	Liberated insect	FREE BEE
486 .	Life fluid friend	BLOOD BUD
487 .	Light fixture holder	LAMP CLAMP
488 .	Light headed holy person	FAINT SAINT
489 .	Light red decorative fur	PINK MINK
490 .	Light red psychiatrist	PINK SHRINK
491 .	Lime body organ	GREEN SPLEEN
492 .	Lime lentil	GREEN BEAN
493 .	Linear 4+4	STRAIGHT EIGHT
494 .	Links stress	CHAIN STRAIN
495 .	Lip pecked forearm	KISSED WRIST
496 .	Literary thief	BOOK CROOK
497 .	Little separation	SMALL WALL
498 .	Liver secretion mound.	BILE PILE
499 .	Living plunge	LIVE DIVE
500 .	Loaf cover	BREAD SPREAD
501 .	Lobby, hobo	LOUNGE SCROUNGE
502 .	Lodge light	CAMP LAMP
503 .	Lots of turf.	MASS GRASS
504 .	Loveboat daily.	CRUISE NEWS

505 .	Luggage label	BAG TAG
506 .	Lumbering deer	SLOW DOE
507 .	Luminescent display	GLOW SHOW
508 .	Lunar melody	MOON TUNE
509 .	Lunar, mound of sand	MOON DUNE
510 .	Machinery gas	TOOL FUEL
511 .	Main steer	CHIEF BEEF
512 .	Male deer banner	STAG FLAG
513 .	Malicious pinto	MEAN BEAN
514 .	Mallards good fortune.	DUCK LUCK
515 .	Mandible defect	JAW FLAW
516 .	Maps investigating rod	GLOBE PROBE
517 .	Marked poet	SCARRED BARD
518 .	Masked animals song	COON TUNE
519 .	Massage, baby bear	RUB CUB
520 .	Mean fight.	CRUEL DUEL
521 .	Media anxiety	PRESS STRESS
522 .	Medicine tablet, excitement	PILL THRILL
523 .	Metal cot	LEAD BED
524 .	Metal epdermis	TIN SKIN
525 .	Metal needle	TIN PIN
526 .	Metal tire	STEEL WHEEL
527 .	Metal, storage place	LEAD SHED
528 .	Middle egg pun	YOLK JOKE
529 .	Mind exhaust	BRAIN DRAIN
530 .	Miss the arm of the shirt	GRIEVE SLEEVE
531 .	Mistaken melody	WRONG SONG
532 .	Moist lantern	DAMP LAMP
533 .	Moitionless fish lung	STILL GILL
534 .	Monarch legume	QUEEN BEAN
535 .	Money party	CASH BASH
536 .	Mongrel dog's, house	MUTT HUT
537 .	Monster meal	BEAST FEAST
538 .	Moody American	CRANKY YANKEE

539 .	Mortgage howl	LOAN MOAN
540 .	Mountain proficiency	HILL SKILL
541 .	Movie royalty	SCREEN QUEEN
542 .	Munchie bag	SNACK PACK
543 .	Munchies small cabin	SNACK TRACK
544 .	Musical stlye, headgear	RAP CAP
545 .	Mutual score	JOINT POINT
546 .	Naked guy	NUDE DUDE
547 .	Name of a disease	GERM TERM
548 .	Narrow fish appendage	THIN FIN
549 .	Nasty setting	MEAN SCENE
550 .	Natural remedy	PURE CURE
551 .	Naughty boy	BAD LAD
552 .	Neat dribbles	COOL DROOL
553 .	Neat pond	COOL POOL
554 .	Neat stage setting	CLEAN SCENE
555 .	Needle and yarn basket	KNIT KIT
556 .	Nervous picket barrier	TENSE FENCE
557 .	Nice fancy hotel room	NEAT SUITE
558 .	Nice poster	FINE SIGN
559 .	Nightbird grimace	OWL SCOWL
560 .	Nightmare squad	DREAM TEAM
561 .	No cost dog bug	FREE FLEA
562 .	No more fiber.	BRAN BAN
563 .	No victor	NONE WON
564 .	No way to make a mistake	GOOF PROOF
565 .	Nocturnal battle	NIGHT FIGHT
566 .	Non-feeling, finger	NUMB THUMB
567 .	Not a fake tire.	REAL WHEEL
568 .	Not a false turquoise	TRUE BLUE
569 .	Not a very high toss	LOW THROUGH
570 .	Not a very strong pinch on the cheek.	WEAK TWEAK
571 .	Not a very strong stream.	WEAK CREEK
572 .	Not as good poem	WORSE VERSE

573 .	Not fresh story	STALE TALE
574 .	Not narrow hips	WIDE THIGHED
575 .	Not why...	BUT WHAT
576 .	Notched long knife	SCORED SWORD
577 .	Noxious plant's fruits	WEED SEED
578 .	Nude rabbit	BARE HARE
579 .	Number 3 part of a sentence	THIRD WORD
580 .	Number flood	MATH BATH
581 .	Number one asscent	PRIME CLIMB
582 .	Obese cap	FAT HAT
583 .	Obese rodent.	FAT RAT
584 .	Obscene guy	LEWD DUDE
585 .	Obscure epidemic	VAGUE PLAGUE
586 .	Obvious terror	CLEAR FEAR
587 .	Odd alteration	STRANGE CHANGE
588 .	Oily punt	SLICK KICK
589 .	One more than four go head first.	FIVE DIVE
590 .	Opposite of a sharp back.	BLUNT FRONT
591 .	Orca story	WHALE TALE
592 .	Ordained dog.	CROWNED HOUND
593 .	Otopuss slipped	SQUID SLID
594 .	Outer perimeter of the row of plants	HEDGE EDGE
595 .	Outstanding cargo	GREAT FRIGHT
596 .	Paddle shop	OAR STORE
597 .	Pale lacquer	FAINT PAINT
598 .	Pale man in armor	WHITE KNIGHT
599 .	Pale rabbit	FAIR HAIR
600 .	Paperback corner	BOOK NOOK
601 .	Parched cornea	DRY EYE
602 .	Park seating made in France	FRENCH BENCH
603 .	Passed up, to-do note	MISSED LIST
604 .	Past tense of eating wonderfully.	ATE GREAT
605 .	Pasta pastry	NOODLE STRUDEL
606 .	Pastel red kitchen basin	PINK SINK

607 .	Pebble supply	ROCK STOCK
608 .	Penitentiary letters	JAIL MAIL
609 .	Pennant tear	FLAG SNAG
610 .	People die.	FOLK CROAK
611 .	Pet the bike wheels	STROKE SPOKE
612 .	Pheasant prison	QUAIL JAIL
613 .	Phoney pain	FAKE ACHE
614 .	Pick up the present	LIFT GIFT
615 .	Picked what you are going to wear.	CHOSE CLOTHES
616 .	Pier apron	DOCK SMOCK
617 .	Pier stocking	DOCK SOCK
618 .	Pig squeal	SWINE WHINE
619 .	Pig utensil	PORK FORK
620 .	Pig's peat pond	HOG BOG
621 .	Pigeon adoration	DOVE LOVE
622 .	Plane mortgage	JET DEBT
623 .	Plant the line	SOW ROW
624 .	Plasma inundation	BLOOD FLOOD
625 .	Pleasant frozen water	NICE ICE
626 .	Poem hour	RHYME TIME
627 .	Pokey raven	SLOW CROW
628 .	Pompus, cumulous	PROUD CLOUD
629 .	Pony route	HORSE COURSE
630 .	Poorly lit school athletic room.	DIM GYM
631 .	Position taken when mesmerized.	TRANCE STANCE
632 .	Postage winner	STAMP CHAMP
633 .	Potato junk	SPUD CRUD
634 .	Powerful melody	STRONG SONG
635 .	Pressed rug	FLAT MAT
636 .	Primary feed	MAIN GRAIN
637 .	Primary hoist	MAIN CRANE
638 .	Prison deposit	JAIL BAIL
639 .	Prison ointment	CELL GEL
640 .	Prison story	JAIL TALE

641 .	Professional, enemy	PRO FOE
642 .	Propeller prohibition	FAN BAN
643 .	Prying, boy scout team	SNOOP TROOP
644 .	Pulled freight	TOWED LOAD
645 .	Purple fruit in a French pancake.	GRAPE CREPE
646 .	Purple fruit, chewing stick	PLUM GUM
647 .	Put fire to the frond.	BURN FERN
648 .	Put in the cabinets, one dozen	SHELVE TWELVE
649 .	Putty sled	CLAY SLEIGH
650 .	Quiet informer	SHY SPY
651 .	Rabbit garments	HARE WEAR
652 .	Rainless spell.	DROUGHT BOUT
653 .	Raised patio inspection.	DECK CHECK
654 .	Ran after the flavor	CHASED TASTE
655 .	Ranch appeal	FARM CHARM
656 .	Rapid selection	QUICK PICK
657 .	Really dislike the worms used for fishing.	HATE BAIT
658 .	Rectangular couple	SQUARE PAIR
659 .	Red vegetable Avenue	BEET STREET
660 .	Reddish snowsled	ROUGE LUGE
661 .	Redish nylons	ROSE HOSE
662 .	Relaxed poem	CALM PSALM
663 .	Rent sister's daughter	LEASE NIECE
664 .	Rock area	STONE ZONE
665 .	Rodent head bug	MICE LICE
666 .	Rodent home	MOUSE HOUSE
667 .	Rodent's head gear	RAT'S HATS
668 .	Rollerblading in line.	SKATE STRAIGHT
669 .	Rookie team	NEW CREW
670 .	Rough pony	COURSE HORSE
671 .	Royal chair area	THRONE ZONE
672 .	Rub the tubing	WIPE PIPE
673 .	Ruin the grease	SPOIL OIL
674 .	Ruler's finger jewelry	KING'S RINGS

675 .	Sad church song	GRIM HYMN
676 .	Safe terrain	SOUND GROUND
677 .	Sailboat rope tie	YACHT KNOT
678 .	Salary madness	WAGE RAGE
679 .	Saliva short play	SPIT SKIT
680 .	Salmon plate.	FISH DISH
681 .	Sanctify the Kings game.	BLESS CHESS
682 .	Sap tickle	PITCH ITCH
683 .	Satchel prank	BAG GAG
684 .	Saying confusion	PHRASE DAZE
685 .	Scaenge, citrus	LOOT FRUIT
686 .	Scalding cauldron	HOT POT
687 .	School transportation hassle.	BUS FUSS
688 .	Scold the lady who's getting married	CHIDE BRIDE
689 .	Scour the bath	SCRUB TUB
690 .	Sea Lion cry	SEAL SQUEAL
691 .	Season's light toss	SPRING FLING
692 .	Secure vagabond	SAFE WAIF
693 .	Sediment, overflow	MUD FLOOD
694 .	Send Uncles Sam's potion of the phone lines.	FAX TAX
695 .	Separated peach seed	SPLIT PIT
696 .	Serpent dessert	SNAKE CAKE
697 .	Seven days of being cool in France.	CHIC WEEK
698 .	Sharp speech impediment.	CRISP LISP
699 .	Sheared creature	FLEECED BEAST
700 .	Sheep jelly	LAMB JAM
701 .	Ship bouy	BOAT FLOAT
702 .	Ship canal around a castle	BOAT MOAT
703 .	Ship saying	BOAT QUOTE
704 .	Ship suggestion	SHIP TIP
705 .	Shoe money	BOOT LOOT
706 .	Shoreline cheers	COAST TOAST
707 .	Short sorrow	BRIEF GRIEF
708 .	Should refrain	OUGHT NOT

709 . Shove shrub	PUSH BUSH
710 . Shovel up the droppings	SCOOP POOP
711 . Sick want	ILL WILL
712 . Sightless brain	BLIND MIND
713 . Sightless discovery	BLIND FIND
714 . Silent fighting	QUIT RIOT
715 . Silent performer poem	MIME RHYME
716 . Silent piccolo	MUTE FLUTE
717 . Silicon acres	SAND LAND
718 . Silvery covered stadium	CHROME DOME
719 . Simmered grub	STEWED FOOD
720 . Single, 2000 lbs.	ONE TON
721 . Skillful robbery	DEFT THEFT
722 . Skinny adolescent	LEAN TEEN
723 . Skinny smile	THIN GRIN
724 . Small bread loaf basket	ROLL BOWL
725 . Small harbor.	DWARF WHARF
726 . Small pigeon's mitten.	DOVE GLOVE
727 . Smart award	WISE PRIZE
728 . Smooch my sister	KISS SIS
729 . Smoother shoe	SLEEKER SNEAKER
730 . Snail pace performance	SLOW SHOW
731 . Snail, squeeze	SLUG HUG
732 . Sneaky, detective	SLY SPY
733 . Sniff, great	SMELL SWELL
734 . Snippy wife to be	SNIDE BRIDE
735 . Soar above the clouds.	FLY HIGH
736 . Soda store	POP SHOP
737 . Sodium safe	SALT VAULT
738 . Sofa pocket	COUCH POUCH
739 . Sofa slump	COUCH SLOUCH
740 . Sofa's grumpy person	COUCH GROUCH
741 . Solar enjoyment	SUN FUN
742 . Solar joke	SUN PUN

743 .	Somber fancy	GRIM WHIM
744 .	Soul transmitter	LOAN PHONE
745 .	Sour beginning	TART START
746 .	Southpaw, split	LEFT CLEFT
747 .	Sparse bush	SCANT PLANT
748 .	Speeding hair	FUR BLUR
749 .	Sphere fight	BALL BRAWL
750 .	Spherical ground	ROUND GROUND
751 .	Spirit party giver	GHOST HOST
752 .	Splendid alter	FINE SHRINE
753 .	Spouse's characteristics	MATES TRAITS
754 .	Sprint offspring	RUN SON
755 .	Squashes weapon	GOURD SWORD
756 .	Squeeze herring	SQUISH FISH
757 .	Sream, "NOT SAFE"	SHOUT OUT
758 .	Stag vehicle	BUCK TRUCK
759 .	Steak chair	MEAT SEAT
760 .	Steal from Robert	ROB BOB
761 .	Stiff hair curls.	FIRM PERM
762 .	Stiff letter	HARD CARD
763 .	Stir together, limbs	MIX STICKS
764 .	Stop the fad.	END TREND
765 .	Stop the non-violence.	CEASE PEACE
766 .	Stop the oil.	CEASE GREASE
767 .	Store idiot	CLERK JERK
768 .	Store policeman	SHOP COP
769 .	Strange goatee	WEIRD BEARD
770 .	Strange seed	ODD POD
771 .	Street frog	ROAD TOAD
772 .	Stripped animal smelled	SKUNK STUNK
773 .	Stubby tree house	SHORT FORT
774 .	Stubby, tennis area	SHORT COURT
775 .	Stuffed male cow	FULL BULL
776 .	Stupid fruit	DUMB PLUM

777 .	Sturdy summer footwear	STRONG THONG
778 .	Stylish onion	CHIC LEEK
779 .	Submarine food	SUB GRUB
780 .	Sugary beef	SWEET MEAT
781 .	Sugary red vegetable	SWEET BEET
782 .	Superb evergreen	FINE PINE
783 .	Surprise pistol	STUN GUN
784 .	Survey objective	POLL GOAL
785 .	Swallow OJ fiber	GULP PULP
786 .	Sweatshirt swatch.	FLEECE PIECE
787 .	Sweeper chamber	BROOM ROOM
788 .	Sweet condiment	NICE SPICE
789 .	Swift hoax	QUICK TRICK
790 .	Syrup collector	SAP TRAP
791 .	Take the rudder	STEEL KEEL
792 .	Tanned circus entertainer	BROWN CLOWN
793 .	Tardy escort	LATE DATE
794 .	Team leader's pin	COACH BROACH
795 .	Ten cent violation.	DIME CRIME
796 .	Tentsite winner	CAMP CHAMP
797 .	Termite haven	PEST NEST
798 .	Termite, evaluation	PEST TEST
799 .	Terrific escort	GREAT DATE
800 .	Test expert	QUIZ WIZ
801 .	The best vocal chords	CHOICE VOICE
802 .	The boy's test	HIS QUIZ
803 .	The dislike of extra pounds.	HATE WEIGHT
804 .	The entire telephone wire holder	WHOLE POLE
805 .	The floppies potential harm.	DISK RISK
806 .	The greens do well	CHIVE THRIVE
807 .	The groups long-term goal.	TEAM DREAM
808 .	The large-toothed group.	FANG GANG
809 .	The most terrible craving for water	WORST THIRST
810 .	The number of pounds of what is being shipped.	FREIGHT WEIGHT

811 .	The number one lung holder.	BEST CHEST
812 .	The picnic pest is unable.	ANT CAN'T
813 .	The section in the contract that let's you rest.	PAUSE CLAUSE
814 .	The specific cap.	THAT HAT
815 .	Thick enclosure	DENSE FENCE
816 .	Thick, hair tool	LUSH BRUSH
817 .	Thin border.	FINE LINE
818 .	Thin college president	LEAN DEAN
819 .	Thin Highness	LEAN QUEEN
820 .	Thin James	SLIM JIM
821 .	Thin pancake overcoat	CREPE CAPE
822 .	Thin rope stuff	STRING THING
823 .	Thorny flower's ribbons	ROSE BOWS
824 .	Thorough slumber.	DEEP SLEEP
825 .	Through royalty.	FLING KING
826 .	Throw supervisor	TOSS BOSS
827 .	Tight carpet	SNUG RUG
828 .	Timid insect	SHY FLY
829 .	Timid man	SHY GUY
830 .	Tiny sphere	SMALL BALL
831 .	Tired king	BORED LORD
832 .	Title contest	NAME GAME
833 .	To bring dirt to 212 degrees.	BOIL SOIL
834 .	To burn a mark on the end of your arm.	BRAND HAND
835 .	To chew on an animals foot.	GNAW PAW
836 .	To crush garbage.	SMASH TRASH
837 .	To instruct others how to talk publically.	TEACH SPEECH
838 .	Top exam	BEST TEST
839 .	Toss batter	THROW DOUGH
840 .	Tossed worker bee	THROWN DRONE
841 .	Transparent ball	CLEAR SPHERE
842 .	Transparent epidermis	THIN SKIN
843 .	Trap door handle	HATCH LATCH
844 .	Trendy person from Athens	CHIC GREEK

845 . Tripped nicely.	FELL WELL
846 . Trophy, largeness	PRIZE SIZE
847 . Trout plate	FISH DISH
848 . True bargain	REAL DEAL
849 . Tug, sheep's hair	PULL WOOL
850 . Turf ball	SOD WAD
851 . Turn clenched hand	TWIST FIST
852 . Turquoise footwear	BLUE SHOE
853 . Twist the broken arm holder	WRING SLING
854 . Twist the female	TWIRL GIRL
855 . Unchained deer-like animal	LOOSE MOOSE
856 . Uncommon couple	RARE PAIR
857 . Underground animals tunnel	MOLE HOLE
858 . Understood color	KNEW HUE
859 . Unfocussed mist	STRAY SPRAY
860 . Unintelligent finger	DUMB THUMB
861 . Unite, desire	MERGE URGE
862 . Unmovable vehicle	STUCK TRUCK
863 . Unrefined young guy.	CRUDE DUDE
864 . Unspeaking, giant	MUTE BRUTE
865 . Untamed youngster	WILD CHILD
866 . Unusual fish	ODD COD
867 . Unusual seat	RARE CHAIR
868 . Unwritten board	BLANK PLANK
869 . Upper bodywear soil.	SHIRT DIRT
870 . Used honker	WORN HORN
871 . Used penny	SPENT CENT
872 . Valentine piece	HEART PART
873 . Van commotion	BUS FUSS
874 . Vast country	GRAND LAND
875 . Veranda flame	PORCH TORCH
876 . Very Nice and subdued wall pigment.	QUAINT PAINT
877 . Vibrant bee home	LIVE HIVE
878 . Vicious empress	MEAN QUEEN

879 .	Village jester	TOWN CLOWN
880 .	Vulgar amount of medicine	GROSS DOSE
881 .	Wander to your house	ROAM HOME
882 .	Wash the magnifying glass	CLEANSE LENS
883 .	Washed Chromosome	CLEAN GENE
884 .	Washed empress	CLEAN QUEEN
885 .	Waterfront fruit	BEACH PEACH
886 .	Weak man	FRAIL MALE
887 .	Wealthy segment	RICH NICHE
888 .	Wealthy sorceress	RICH WITCH
889 .	Wealthy, marriage	RICH HITCH
890 .	Well fitting, coffee mug	SNUG MUG
891 .	Wet postage	DAMP STAMP
892 .	Wet pulley	MOIST HOIST
893 .	Wet winner	DAMP CHAMP
894 .	Wharf latch	DOCK LOCK
895 .	What happened to Kennedy. He _____	GOT SHOT
896 .	What keeps me up at night	YOUR SNORE
897 .	What the frozen water costs	ICE PRICE
898 .	What you do when you want something	I BUY
899 .	What you say when you want the feline to leave	SCAT CAT
900 .	What young ponies do when scared	COLT BOLT
901 .	Where ghosts go to learn	GHOUL SCHOOL
902 .	Whip or hit the bread grain	BEAT WHEAT
903 .	White lake birds sleepy breath	SWAN YAWN
904 .	Wind toy altitude	KITE HEIGHT
905 .	Wine-fruit curtain	GRAPE DRAPE
906 .	Wish hill	HOPE SLOPE
907 .	Wolf container	FOX BOX
908 .	Wonderful partner	GREAT MATE
909 .	Wood chapel	BIRCH CHURCH
910 .	Young dogs mug	PUP CUP
911 .	Youngster honesty	YOUTH TRUTH
912 .	Your marshmallow were black but mine...	WEREN'T BURNT

RHYME TIME - 2 Syllable

CLUE

ANSWER

1 . "Blah" tile or carpeting — BORING FLOORING

2 . "Gee whiz" Miss Ringwald — GOLLY MOLLY

3 . "More please", Mexican man — ENCORE SENIOR

4 . A battalion area — LEGION REGION

5 . A boat captain — CLIPPER SKIPPER

6 . A crow with no 5 O'clock shadow — SHAVEN RAVEN

7 . A fence to prevent pinball playing — ARCADE BLOCKADE

8 . A folk dance sung at skating rinks — HOKEY POKEY

9 . A food server that's joined the other side — WAITER TRAITOR

10 . A golf club CARRIER for a father — DADDY CADDY

11 . A goofy Mt. cat with no tail — DINGBAT BOBCAT

12 . A large sign about the bread browner — TOASTER POSTER

13 . A more easily seen reflecting glass — CLEARER MIRROR

14 . A *more* upset, organ close to the kidneys — MADDER BLADDER

15 . A person who bags saltines — CRACKER PACKER

16 . A person who hangs around downstairs — CELLAR DWELLER

17 . A precise offensive move — EXACT ATTACK

18 . A racket to use while sitting on a horse — SADDLE PADDLE

19 . A small binding document — COMPACT CONTRACT

20 . A top-of-the-line prisoner — FIRST-RATE INMATE

21 . A very lean stray boy feline — NON-FAT TOM CAT

22 . Abductor hitter — MUGGER SLUGGER

23 . Able to buy the synthesizer — AFFORD KEYBOARD

24 . Admit too much — CONFESS EXCESS

25 . Advertise, TV clicker — PROMOTE REMOTE

26 . Aerodynamic cat — STREAMLINE FELINE

27 . Agile wood — LIMBER TIMBER

28 . Alcohol, tiff	LIQUEUR BICKER
29 . Alien peril	STRANGER DANGER
30 . Alien, rabbit pen	FOREIGN WARREN
31 . Almost, every year	NEARLY YEARLY
32 . Alphabet cardigan	LETTER SWEATER
33 . Alternate sibling	OTHER BROTHER
34 . Amazing jogging	STUNNING RUNNING
35 . Angrier combiner	MADDER ADDER
36 . Animal watcher	CRITTER SITTER
37 . Annuity anxiety	PENSION TENSION
38 . Anxious, religious ceremony	NERVOUS SERVICE
39 . Appreciate clothes	ADMIRE ATTIRE
40 . Arachnid juice	SPIDER CIDER
41 . Arctic tooth	POLAR MOLAR
42 . Arctic, baby carriage	POLAR STROLLER
43 . Arguing sister	QUIBBLING SIBLING
44 . Artillery, collater	MORTAR SORTER
45 . Ask the witches	CONSULT OCCULT
46 . Atom splitting, dream	FISSION VISION
47 . Attempting pouting	TRYING CRYING
48 . Attract, wood eating bug	INVITE TERMITE
49 . Attractive kidnapping payment	HANDSOME RANSOM
50 . Avoid the sweets	AVERT DESSERT
52 . Bad, beam me up man	NAUGHTY SCOTTY
53 . Barbecue the entry statue	CHARBROIL GARGOYLE
54 . Barn tale	STABLE FABLE
55 . Bass violin man	CELLO FELLOW
56 . Bat away, the bug	DEFLECT INSECT
57 . Bathing time	SHOWER HOUR
58 . Beautiful town	PRETTY CITY
59 . Bee's sweet cash	HONEY MONEY
60 . Betrayal period	TREASON SEASON
61 . Big toothpick, muncher	SKEWER CHEWER
62 . Big van driver, gullible person	TRUCKER SUCKER

63 .	Bleeding friend	BLOODY BUDDY
64 .	Blessed hockey player	HOLY GOALIE
65 .	Bloody tale	GORY STORY
66 .	Blossom precipitation	FLOWER SHOWER
67 .	Blue sauce	NAVY GRAVY
68 .	Bluegreen herb	HAZEL BASIL
69 .	Body shape, review	PHYSIQUE CRITIQUE
70 .	Bold shriveled grape	BRAZEN RAISIN
71 .	Bother hotel worker	ANNOY BELLBOY
72 .	Boundary direction	BORDER ORDER
73 .	Bovine war	CATTLE BATTLE
74 .	Bread producer, teacher	BAKER MAKER
75 .	Breakable pan	BRITTLE SKITTLE
76 .	Brighter sacrificer	SMARTER MARTYR
77 .	Brochure evaporator	FLIER DRIER
78 .	Buck-tooth mourner	BEAVER GRIEVER
79 .	Building energy	TOWER POWER
80 .	Bum's, woodwind instrument	HOBO OBOE
81 .	Bumper twister	FENDER BENDER
82 .	Bunny routine	RABBIT HABIT
83 .	Burdened girl	LADEN MAIDEN
84 .	Busted bus coin	BROKEN TOKEN
85 .	Caesar's curse	ROMAN OMEN
86 .	Calm chemical	PLACID ACID
87 .	Calm color	MELLOW YELLOW
88 .	Calm guy	MELLOW FELLOW
89 .	Calm, lemon hue	MELLOW YELLOW
90 .	Cancer gossip	TUMOR RUMOR
91 .	Car raffle	AUTO LOTTO
92 .	Car, salesman	WHEELER DEALER
93 .	Careful pupil	PRUDENT STUDENT
94 .	Careless jewelry	RECKLESS NECKLACE
95 .	Caribbean Islands, gas pump	HAITIAN STATION
96 .	Caribbean subject	TROPIC TOPIC

97 . Carrying the trim		HOLDING MOLDING
98 . Casinova protection		CHARMER ARMOR
99 . Cat's gloves		KITTEN'S MITTENS
100 . Catwalker, wiggle		MODEL WADDLE
101 . Cave , guide rule		GROTTO MOTTO
102 . Cave saloon		CAVERN TAVERN
103 . Cement expert		PLASTER MASTER
104 . Central violin		MIDDLE FIDDLE
105 . Chain contraction		LINKAGE SHRINKAGE
106 . Change the musical repetition		REVISE REPRISE
107 . Change to blah		BECOME HO-HUM
108 . A person who switches things, tattletale		SWITCHER SNITCHER
109 . Cheerful car carrying boat		MERRY FERRY
110 . Cheese dip, opening act		FONDUE DEBUT
111 . Cherish job		REVERE CAREER
112 . Chinook starvation		SALMON FAMINE
113 . Chivalrous ability		GALLANT TALENT
114 . City Arabian headgear		URBAN TURBAN
115 . City leader killer		MAYOR SLAYER
116 . City liquor		URBAN BOURBON
117 . Clarify ending		DEFINE DEADLINE
118 . Clean, day after Thursday		TIDY FRIDAY
119 . Clear and short, suggestion		CONCISE ADVISE
120 . Clever cat		WITTY KITTY
121 . Clever short song		WITTY DITTY
122 . Close down the frequency modulation		CONDEMN FM
123 . Close to the seventh month		NEARBY JULY
124 . Close, hog pen		NEARBY PIGSTY
125 . Clothes fastener cutter		ZIPPER CLIPPER
126 . Cloud clapping, awe		THUNDER WONDER
127 . Club the thief		CLOBBER ROBBER
128 . Coastal, land movement		SEASIDE LANDSLIDE
129 . Cold, Easter flower		CHILLY LILY
130 . Colored gelatin		YELLOW JELL-O

131 .	Come to the party not dead	ARRIVE ALIVE
132 .	Comic strip monkey	CARTOON BABOON
133 .	Competent old story	ABLE FABLE
134 .	Complete county	THOROUGH BOROUGH
135 .	Confident horse rider	COCKY JOCKEY
136 .	Congenial grouse	PLEASANT PHEASANT
137 .	Connection purpose	JUNCTION FUNCTION
138 .	Corset barrier	GIRDLE HURDLE
139 .	Countryside, wall painting	RURAL MURAL
140 .	Cow gossip	CATTLE TATTLE
141 .	Cow's bathroom	HOLSTEIN LATRINE
142 .	Crazy political running	INSANE CAMPAIGN
143 .	Create concrete	INVENT CEMENT
144 .	Creative way of doing something	UNIQUE TECHNIQUE
145 .	Critical name	VITAL TITLE
146 .	Crow refuge	RAVEN HAVEN
147 .	Crushed wheat silo	FLOUR TOWER
148 .	Crustacean, bad guy	LOBSTER MOBSTER
149 .	Cucumber cutter	PICKLE SICKLE
150 .	Cute cat	PRETTY KITTY
151 .	Daisy strength	FLOWER POWER
152 .	Damp and cool, soft leather	CLAMMY CHAMOIS
153 .	Dance flowers, mural	CORSAGE COLLAGE
154 .	Dark hair singers (2)	BRUNET DUET
155 .	Dark red, inflatable bag	MAROON BALLOON
156 .	Dawn caution	MORNING WARNING
157 .	Deal talk	BARGAIN JARGON
158 .	Decimal movement	FRACTION ACTION
159 .	Declare achievement	PROFESS SUCCESS
160 .	Dedicated highness	LOYAL ROYAL
161 .	Defeat the horn blower	CONQUER HONKER
162 .	Dehydrated miniature plant	BONE-DRY BONSAI
163 .	Delicate bumper	TENDER FENDER
164 .	Delicate, teeth work	GENTLE DENTAL

165 .	Delicious drink, area	NECTAR SECTOR
166 .	Delightful confection	DANDY CANDY
167 .	Deplore, calcium deposits	BEMOAN GALLSTONE
168 .	Deutschland, Homely	GERMAN SERMON
169 .	Dig up, the man getting married	EXHUME BRIDEGROOM
170 .	Dimensional tent	3-D MARQUEE
171 .	Dirty husband	GRUBBY HUBBY
172 .	Dirty small fish	UNCLEAN SARDINE
173 .	Discover, disregard	DETECT NEGLECT
174 .	Discovered park	NEWFOUND PLAYGROUND
175 .	Discreet quarterback meeting	SUBTLE HUDDLE
176 .	Dish talk	PLATTER CHATTER
177 .	Dismal question	DREARY QUERY
178 .	Displaying quilt	SHOWING SEWING
179 .	Do it again, erase	REPEAT DELETE
180 .	Do well, for sure	SUCCEED INDEED
181 .	Dogs hips	CANINE WAISTLINE
182 .	Dormitory leader	RESIDENT PRESIDENT
183 .	Dove bit	PIGEON SMIDGEN
184 .	Dreadful, monastery brother	DIRE FRIAR
185 .	Drivers shoes	CHAUFFEURS LOAFERS
186 .	Drunk nomad	TIPSY GYPSY
187 .	Dumb matchmaker	STUPID CUPID
188 .	Easily impregnated, shelled animal	FERTILE TURTLE
189 .	Eery, Plains Indian home	CREEPY TEEPEE
190 .	Elaborate back-end of the car	ORNATE TAILGATE
191 .	Elegant, car body	CLASSY CHASSIS
192 .	Elevated pilot	HIGHER FLIER
193 .	Eloquent absentee	FLUENT TRUANT
194 .	Elusive hug	SUBTLE CUDDLE
195 .	Employ, local magistrate	HIRE SQUIRE
196 .	Empty ingestion	HALLOW SWALLOW
197 .	Empty, the van	UNLOAD TRUCKLOAD
198 .	Energetic snake	HYPER VIPER

199 .	Enjoyable gift	PLEASANT PRESENT
200 .	Enjoyable plebeian	PLEASANT PEASANT
201 .	Enormous customer	GIANT CLIENT
202 .	Estate organizer	MANOR PLANNER
203 .	Estimate fun	MEASURE PLEASURE
204 .	Even continuation	EQUAL SEQUEL
205 .	Evil castle	MALICE PALACE
206 .	Exact tool	PRECISE DEVICE
207 .	Excuse, special treatment	WAIVER FAVOR
208 .	Execute the marital split	ENFORCE DIVORCE
209 .	Exercise, proof bearer	FITNESS WITNESS
210 .	Expert demolitionist	MASTER BLASTER
211 .	Explore, over there	WANDER YONDER
212 .	Expose the squirrel like animal	DEBUNK CHIPMUNK
213 .	Expression show	CLICHE' DISPLAY
214 .	Extreme protection	INTENSE DEFENSE
215 .	Extreme, polymers	DRASTIC PLASTIC
216 .	Faithful, quitter	DEVOUT DROPOUT
217 .	Fake Anthony	PHONY TONY
218 .	Fake attraction	UNREAL APPEAL
219 .	Fake pressed meat.	PHONEY BOLOGNA
220 .	Fake stallion	PHONY PONY
221 .	False teeth, journey	DENTURE VENTURE
222 .	Faltering bannister	FAILING RAILING
223 .	Fame tale	GLORY STORY
224 .	Fancy red fish	DAPPER SNAPPER
225 .	Fantastic wise saying	SUPERB PROVERB
226 .	Fast cat, pocket sandwich	CHEETAH PITA
227 .	Faster booze	QUICKER LIQUOR
228 .	Fat ape	CHUNKY MONKEY
229 .	Fat cops	OBESE POLICE
230 .	Fat tariff	HEAVY LEVY
231 .	Fatal Illusion	TRAGIC MAGIC
232 .	Fatal tune	DEADLY MEDLEY

233 .	Fatten the scardy cat	THICKEN CHICKEN
234 .	Feebler footwear	WEAKER SNEAKER
235 .	Feed box, risk	MANGER DANGER
236 .	Figure, the car ride to work	COMPUTE COMMUTE
237 .	Finished nicely	ENDED SPLENDID
238 .	Fish doctor	STURGEON SURGEON
239 .	Flaky, overhead wall	PEELING CEILING
240 .	Flaming desire	BURNING YEARNING
241 .	Flesh rotting, immunization	GANGRENE VACCINE
242 .	Flowered reef	FLORAL CORAL
243 .	Fluorescent, rely race stick	NEON BATON
244 .	Food consuming, gathering	EATING MEETING
245 .	Foresee, fight	PREDICT CONFLICT
246 .	Forest blunder	JUNGLE BUNGLE
247 .	Fortunate quaker	LUCKY DUCKY
248 .	Freezing plank	ICE-COLD SCAFFOLD
249 .	Frenzied caper	FRANTIC ANTIC
250 .	Frenzied fear	MANIC PANIC
251 .	Fresh air, commotion	OUTDOOR UPROAR
252 .	Friendlier chopper	NICER DICER
253 .	Friendly idiot	CHUMMY DUMMY
254 .	Frightening tooth goddess	SCARY FAIRY
255 .	Front of the church, mistake	ALTAR FALTER
256 .	Fruit boat	BERRY FERRY
257 .	Funky mule	HONKEY DONKEY
258 .	Furnace measuring device	HEATER METER
259 .	Furry fruit	HAIRY BERRY
260 .	Gangly American	LANKY YANKEE
261 .	Gather admiration	COLLECT RESPECT
262 .	Genuine, money taker	SINCERE CASHIER
263 .	Give respect to the dead man	HONOR GONER
264 .	Glad father	HAPPY PAPPY
265 .	Glass gun	CRYSTAL PISTOL
266 .	Good-bye, antelope	FAREWELL GAZELLE

267 .	Goofy flower	SILLY LILY
268 .	Goofy, salt-water candy	DAFFY TAFFY
269 .	Goofy, spicy beans	SILLY CHILI
270 .	Grainy metropolis	GRITTY CITY
271 .	Grainy sweets	SANDY CANDY
272 .	Grasshoppers, small door	CRICKET WICKET
273 .	Greasy napkin	OILY DOILY
274 .	Greasy uncooked burger	FATTY PATTY
275 .	Great cop	SUPER TROOPER
276 .	Great goof	SUPER BLOOPER
277 .	Great horned, moan	OWL HOWL
278 .	Green-back, researcher	DOLLAR SCHOLAR
279 .	Greeting goof	HANDSHAKE MISTAKE
280 .	Grizzly duo	GRUESOME TWOSOME
281 .	Groovy chimp	FUNKY MONKEY
282 .	Growing flames	HIGHER FIRE
283 .	Growling, nighttime breathing	ROARING SNORING
284 .	Grumpy female domestic cat	CRABBY TABBY
285 .	Guarantee Tom	PROMISE THOMAS
286 .	Guard door	SENTRY ENTRY
287 .	Guiding, word assimilation	LEADING READING
288 .	Gun teacher	SHOOTER TUTOR
289 .	Gym closet inhibitor	LOCKER BLOCKER
290 .	Halley's barf	COMET VOMIT
291 .	Handsome early Norwegian	STRIKING VIKING
292 .	Haphazard dual bicycle	RANDOM TANDEM
293 .	Happy captain	CHIPPER SKIPPER
294 .	Happy maraschino	MERRY CHERRY
295 .	Happy question	CHEERY QUERY
296 .	Happy trio	GLEESOME THREESOME
297 .	Happy, Lassie	JOLLY COLLIE
298 .	Hardened castle	CALLOUS PALACE
299 .	Hate, the mask	DESPISE DISGUISE
300 .	Hating garments	LOATHING CLOTHING

301 .	Heavier baseball hitter	FATTER BATTER
302 .	Herb used in the nose	NASAL BASIL
303 .	Hide, the admiration	CONCEAL APPEAL
304 .	Hilarious cash	FUNNY MONEY
305 .	Hire, ranch hand	EMPLOY COWBOY
306 .	Hot cereal, trial	OATMEAL ORDEAL
307 .	How old is an Australian after 79?	80 MATEY
308 .	Huge cost	IMMENSE EXPENSE
309 .	Human produced hand bomb	MAN-MADE GRENADE
310 .	Human spire	PEOPLE STEEPLE
311 .	Humorous hare	FUNNY BUNNY
312 .	Ice-box delight	FREEZER PLEASER
313 .	Icebox hugger	FREEZER SQUEEZER
314 .	Illegal alcohol, cutback	MOONSHINE DECLINE
315 .	Imitate trick	MIMIC GIMMICK
316 .	Improved correspondence	BETTER LETTER
317 .	Improved yellow cheese	BETTER CHEDDAR
318 .	In the middle of coffee	BETWEEN CAFFEINE
319 .	In the womb, lady bug	FETAL BEETLE
320 .	Inactive harness	IDLE BRIDLE
321 .	Inconspicuous rain pool	SUBTLE PUDDLE
322 .	Individual, horse and mallet game	SOLO POLO
323 .	Industrialist, spit bowl	TYCOON SPITTOON
324 .	Inexperienced snickerdoodle	ROOKIE COOKIE
325 .	Infants hydrophobia	BABIES RABIES
326 .	Inflamed intestine	SWOLLEN COLON
327 .	Inner-city, closure	DOWNTOWN SHUTDOWN
328 .	Insurgent stone	REBEL PEBBLE
329 .	Intellectual yell	SCHOLAR HOLLER
330 .	Intense recover	PROFOUND REBOUND
331 .	Intense, high regard	EXTREME ESTEEM
332 .	Intricate, outerlayer of brain	COMPLEX CORTEX
333 .	Iron, lever worked by the foot	METAL PEDAL
334 .	Irritable paid driver	CRABBY CABBY

335 .	Irritate dad	BOTHER FATHER
336 .	Jail money problems	BAILMENT AILMENT
337 .	Jam stomach	JELLY BELLY
338 .	Java candy	COFFEE TOFFEE
339 .	Jester agent	JOKER BROKER
340 .	Jewish toy, manger	DRIEDEL CRADLE
341 .	Joker proctor	JESTER TESTER
342 .	Judging committee, rage	JURY FURY
343 .	June 21, pipe fixer	SUMMER PLUMBER
344 .	Keep still, Edward	STEADY EDDIE
345 .	Kick out, the idiot	EXPEL DUMBBELL
346 .	Kick-ball, changing room	SOCCER LOCKER
347 .	Kind, writer of plays	POLITE PLAYWRIGHT
348 .	King's Barbecue	ROYAL BROIL
349 .	Knowledge desire	LEARNING YEARNING
350 .	Land grabber	ACRE TAKER
351 .	Larger gun lever	BIGGER TRIGGER
352 .	Larger shoveler	BIGGER DIGGER
353 .	Laughter movement	GIGGLE WIGGLE
354 .	Lawful "bald" bird	LEGAL EAGLE
355 .	Lazier oarsman	SLOWER ROWER
356 .	Leaner bather	TRIMMER SWIMMER
357 .	Leave out, quick meal	EXCLUDE FAST-FOOD
358 .	Lengthen, Saturday and Sunday	EXTEND WEEKEND
359 .	Less heavy, bishops head dress	LIGHTER MITER
360 .	Let go of, the traveling bag	RELEASE VALISE
361 .	Light it, this evening	IGNITE TONIGHT
362 .	Light snowfall, worry	FLURRY WORRY
363 .	Like the table cleaner	ENJOY BUSBOY
364 .	Live through, the honey comb	SURVIVE BEEHIVE
365 .	Lock up the cows	CONFINE BOVINE
366 .	Loveliness job	CUTEY DUTY
367 .	Lower the ranks of the British soldier	DEMOTE REDCOAT
368 .	Lunatic flower	CRAZY DAISY

369 . Mad friend	IRATE PLAYMATE
370 . Made it through the pamphlet	ENDURE BROCHURE
371 . Majestic hound	REGAL BEAGLE
372 . Make, the end of the train	PRODUCE CABOOSE
373 . Manger made of evergreen wood	CEDAR FEEDER
374 . Maraschino boat	CHERRY FERRY
375 . Margarine slicer	BUTTER CUTTER
376 . Marriage covers	WEDDING BEDDING
377 . Masked animal, tavern	RACCOON SALOON
378 . Meaner monarch	CRUELER RULER
379 . Median word puzzle	MIDDLE RIDDLE
380 . Medium, skyscraper	MID-SIZE HIGH-RISE
381 . Mellow valley	SERENE RAVINE
382 . Mending emotion	HEALING FEELING
383 . Messy ditto	SLOPPY COPY
384 . Messy opium flower	SLOPPY POPPY
385 . Metallic, push bike	PEWTER SCOOTER
386 . Metropolis sympathy	CITY PITY
387 . Midnight till morning happiness	ALL-NIGHT DELIGHT
388 . Missile gear	ROCKET SPROCKET
389 . Missile outlet	ROCKET SOCKET
390 . Mistake bringer	ERROR BEARER
391 . Mistake fright	ERROR TERROR
392 . Mixed-up, baseball referee	HAYWIRE UMPIRE
393 . Mob joker	GANGSTER PRANKSTER
394 . Modest dropping of a ball	HUMBLE FUMBLE
395 . Money banker	TENDER LENDER
396 . Monster cart	DRAGON WAGON
397 . Monster minister	CREATURE PREACHER
398 . Moody American	CRANKY YANKEE
399 . Moon ship	LUNAR SCHOONER
400 . More coarse, smoker	ROUGHER PUFFER
401 . More domesticated, carpenter	TAMER FRAMER
402 . More fit landlord	TONER OWNER

403 .	More relaxed bomb dropper	CALMER BOMBER
404 .	More shy orator	MEEKER SPEAKER
405 .	More stupid pipe repairman	DUMBER PLUMBER
406 .	Morning amazement	SUNRISE SURPRISE
407 .	Mother, Alpaca	MAMMA LLAMA
408 .	Motorcycle thief	SCOOTER LOOTER
409 .	Movement cream	MOTION LOTION
410 .	Naked Buddha follower	NUDIST BUDDHIST
411 .	Nastier detergent	MEANER CLEANER
412 .	Neat, number of states	NIFTY FIFTY
413 .	Neater clothes fastener	HIPPER ZIPPER
414 .	Never before used, cane grass	BRAND-NEW BAMBOO
415 .	Next stitch	FUTURE SUTURE
416 .	Nibbled cat	BITTEN KITTEN
417 .	Nicer cardigan	BETTER SWEATER
418 .	Nicer eater	FINER DINER
419 .	Non-malignant, raisin branch	BENIGN GRAPEVINE
420 .	Non-military twist	CIVIL SWIVEL
421 .	Non-spoiled skin	FRESH FLESH
422 .	Non-transparent, breakfast item	OPAQUE PANCAKE
423 .	O3, tornado	OZONE CYCLONE
424 .	Oatmeal search	PORRIDGE FORAGE
425 .	Off limit, skin art	TABOO TATTOO
426 .	Offend elder	INSULT ADULT
427 .	Officer's diary's	COLONEL'S JOURNAL'S
428 .	Ok the men's fragrance	CONDONE COLOGNE
429 .	Old Faithful, hat	GEYSER VISOR
430 .	Old McDonald shield	FARMER ARMOR
431 .	Old, metal fuser	ELDER WELDER
432 .	On no occasion, witty	NEVER CLEVER
433 .	One ditty	SINGLE JINGLE
434 .	Order, police	CONTROL PATROL
435 .	Ordering Australian	BOSSY AUSSIE
436 .	Organ tremor	LIVER QUIVER

437 . Ostentatious physique	GAUDY BODY
438 . Outback community scriptures	TRIBAL BIBLE
439 . Outspoken native	VOCAL LOCAL
440 . Overly energetic rifleman	HYPER SNIPER
441 . Overweight husband	CHUBBY HUBBY
442 . Own, tact	POSSES FINESSE
443 . Pacific brew	OCEAN POTION
444 . Pale lettuce	PALLID SALAD
445 . Paler boxer	WHITER FIGHTER
446 . Pant pouch, necklace	POCKET LOCKET
447 . Parchment cleaning tool	PAPER SCRAPER
448 . Parchment escapade	PAPER CAPER
449 . Parchment hanger	PAPER DRAPER
450 . Parchment, molder	PAPER SHAPER
451 . Peaceful appliance	SERENE MACHINE
452 . Peppy gobbler	PERKY TURKEY
453 . Percussionist disappointment	DRUMMER BUMMER
454 . Person who collects people who owe	DEBTOR GETTER
455 . Pessimist hospital	CYNIC CLINIC
456 . Pet stylist comedy	GROOMER HUMOR
457 . Philanthropist, whiner	DONOR GROANER
458 . Plaid, TV frequency	FLANNEL CHANNEL
459 . Plain plaid	SPARTAN TARTAN
460 . Plan, the mask	DEVISE DISGUISE
461 . Plane terminal, date	AIRPORT ESCORT
462 . Planet's repeating designs	SATURN'S PATTERNS
463 . Planning on oaring	GOING ROWING
464 . Pontifical tree	PAPAL MAPLE
465 . Pool chemical, water container	CHLORINE CANTEEN
466 . Practice swivel	REHEARSE TRAVERSE
467 . Previous singers	PRIOR CHOIR
468 . Prideless mistake	HUMBLE BUMBLE
469 . Prolong, taste	SAVOR FLAVOR
470 . Protection series	DEFENSE SEQUENCE

471 . Put in, the wallboard	INSTALL DRYWALL
472 . Quicker plaster	FASTER PLASTER
473 . Race announcer	GRAND-PRIX M-C
474 . Rancid fiber	ROTTEN COTTON
475 . Red delicious small church	APPLE CHAPEL
476 . Reddish caricature	MAROON CARTOON
477 . Reddish squadron	MAROON PLATOON
478 . Refuse response	DENY REPLY
479 . Refuse, center hit	DENY BULL'S-EYE
480 . Relaxed coach	LOW-KEY TRAINEE
481 . Remember, the precipitation	RECALL RAINFALL
482 . Reptiles, second stomachs	LIZARDS' GIZZARDS
483 . Reveal the manufacturers price	UNVEIL WHOLESALE
484 . Rich dirt, confusion	TOPSOIL TURMOIL
485 . Riches delight	TREASURE PLEASURE
486 . Ridiculous word puzzle	ABSURD CROSSWORD
487 . Rigid shuttlecock	STURDY BIRDIE
488 . Risky whim	CHANCY FANCY
489 . Robbed intestine	STOLEN COLON
490 . Rock carrier	BOULDER HOLDER
491 . Rodents shoes	GOPHERS LOAFERS
492 . Rookie pursuit	RECRUIT PURSUIT
493 . Rowdy assembly	RAUCOUS CAUCUS
494 . Rub down, area of the house	MASSAGE GARAGE
495 . Rude soldier	OBSCENE MARINE
496 . Sad demand	DEPRESSED REQUEST
497 . Saucy, Swiss girl	SASSY LASSIE
498 . Scavenger birds way of life	VULTURE CULTURE
499 . Scented rodent	HERBAL GERBIL
500 . Sea movement	OCEAN MOTION
501 . Sealer bowl	GASKET BASKET
502 . Seamstress van	TAILOR TRAILER
503 . Seaport haircutter	HARBOR BARBER
504 . Search, literary sales place	EXPLORE BOOKSTORE

505 .	Selection accuracy	DECISION PRECISION
506 .	Seller bliss	VENDOR SPLENDOR
507 .	Senior stone	OLDER BOULDER
508 .	Sexy chicken	SULTRY POULTRY
509 .	Shamrock wanderer	CLOVER ROVER
510 .	Share upholding	REPORT SUPPORT
511 .	Shelter flooding	REFUGE DELUGE
512 .	Ship weight	TANKER ANCHOR
513 .	Sick poultry	STRICKEN CHICKEN
514 .	Sign up for, the before meal snack	RESERVE HOR'S D' OEURVE
515 .	Significant wager	MAJOR WAGER
516 .	Silent weight program	QUIET DIET
517 .	Silly playdough	NUTTY PUTTY
518 .	Singing verses with lots of holes	POROUS CHORUS
519 .	Skinnier frankfurter	LEANER WIENER
520 .	Skinnier, law breaker	THINNER SINNER
521 .	Skinny javelin	NARROW ARROW
522 .	Skinny small horse	BONY PONY
523 .	Skyscraper sprinkle	TOWER SHOWER
524 .	Slim Finch	NARROW SPARROW
525 .	Slim loaner	SLENDER LENDER
526 .	Sluggish lawn cutter	SLOWER MOWER
527 .	Small frankfurter	TEENY WEENIE
528 .	Small jock	PETITE ATHLETE
529 .	Small motorcycle thief	SCOOTER LOOTER
530 .	Smarter frugal person	WISER MISER
531 .	Smarter author	BRIGHTER WRITER
532 .	Smarter cheapskate	WISER MISER
533 .	Smelly finger	STINKY PINKY
534 .	Smelly washcloth	FOUL TOWEL
535 .	Snow storm magician	BLIZZARD WIZARD
536 .	Soft color, almond cover	PASTEL NUTSHELL
537 .	Soft grandeur	TENDER SPLENDOR
538 .	Sour pastry	BITTER FRITTER

539 . Speckled rock planet	GRANITE PLANET
540 . Spice up the love life	ENHANCE ROMANCE
541 . Spotted panther	PEPPERED LEOPARD
542 . Spread out, protective escort	DEPLOY CONVOY
543 . Spread, cookie dough around	SCATTER BATTER
544 . Starvation, dealer	HUNGER MONGER
545 . Starve the lettuce	DEPRIVE ENDIVE
546 . Stay away from the robot	AVOID ANDROID
547 . Steel , part of a flower	METAL PETAL
548 . Steel teapot	METAL KETTLE
549 . Stinky delicatessen	SMELLY DELI
550 . Stinky stomach	SMELLY BELLY
551 . Stop the gun	STIFLE RIFLE
552 . Stopping the sodium chloride	HALTING SALTING
553 . Stout left paw	HEFTY LEFTY
554 . Straight-forward, result	DIRECT EFFECT
555 . Strange gobbler	QUIRKY TURKEY
556 . Streetcar foolishness	TROLLEY FOLLY
557 . Strong celebration	HEARTY PARTY
558 . Stubbier bellhop	SHORTER PORTER
559 . Student's money	SCHOLAR'S DOLLARS
560 . Style fervor	FASHION PASSION
561 . Substantive contract	MEATY TREATY
562 . Suede plumage	LEATHER FEATHER
563 . Sufficient defense	ENOUGH REBUFF
564 . Sufficient portion	AMPLE SAMPLE
565 . Suffocate, male sibling	SMOTHER BROTHER
566 . Suggest death	ADVISE DEMISE
567 . Sunny bear	SOLAR POLAR
568 . Superior dog	BETTER SETTER
569 . Supper, prize getter	DINNER WINNER
570 . Sure drape	CERTAIN CURTAIN
571 . Surprising long sock	SHOCKING STOCKING
572 . Sweepstake slogan	LOTTO MOTTO

573 .	Sweet rabbit	HONEY BUNNY
574 .	Swift encounter	FLEETING MEETING
575 .	Swifter clergyman	FASTER PASTOR
576 .	Syntax outcry	GRAMMAR CLAMOR
577 .	Syntax tool	GRAMMAR HAMMER
578 .	Talcum clam soup	POWDER CHOWDER
579 .	Talk about, stress	MENTION TENSION
580 .	Talkative hamster	VERBAL GERBIL
581 .	Talkative, person from North India	WINDY HINDI
582 .	Tart rose	SOUR FLOWER
583 .	Temperate kid	MILD CHILD
584 .	Tennis shoe, hunter	SNEAKER SEEKER
585 .	Terrible inferno	DIRE FIRE
586 .	The best, frozen milk	SUPREME ICE CREAM
587 .	The next kisser	FUTURE SMOOCHER
588 .	Thicker, serving plate	FATTER PLATTER
589 .	Thief drool	ROBBER SLOBBER
590 .	Thinner boxer	SLIGHTER FIGHTER
591 .	Three, small waves	TRIPLE RIPPLE
592 .	Thrifty trumpet	FRUGAL BUGLE
593 .	Tidier, food consumer	NEATER EATER
594 .	Time of year, explanation	SEASON REASON
595 .	To argue about the ending of a chess game.	DEBATE CHECKMATE
596 .	To squish one of the oldest languages.	FLATTEN LATIN
597 .	Toilet paper topic	TISSUE ISSUE
598 .	Tornado callous	TWISTER BLISTER
599 .	Town robbery	VILLAGE PILLAGE
600 .	Trade beginner	BARTER STARTER
601 .	Tradition scavenger (bird)	CULTURE VULTURE
602 .	Tranquil Seaman	SERENE MARINE
603 .	Trendy, red vegetable	FADDISH RADISH
604 .	Trial information	BETA DATA
605 .	Tropical fruit dance	MANGO TANGO
606 .	Try disdain	ATTEMPT CONTEMPT

607 .	TV wire name	CABLE LABEL
608 .	Twin calamity	DOUBLE TROUBLE
609 .	Twin, air pockets	DOUBLE BUBBLE
610 .	Twist the hot dish plate	PIVOT TRIVET
611 .	Twist together the cord for drying	ENTWINE CLOTHESLINE
612 .	Under legal age, complainer	MINOR WHINER
613 .	Under the ocean , wine	DEEP-SEA CHABLIS
614 .	Undercover, ocean front	INDOOR SEASHORE
615 .	Unethical woman	SHADY LADY
616 .	University information	COLLEGE KNOWLEDGE
617 .	Unkempt driver	SHABBY CABBY
618 .	Unobvious, getaway	SUBTLE SCUTTLE
619 .	Use up the podded plant	CONSUME LEGUME
620 .	Verbalize anguish	EXPRESS DISTRESS
621 .	Very mountainous	REALLY HILLY
622 .	Very old, store	ANTIQUE BOUTIQUE
623 .	Vivid flow or cars	GRAPHIC TRAFFIC
624 .	Waiting room, pastime	LOBBY HOBBY
625 .	Wandering guardian	ERRANT PARENT
626 .	Want, the bat	DESIRE VAMPIRE
627 .	War noise maker	BATTLE RATTLE
628 .	Waste water, sight seeing	SEWER TOUR
629 .	Watching, snow sport	SEEING SKIING
630 .	Water-down, argument	DILUTE DISPUTE
631 .	Waterways feelings	CANAL MORAL
632 .	Wax holder	CANDLE HANDLE
633 .	Waxy disgrace	CANDLE SCANDAL
634 .	Weaker seamstress	FRAILER TAILOR
635 .	Weasel worth	FERRET MERIT
636 .	Wedding transportation	MARRIAGE CARRIAGE
637 .	Weighty Cheverolet	HEAVY CHEVY
638 .	Weirder hay	ODDER FODDER
639 .	Weirder, forest guide	STRANGER RANGER
640 .	Well-known, pajamas	RENOWN NIGHTGOWN

641 . Whale fat sponge	BLUBBER SCRUBBER
642 . Wheels burning	TIRE FIRE
643 . Whole, verification of purchase	COMPLETE RECEIPT
644 . Wicked joust	CRUEL DUEL
645 . Widest woodchip	BROADEST SAWDUST
646 . Wingless plane, passenger	GLIDER RIDER
647 . Witty switch	CLEVER LEVER
648 . Women from hell.	HADES LADIES
649 . Wood numeral	LUMBER NUMBER
650 . Woodcutter runner	LOGGER JOGGER
651 . Wool women's undergarment	CASHMERE BRASSIERE
652 . Would prefer to collect	RATHER GATHER
653 . Wretched court hearing	VILE TRIAL
654 . Yellow cheese grater	CHEDDAR SHREDDER
655 . Young urban dog	YUPPIE PUPPY
656 . Yucky, kiss mark	ICKY HICKEY
657 . Zit pit	PIMPLE DIMPLE

RHYME TIME - 3 Syllable

CLUE

CLUE	ANSWER
1 . "And now...a very bright star..."	INTRODUCE BETELGEUSE
2 . 101, pregnancy time	DALMATIAN GESTATION
3 . 20 + 2 Australian animal	TWENTY-TWO WALLAROO
4 . A certain lizards heaven	IGUANA NIRVANA
5 . A smart-alek in a canoe-like boat	WISECRACKER KAYAKER
6 . A wood-cutters house on a turn around	LUMBERJACK CUL-DE-SAC
7 . Act, request	RENDITION PETITION
8 . Activist dodger	CRUSADER EVADER
9 . Actor follower	PERFORMER CONFORMER
10 . Advancement disorder	PROMOTION COMMOTION
11 . All town personal ad	CITYWIDE CLASSIFIED
12 . An airless sealed antiquity	VACUUM-PACKED ARTIFACT
13 . Awareness meeting	ATTENTION CONVENTION
14 . Awful clothing	TERRIBLE WEARABLE
15 . Base annoyment	FOUNDATION FRUSTRATION
16 . Believable food	CREDIBLE EDIBLE
17 . Blood sucking animals Mexican food	MOSQUITO BURRITO
18 . Bother the barn hand	IRRITATE STABLEMATE
19 . Bouyancy bothering	FLOTATION FRUSTRATION
20 . Bring back the regional variety of language	RESURRECT DIALECT
21 . Building show	CONSTRUCTION PRODUCTION
22 . Bye bye, fat	ADIOS ADIPOSE
23 . Cautious leader	HESITANT PRESIDENT
24 . Cautious occupant	HESITANT RESIDENT
25 . Ceramic sweepstakes	POTTERY LOTTERY
26 . Change the American dessert	MODIFY APPLE-PIE
27 . Change the monster	REDESIGN FRANKENSTEIN

28 . Cheater environment	COPYCAT HABITAT
29 . Choosey outlook	SELECTIVE PROSPECTIVE
30 . Choosy investigator	SELECTIVE DETECTIVE
31 . Clean the neck covering shirt	DISINFECT TURTLE NECK
32 . Cold storage way of remembering	CRYONICS MNEMONICS
33 . Combine, government	INTERMIX POLITICS
34 . Common design with tiles	PROSAIC MOSAIC
35 . Commonly dirty	ROUTINELY UNCLEANLY
36 . Comprehend childraising	UNDERSTOOD PARENTHOOD
37 . Confirm the runs batted in	VERIFY RBI
38 . Contempt suggestion	DESPISEMENT ADVISEMENT
39 . Costly rude behavior	EXPENSIVE OFFENSIVE
40 . Cow-pie, gatherer	MANURE PROCURER
41 . Crash ruling	COLLISION DECISION
42 . Creator stopper	INVENTOR PREVENTOR
43 . Short pre-school	CURSORY NURSERY
44 . Custom, fruit drink	TAILOR-MADE LEMONADE
45 . Dark ages, revolution	MEDIEVAL UPHEAVAL
46 . Decoding frazzlement	TRANSLATION FRUSTRATION
47 . Delinquent bill	OVERDUE IOU
48 . Detective, manager	INSPECTOR DIRECTOR
49 . Devouring belief	CONSUMPTION ASSUMPTION
50 . Dietary, knowledge	NUTRITION COGNITION
51 . Diffusion outlook	OSMOSIS PROGNOSIS
52 . Doctor illusionist	PHYSICIAN MAGICIAN
53 . Doctor's ok	PHYSICIAN PERMISSION
54 . Don't forget month number 9	REMEMBER SEPTEMBER
55 . Downsizing direction	REDUCTION INSTRUCTION
56 . Dream of the divide	ENVISION DIVISION
57 . Drink advantage	BEVERAGE LEVERAGE
58 . Drink server disgracer	BARTENDER OFFENDER
59 . Dutchman strainer	HOLLANDER COLANDER
60 . Earthenware imitation	CROCKERY MOCKERY
61 . Embalmer , custom	MORTICIAN TRADITION

62 . Emphasis meat-eater	UNDERSCORE CARNIVORE
63 . Endurable story	BEARABLE PARABLE
64 . Enticement saving	TEMPTATION SALVATION
65 . Evaluate Star Trek ship	CRITICIZE ENTERPRISE
66 . Everyday cushion covering	COMMONPLACE PILLOWCASE
67 . Evil disturbance	CORRUPTION DISRUPTION
68 . Evil memory technique	DEMONIC MNEMONICS
69 . Evil preacher	SINISTER MINISTER
70 . Evolution place	MUTATION LOCATION
71 . Exact change	PRECISION REVISION
72 . Exoskeleton movement	CRUSTACEAN MIGRATION
73 . Exposing calmness	DISCLOSURE COMPOSURE
74 . Faulty investigator	DEFECTIVE DETECTIVE
75 . Feelings emphasis	EMOTION PROMOTION
76 . Fence baggage	BARRIER CARRIER
77 . Flaming journal	FIERY DIARY
78 . Flooding outcome	DELUSION CONCLUSION
79 . Fluttering tariff	VIBRATION TAXATION
80 . Food energy, display	CALORIE GALLERY
81 . Foolish needled animal	ASININE PORCUPINE
82 . Frosted tributary-ship	SUGARCOAT RIVERBOAT
83 . Garbage man, traitor	COLLECTOR DEFECTOR
84 . Gather the diamond shaped pattern	COMPILE ARGYLE
85 . Gear hunch	TRANSMISSION SUSPICION
86 . Get the blue Jewel	ACQUIRE SAPPHIRE
87 . Give up, heaven	SACRIFICE PARADISE
88 . Giving happiness	DONATION ELATION
89 . Graduation paper smell	DIPLOMA AROMA
90 . Grouping suggestion	DIVISOR ADVISOR
91 . Guide chooser	DIRECTOR SELECTOR
92 . Haphazard journey	WHATEVER ENDEAVOR
93 . Happier Yorkshire	MERRIER TERRIER
94 . Hasty baby-room	CURSORY NURSERY
95 . Head injury talk	CONCUSSION DISCUSSION

96 . Help endurance	ASSISTANCE PERSISTENCE
97 . Hiker assailant	BACKPACKER ATTACKER
98 . Homecoming existence	ARRIVAL SURVIVAL
99 . Huge disciple	COLOSSAL APOSTLE
100 . Huge, sentimentalist	GIGANTIC ROMANTIC
101 . Hunger feeling	STARVATION SENSATION
102 . I think I've seen this cookout...	DEJA' VU BARBECUE
103 . Impartial courtroom authority	JUDICIAL OFFICIAL
104 . Inconsistent zealot	ERRATIC FANATIC
105 . Increase volume of baby song	AMPLIFY LULLABY
106 . Infirmary, pardon	HOSPITAL REMITTAL
107 . Instrument player, learning fee	MUSICIAN TUITION
108 . Invention place	CREATION LOCATION
109 . Jail money problems	BAILMENT AILMENT
110 . Jell-o bones	GELATIN SKELETON
111 . Joining in resistance	COMPLIANCE DEFIANCE
112 . Knitter traitor	CROCHETER BETRAYER
113 . Language facts	LINGUISTICS STATISTICS
114 . Lazy-Boy creator	RECLINER DESIGNER
115 . Less noisy starver	QUIETER DIETER
116 . limitation forecast	RESTRICTION PREDICTION
117 . Litter answer	POLLUTION SOLUTION
118 . Love meeting	AFFECTION CONNECTION
119 . Lumberjack dancer, manager	LOGROLLER CONTROLLER
120 . Magic bewilderment	ILLUSION CONFUSION
121 . Mark up the goods, too much	OVERPRICE MERCHANDISE
122 . Market agreement	ADVERTISE COMPROMISE
123 . Melanin adjustment	COMPLEXION CORRECTION
124 . Mesmerizing, addictive drug	HYPNOTIC NARCOTIC
125 . Message bearer fretter	COURIER WORRIER
126 . Mexican food ending	TAMALE FINALE
127 . Mirror opposer	REFLECTOR OBJECTOR
128 . Mirrored point of view	REFLECTIVE PERSPECTIVE
129 . Missile data	BALLISTIC STATISTIC

130 . Most likely wiggly	PROBABLY WOBBLY
131 . Movie machine chooser	PROJECTOR SELECTOR
132 . Native Alaskan hang-out	ESKIMO BUNGALOW
133 . Necessary certificate	ESSENTIAL CREDENTIAL
134 . Non-digital conversation	ANALOG DIALOGUE
135 . Non-military shopping center	CIVILIAN PAVILION
136 . Nuclear religious person	ATOMIC ISLAMIC
137 . Obese parchment holder	OVERWEIGHT PAPERWEIGHT
138 . Occupant leader	RESIDENT PRESIDENT
139 . October 31, toy statue	HALLOWEEN FIGURINE
140 . Only undergarments	SOLITAIRE UNDERWEAR
141 . Orchestra leader teacher	CONDUCTOR INSTRUCTOR
142 . Past suspense	HISTORY MYSTERY
143 . PC pledger	COMPUTER SALUTER
144 . Person who gets "the buyer" out of the grave	CONSUMER EXHUMER
145 . Persuade, symmetry	INFLUENCE CONGRUENCE
146 . Projectile transportation	BALLISTICS LOGISTICS
147 . Promote fitness	EMPHASIZE EXERCISE
148 . Proofer hunter	EDITOR PREDATOR
149 . Question the Joey	INTERVIEW KANGAROO
150 . Quick read denial	PERUSAL REFUSAL
151 . Rally person, winner	CHEERLEADER SUCCEEDER
152 . Reading statement	NARRATION QUOTATION
153 . Relying son	DEPENDANT DESCENDANT
154 . Remedy short story	ANTIDOTE ANECDOTE
155 . Removal suggestion	DISPOSAL PROPOSAL
156 . Request divide	COMMISSION PARTITION
157 . Rotting test model	OVER-RIPE PROTOTYPE
158 . Rust burst	CORROSION EXPLOSION
159 . Rusty dynamite	CORROSIVE EXPLOSIVE
160 . Sacred oil application meeting	ANOINTMENT APPOINTMENT
161 . Sadness statement	DEPRESSION CONFESSION
162 . Salty lotion	ALKALINE CALAMINE
163 . Scare the Japanese wrestler	PETRIFY SAMURAI

164 . School skipping expertise	TRUANCY FLUENCY
165 . Secret bowels	CLANDESTINE INTESTINE
166 . Semi-conductor, opposer	TRANSISTOR RESISTOR
167 . Settlers memento	PIONEER SOUVENIR
168 . Shareholder mugger	INVESTOR MOLESTER
169 . Shot Dr., proofer	INJECTOR CORRECTOR
170 . Sky-tram, trail mix	GONDOLA GRANOLA
171 . Sleepover fat	OVERNIGHT CELLULITE
172 . Small particle	MINISCULE MOLECULE
173 . Smoker's politeness	CIGARETTE ETIQUETTE
174 . Soft badger	VELVETEEN WOLVERINE
175 . Sparkling name celebration	GLISTENING CHRISTENING
176 . Spinning feeling	ROTATION SENSATION
177 . Spotted, orange fruit	POLK-A-DOT APRICOT
178 . Squash alcoholic drink	ZUCCHINI MARTINI
179 . Squash pasta	ZUCCHINI LINGUINE
180 . Stamina protection	ENDURANCE INSURANCE
181 . Start-up engineer	IGNITION TECHNICIAN
182 . Stop the display	PROHIBIT EXHIBIT
183 . Stretch car fuel	LIMOUSINE GASOLINE
184 . Stunning blueprint	DRAMATIC SCHEMATIC
185 . Stylist try-out	BEAUTICIAN AUDITION
186 . Sum illusionist	ADDITION MAGICIAN
187 . Supportive craftsman	PARTISAN ARTISAN
188 . Switch-over influence	CONVERSION COERCION
189 . Take apart month 12	DISMEMBER DECEMBER
190 . Talkers dilemma	CHATTERBOX PARADOX
191 . Tariff anger	TAXATION FRUSTRATION
192 . Tarrif holiday	TAXATION VACATION
193 . Thrill, grand jury charge	EXCITEMENT INDICTMENT
194 . Thrilled zealot	ECSTATIC FANATIC
195 . Thrilling penmanship	EXCITING HANDWRITING
196 . Thrown-out guidance	EJECTION DIRECTION
197 . TNT hunger	DYNAMITE APPETITE

198 . Too much food for the 1000 footer	OVER-FEED MILLIPEDE
199 . Torture, certain dog	PERSECUTE MALAMUTE
200 . Treason legacy	SEDITION TRADITION
201 . Trick accusation	BAMBOOZLE ACCUSAL
202 . Truthful dependence	NON-FICTION ADDICTION
203 . Umbrella characteristic	BUMBERSHOOT ATTRIBUTE
204 . Value determiner teacher	ASSESSOR PROFESSOR
205 . Varied cleanser	DIVERGENT DETERGENT
206 . Voter manager	ELECTOR DIRECTOR
207 . Wealth venture	AFFLUENCE PURSUANCE
208 . Whiner box	COMPLAINER CONTAINER
209 . White-man scratch	CAUCASIAN ABRASION
210 . Wonderful, stretchy material	FANTASTIC ELASTIC
211 . Word scramble picture	ANAGRAM DIAGRAM
212 . Working pleasure	EMPLOYMENT ENJOYMENT
213 . Wrong building designer	INCORRECT ARCHITECT
214 . Wrong, Catholic bow	INCORRECT GENUFLECT
215 . Yellow fruit headgear	BANANA BANDANA

RHYME TIME - 4 Syllable

CLUE

CLUE	ANSWER
1 . Movable flammable material	ADJUSTABLE COMBUSTIBLE
2 . Teen energy	ADOLESCENCE EFFERVESCENCE
3 . Divorce payment party	ALIMONY CEREMONY
4 . Accusing debate	ALLEGATION ARBITRATION
5 . Pension show of thanks	ANNUITY GRATUITY
6 . unmotivated insulin dependent	APATHETIC DIABETIC
7 . Getting use to the mountains in Eastern USA	APPALACHIAN ACCLIMATION
8 . Catholic leaders skin problem	ARCHDIOCESE PSORIASIS
9 . Zodiac forgiveness	ASTROLOGY APOLOGY
10 . Command, tenure	AUTHORITY SENIORITY
11 . Infected fabric	BACTERIAL MATERIAL
12 . Mean cooling fluid	BELLIGERENT REFRIGERANT
13 . Two-way, security	BILATERAL COLLATERAL
14 . Mathematical party	CALCULATION CELEBRATION
15 . Jailed recreation	CAPTIVITY ACTIVITY
16 . Person who takes pictures of the map maker	CARTOGRAPHER PHOTOGRAPHER
17 . Telling all about the way to open a lock	COMBINATION EXPLANATION
18 . Board member, who seeks request	COMMISSIONER PETITIONER
19 . Towns resistance	COMMUNITY IMMUNITY
20 . Contest explanation	COMPETITION DEFINITION
21 . Essay contest	COMPOSITION COMPETITION
22 . Reliability demand	CONSISTENCY INSISTENCY
23 . Bill of rights, mutation	CONSTITUTION EVOLUTION
24 . Food, big wig	CULINARY DIGNITARY
25 . Government, false pretense	DEMOCRACY HYPOCRISY
26 . Wrecking show	DEMOLITION EXHIBITION
27 . Evil drunkard	DIABOLIC ALCOHOLIC

28 . Certain candy's salt content	DIVINITY SALINITY
29 . College housing, bathroom	DORMITORY LAVATORY
30 . Camel, graveyard	DROMEDARY CEMETERY
31 . Environmental advancements	ECOLOGY TECHNOLOGY
32 . Touching daily religious reading	EMOTIONAL DEVOTIONAL
33 . ecological mandate	ENVIRONMENT REQUIREMENT
34 . Projected possibility	EVENTUAL POTENTIAL
35 . Displayer, donator	EXHIBITOR CONTRIBUTOR
36 . Joyous, bulge	EXUBERANT PROTUBERANT
37 . Plant food, entrepreneur	FERTILIZER ENTERPRISER
38 . English structure leave of study	GRAMMATICAL SABBATICAL
39 . Steam dumbness	HUMIDITY STUPIDITY
40 . Drawing teacher	ILLUSTRATOR EDUCATOR
41 . Required statement	IMPERATIVE DECLARATIVE
42 . Person in charge of the chick hatchery	INCUBATOR OPERATOR
43 . Not the best backend	INFERIOR POSTERIOR
44 . Corporation, rebellion	INSTITUTION REVOLUTION
45 . Between the stars author	INTERSTELLAR STORYTELLER
46 . Unseen quotient	INVISIBLE DIVISIBLE
47 . Young alligator cousin	JUVENILE CROCODILE
48 . Metric car distance instrument	KILOMETER ODOMETER
49 . Number cruncher resistance	MATHEMATICIAN OPPOSITION
50 . Marriage statement	MATRIMONY TESTIMONY
51 . Age insurance	MATURITY SECURITY
52 . Statues, photo display	MEMORIAL PICTORIAL
53 . Small part of population, precedence	MINORITY PRIORITY
54 . Prehistoric HDL	NEANDERTHAL CHOLESTEROL
55 . Needed definition book	NECESSARY DICTIONARY
56 . Rule following part of the mixture	OBEDIENT INGREDIENT
57 . Usual funeral house	ORDINARY MORTUARY
58 . Torture, scattering	PERSECUTION DISTRIBUTION
59 . Public official identification	POLITICIAN RECOGNITION
60 . Hindrance, spiff	PREVENTATIVE INCENTIVE
61 . No alcohol, resistance	PROHIBITION OPPOSITION

62 . Build again, prologue	RECONSTRUCTION INTRODUCTION
63 . Retaliation, replacement	RETRIBUTION SUBSTITUTION
64 . Radical change, payback	REVOLUTION RETRIBUTION
65 . Very lazy office clerk	SEDENTARY SECRETARY
66 . On the wagon nervousness	SOBRIETY ANXIETY
67 . Culture differences	SOCIETY VARIETY
68 . Single, letterhead	SOLITARY STATIONARY
69 . Fantastic dialect	SPECTACULAR VERNACULAR
70 . Undersea navel persons infraction	SUBMARINER MISDEMEANOR
71 . Really good parachutist	SUPER-DOOPER PARATROOPER
72 . The best insides	SUPERIOR INTERIOR
73 . Boss, destroyer	SUPERVISOR VAPORIZER
74 . Keyboard, steadier	SYNTHESIZER STABILIZER
75 . TV indecisiveness	TELEVISION INDECISION
76 . Short term army	TEMPORARY MILITARY
77 . Hot tempered Asian	TEMPERAMENTAL ORIENTAL
78 . Unusual kids pop-up toy	UNORTHODOX JACK-IN-THE-BOX
79 . Archies' favorite girls small wind instument	VERONICA'S HARMONICAS
80 . Love, self confirmation	ADORATION AFFIRMATION
81 . Acquiring ambition	ANNEXATION ASPIRATION
82 . Computation, discontinue	CALCULATION CANCELLATION
83 . Payment party	COMPENSATION CELEBRATION
84 . Grouping intrigue	COMBINATION CAPTIVATION
85 . Calculation, mental focus	COMPUTATION CONCENTRATION
86 . Water build up, supporting evidence	CONDENSATION CONFIRMATION
87 . Big Dipper, pondering	CONSTELLATION CONTEMPLATION
88 . Teaching show	EDUCATION DEMONSTRATION
89 . Loss of water, knowledge	DEHYDRATION INFORMATION
90 . Drawing forgery	ILLUSTRATION IMITATION
91 . School completion laws	GRADUATION LEGISLATION
92 . Surgery pause	OPERATION HESITATION
93 . Pills annoyance	MEDICATION IRRITATION
94 . School completion, inspiration	GRADUATION MOTIVATION

95 . Changing, visual recording	FLUCTUATION OBSERVATION
96 . Cold barrier, company	INSULATION CORPORATION
97 . Foreign influx, quota	IMAGINATION LIMITATION
98 . Invention, put in	INNOVATION INSTALLATION
99 . Job ending	OCCUPATION CULMINATION
100 . Party definition	CELEBRATION EXPLANATION
101 . Number of people, problems	POPULATION COMPLICATION
102 . Flora, control	VEGETATION REGULATION
103 . Temporary stay, sign-up	VISITATION REGISTRATION
104 . Advice meeting	CONSULTATION RESERVATION
105 . Searching increase	EXPLORATION ESCALATION
106 . Smothering, finger pointing	SUFFOCATION ACCUSATION
107 . Limb removal, pills	AMPUTATION MEDICATION
108 . Bee's work, prevention	POLLINATION DEPRAVATION

RHYME TIME - 5 Syllable

CLUE

#	CLUE	ANSWER
1	Cleaning up, teamwork	BEAUTIFICATION COOPERATION
2	Creativity, destruction	IMAGINATION ANNIHILATION
3	Custodians personal views in the newspaper	JANITORIAL EDITORIAL
4	Darwinian radical changer	EVOLUTIONIST REVOLUTIONIST
5	Detective work, planning	INVESTIGATION ORGANIZATION
6	Dry up, records	EVAPORATION DOCUMENTATION
7	Fast adding, fear	MULTIPLICATION INTIMIDATION
8	Flirtatious, confusion	PROMISCUITY AMBIGUITY
9	Formal, personal statement	CEREMONIAL TESTIMONIAL
10	Freedom involvement	EMANCIPATION PARTICIPATION
11	Innovation empathy	CREATIVITY SENSITIVITY
12	Inquisitive about the anger	ANIMOSITY CURIOSITY
13	Murder, link	ASSASSINATION ASSOCIATION
14	Person who wants to abolish public disrober	EXHIBITIONIST ABOLITIONIST
15	Peter Piper picked..., Go on	ALLITERATION CONTINUATION
16	Pollution, teamwork	CONTAMINATION COLLABORATION
17	Put-it-off, awareness	PROCRASTINATION REALIZATION
18	Settling, puppy love	COLONIZATION INFATUATION
19	Sorting test	CLASSIFICATION EVALUATION
20	Upgrading check-up	MODERNIZATION EXAMINATION

ASK ME MORE!

Developing good questioning skills requires good thinking. Old time games such as 20 Questions and I Spy are a great way to get people to formulate questions to help them discover an unknown person, place or thing. We take that a step farther in this activity. Players must continue to ask questions until a scenario can be fully explained. Only YES or NO questions can be asked. (There are always exceptions to this rule so "maybe", "sometimes", "probably", "it doesn't matter" and other responses can be used if needed.) Encourage those who have heard the scenario before or who "know" the answer to remain quiet and let others figure it out.

ASK ME MORE...

Julie, Bob and Nicole went to a movie. They left Sam and Fred at home. When they came home, there was water and glass on the floor and Fred was dead. Sam was sleeping on the couch. The police were not notified. *(Sam is a cat. Fred is a fish.)*

A man and his son were in a car accident. The man brought the boy to a hospital. The surgeon said, "I cannot operate on this boy. He's my son." *(The surgeon is the mother.)*

The man was afraid to go home because the man with the mask was there.
(The man is baseball player afraid to go to home plate. The catcher is there.)

A man, who lives on the 20th floor of an apartment building, doesn't take the elevator unless it's raining. *(The man is a midget and cannot reach the button for the 20th floor unless he has an umbrella.)*

A lady enters a restaurant and asks for a glass of water. The waitress points a gun at her. She says, "Thanks" and leaves. *(The lady had a case of the hiccups. The gun scared them away.)*

A man and a woman order a drink. The woman drinks it quickly and lives, the man drinks it slowly and dies. *(There was poison in the ice. It hadn't melted enough to kill the woman.)*

A man has hung himself in a jail cell with a 10-foot ceiling. Found with him in the cell was a hook on the ceiling, a 3-foot rope, and a large puddle of water.
(The man got to the ceiling on a block of ice.)

It's the beginning of eternity, the end of time and space, the beginning of every end, and the end of every race. *(It's the letter "E".)*

A man is dead in a ring on a sunny afternoon. The man responsible for his death is arrested nearby with a small object in his hand. *(During a bullfight, a man used a mirror to blind either the bull or the bullfighter. If a bull is blinded, he would charge in the direction of the bullfighter's voice.)*

A Japanese executive is shot while giving a speech to a large group of people. The entire audience witnesses the assassination, yet no one lifts a hand to arrest the assassin.
(The assassination took place in Hiroshima, just before the atom bomb was dropped on the city.)

A man, who was told not to eat popcorn, dies in the kitchen while making some.
(The man was making microwave popcorn. The microwave caused his pacemaker to malfunction.)

Lisa lies dead in a ring with Lucy. Rebekah is arrested for Lisa's murder and Lucy goes free.
(Rebekah replaced a tame tiger with Lucy, an untrained tiger, in a circus act.)

A family enjoys fresh eggs every morning. They do not get the eggs from a store.
(The eggs are DUCK eggs.)

A man is found unconscious on the floor. His clothing is scorched.
(Santa Claus has fainted from fireplace fumes as he climbed down a chimney.)

Hundreds of people in many states are dead from poisoning. A woman, who has not left her city, is arrested for the mass murders. *(The woman sent out return envelopes with cyanide laced backing.)*

A man dies in the hospital. The doctor notices something unusual and reports it to the police. Later the man's partner is arrested for murder. *(The man's watch has been tampered with which resulted in him dying from a severe case of the bends.)*

To become President of the United States, a person must be a citizen born in the U.S. who is a least 35 years old and lived in the U.S. for a minimum of 14 years. Despite the law, throughout the course of American history, seven Presidents were NOT born in the United States.
(The Presidents were born in the British colonies since the United States did not exist before 1776.)

A certain lock has no combination or key and does not stop people from reaching the objects inside it. Its owners are pleased with its performance and make no efforts to repair or replace it.
(The locks of the Panama Canal...or any other canal.)

People from around the world attend a sporting event. They know what the outcome will be before they enter. They attend anyway.
(They are watching the Harlem Globetrotters play basketball.)

A man is an expert with knives and uses them to mutilate his victims in a precise manner. The police know where he lives and where he disposes of the limbs and body parts of his victims, but they never arrest him. *(The man is a butcher.)*

A carrot, a pile of pebbles and a pipe lie together in the middle of a field.
(They are the remains of a melted snowman.)

A man, wearing a backpack, is lying dead, face down in a field of snow. There are no footprints.
(His parachute didn't open.)

A naked man is lying face down, dead, in the desert.   A match is near his outstretched hand.
(The people in a descending hot air balloon tossed everything out, including their clothes. Finally, they had to draw matches to see who would have to jump to save the rest. This man lost.)

Deep in a forest is the body of a woman wearing a swimsuit, a snorkel and a facemask. The nearest lake is 10 miles away.   *(A fire-fighting plane, or helicopter, had scooped up water to drop on a fire. The woman was accidentally picked up with the water.)*

It goes up but never comes down.
(Your age.)

It occurs in no month but December.
(The letter D.)

A ball is thrown. Without touching or hitting anything, the ball stops and comes right back to the thrower.   *(The ball was thrown straight up.)*

In the 19th Century, a crowd watched a Queen attack and kill a King.   They then casually continued their party.   *(The crowd was watching a chess match.)*
One dark and stormy night, a man turned off all the lights in the house and went to sleep. The next morning it was discovered that the man's actions resulted in the deaths of several people.
(The man's house was a lighthouse.)

A detective finds Greg lying on his side in a puddle of water and broken glass.   The doctor pronounces him dead. There were no cuts on his body.
(Greg is a goldfish who died from suffocation.)

A professional writer is sitting in her cabin writing a letter. There is a violent electrical storm outside and suddenly she dies.
(She is a professional sky writer and is in the cabin of her plane when it was hit by lightning.)

A woman walked up to a featured exhibit of over-sized prize turkeys at a world fair. She shot the turkeys and then ran out of the building. Although she was known to a number of people, nobody made any attempt to stop her.
(The woman shot the turkeys with a camera. She was a journalist with a deadline.)

A man put a coin into an empty bottle and then inserted a cork into the neck. Later, he needed the coin and was able to remove it without taking out the cork or breaking the bottle.
(The man pushed the cork into the bottle and shook the coin out.)

There is an ancient invention still used in some parts of the world today that allows people to see through walls. *(Windows.)*

A black horse jumped over a tower and landed on a small man, who then disappeared.
(It happened in a chess game. A knight jumped over a rook and landed on a pawn. The pawn, consequently, was removed from the game.)

A black dog stands in the middle of a dark road. None of the streetlights are working due to a power failure caused by a storm. A car with two broken headlights drives towards the dog but is able to avoid hitting it.
(The driver was able to see the dog because it was daylight.)

A man is locked in a windowless bathroom made of concrete blocks. Without thinking, he turned on the taps to take a bath and ponder his escape. When the bathtub was full, he went to turn the taps off, but both were stripped and broken. The room was water tight, and the water was beginning to cover the floor, but the man was able to keep from drowning.
(The man pulled the plug out of the bathtub.)

A woman went for a winter stroll to get some fresh air. That was the last time anyone saw her alive. The autopsy revealed that death was due to the pack on her back.
(It was a pack of wolves.)

A race car driver was in a 500 kilometer race when he blew one of his tires with 200 kilometers to go. He still managed to win the race even though he went 200 kilometers with a flat tire.
(The driver changed his tire and raced the last 200 kilometers with four good tires and one flat one in the trunk.)

A traffic cop was stopped at a red light. A professor, who has his mind on a lecture he was about to give, drove his car right by him and through the light without stopping. The cop witnessed the entire scene but made no attempt to stop him.
(The professor was driving through a green light, in front of the cop who was stopped at the red light.)

Brad was bragging that his hockey team had managed to win without one man scoring a goal. The final score was 5 to 2. *(There were women on the team.)*

Two people played chess. They played five games. They each won the same number of games, and there were no draws or stalemates. *(They were playing different people.)*

A man was shot in a theater during a loud scene.   The murder then took the body out of the theater without anyone stopping him.   *(It was a drive-in theater.)*

An employee told his boss that while he was sleeping last night he had a dream that there was a bomb hidden in one of the company's warehouses. Sure enough, a bomb was found. The following day, the boss fired the employee.
(He was a night watchman, and was sleeping on the job.)

The music stopped and the crowd watched as the blindfolded man fell to his death.
(During a live circus performance, the band conductor prematurely stopped the music. The blind folded high wire walker thought he had reached the end and went to step to the platform.)

A prisoner, who was in a cell 60 feet off the ground, was able to remove one of the bars of his window. He had a rope 30 feet long.   He was able to escape without a dangerous jump of any kind.   *(The prisoner unwound the thick rope and was left with two ropes of 30 feet each, which he tied together.)*

A boy who had been trying to get a hold of a friend on the telephone decided to go to her house.

"How come you didn't answer the phone or return my calls?"
"I've only been home 10 minutes. The car is still warm. Check it."
 Sure enough, the car was warm.
"Your lie won't work this time!" replied the boy.
(It had been raining all day and underneath the car was dry.)

One night, while she was watching TV, the power went out so she decided to read.
(The woman is able to read in Braille.)

A speaker lives in San Diego. He drove to L.A. one day to give a lecture.   When finished he got in his car and continued driving in the same direction that he had drove earlier and managed to get home in time to watch the sunset.   *(He had spent the previous night in a hotel north of L.A.)*

On a plane trip, a man notices an old friend and shout a greeting to him.   Within minutes, he is arrested and handcuffed.   *(He had yelled out..."Hi Jack!")*

A talking parrot was purchased with the guarantee that it would repeat any word it heard. After two weeks, the bird had still not spoken a single word.   *(The bird was deaf.)*

A water glass was filled to the top.   A magician held it up and dropped it to the floor with out a single drop of water spilling.   *(The glass was filled, but not with water.)*

A mother had her two fighting sons stand on the same piece of newspaper in such a way that they couldn't touch each other.   *(The newspaper was slid under a door. The brothers were on either side.)*

Two men were being tried for murder.   The jury found one man guilty and the other innocent.   They were both allowed to go free.   *(They were Siamese twins.)*

Inside a bottle is a ring, hanging from a string that is attached to the cap.   Without touching the bottle, or cap, in any way, a woman is able to make the ring fall to the bottom of the bottle.
(She uses a magnifying glass to burn the string.)

A man hangs up his hat, walks 50 yards blindfolded, then turns and shoots a bullet right through his hat without removing his blindfold.   *(The hat was hung up on the end of his gun.)*

After climbing for several days, the climbers reached the top of the Mountain.   There they found a cabin and four frozen bodies.   When they returned, they proudly claimed to be the first to scale the mountain.   *(They had found an airplane cabin.)*

A man left home one morning. When he returned, a man with a mask was there.
(His house was on fire and a firefighter with an oxygen mask was there.)

A raw egg is falls 4 feet over a concrete sidewalk and does not break.
(After 5 feet it breaks when it hits the ground.)

A boy, who is afraid of monsters under his bed, is able to turn off the light and get into bed before the room is dark.   *(It is still light outside.)*

A young girl was riding a wild horse that wouldn't stop.   She finally did something that caused the horse stop.   *(She covered its eyes. Horses won't run if blinded.)*

Two boys waged a bet on who could stay under water the longest, without the aid of any breathing apparatus.   The first boy managed to stay in the pool for one minute.   The other boy won with a time of 3 minutes.   *(He was under a glass of water.)*

A person driving down the highway is pulled over and given a ticket.
(The driver is driving in the wrong direction.)

A intoxicated man knocked down the First Lady, severely cutting her face.   He was given a stern talk on public drinking but was not arrested.
(It was a picture of the First Lady and the glass cut her face.)

A classical guitarist and his twin brother died in a car wreck. The officer was immediately able to identify who was who. *(The guitarist had the callused fingers.)*

The postal worker had to make a delivery to a house. There was a vicious dog tied to tree. The rope, which was 30 feet long, easily reached the front door. The postal worker past within 10 feet of the tree and calmly placed his package on the front door. *(The postman had circled the tree many times. The dog followed and the rope was shortened on each trip around the tree.)*

A man, late for a meeting, went through a red light and turned down a one-way street in the wrong direction. A police officer observed the entire scene but did nothing about it. *(The man was on foot.)*

A man was found lying dead in the snow. There were no tracks leading to or from the body. He did not die of thirst or hunger. *(The man had fallen out of a plane.)*

An escaped convict saw a police car coming. He ran towards it for a short time, then dashed into the woods. *(He had to run to get off the bridge.)*

A baseball pitcher struck out every batter he faced. He allowed no runs and no hits. His team lost 4 - 0. *(The pitcher came in as a relief pitcher.)*

A horse walks all day long. Strangely enough, two of its legs travel farther than the other two.
(The horse gives kid rides at a fair and travels in a circle. The outer legs travel farther.)

A man points his car North and drives one-mile. He ends up one mile south of where he started.
(The man drove in reverse.)

A man was found sleeping. Fresh blood from this man was found on the ceiling.
(He had killed a mosquito that had been bothering him.)

A woman is found dead on her bed. A pair of scissors lies beside her.
(The scissors were used to cut open the waterbed and drown her.)

A horse, tied to a 10-foot long rope, is able to eat a bale of hay that is 15 feet away.
(The other end of the rope is not tied to anything.)

Regardless of religion or politics, all people agree on what is between Heaven and Earth.
(The word and.)

In Tacoma, Washington, you cannot take a picture of a man with a wooden leg.
(You take a picture of a man, with a camera. Wooden legs don't take pictures.)

A United States Presidential candidate:
1. Must be at least 35 years old.
2. Must be a citizen of the United States.
3. Must have resided in the United States for at least 14 years.
4. Must have been born in the United States.

There is one more requirement.
(Must be elected.)

Forward I'm heavy, backward I'm not.
(The word TON.)

A wealthy King died and left all his wealth to his only son. The whereabouts of this son was unknown. Many boys who fit the description came to claim the wealth. A test was to be given to determine the rightful heir. The only one who refused the test was found to be the son.
(The King's son was a hemophiliac who refused a blood test.)

A customer, who had found a fly in his soup, asked for a new bowl. When the waiter brought back a bowl, the customer said, "I said I wanted a new bowl of soup!"
(The customer had salted his soup.)

A couple was 100 yards apart. Facing each other, and walking in a straight line for 50 yards, they were still 100 yards apart. *(One was walking forward, one was walking back.)*

A woman, washing windows on a 50-foot ladder, slipped and fell onto the concrete sidewalk. She was not injured in any way. *(She was on the first wrung.)*

A child is born in Boston, Massachusetts to parents who were born in Boston, Massachusetts. However, this child is not considered an American citizen.
(The child was born before 1776 and is therefore a British citizen.)

A prison cell measures 10' by 10' by 10'. Two feet of dirt sits on a concrete floor. The only openings are the locked cell door and a skylight. A prisoner begins digging a tunnel and finally escapes. *(The dirt from the tunnel makes a pile. The prisoner climbs the pile to the skylight.)*

At a hardware store, a conversation was overheard.
"How much for 1?"
"Three dollars."
"How much for 25?"
"Six dollars."
"How much for 125?"
"Nine dollars."
(The man was buying house numbers.)

You throw away the outside and cook the inside. You then eat the outside and throw away the inside. *(An ear of corn.)*

Looking through the window on the 30th floor of an office building, the man opened up the window and jumped through. He landed completely unharmed.
(He was a window washer who jumped in.)

A 12-foot tall bus was wedged and stuck in an 11' 10" tunnel. A ten-year-old boy, using no other machinery, was able to get the bus unstuck. *(He let the air out of the tires.)*

A small, injured bird has fallen down a 6" diameter by 5 feet deep hole. Without using sticks or string, the bird is safely rescued. *(Water or sand is slowly poured into the hole.)*

A bank robbery had occurred. The thief ran off through the woods. Five men were brought in as suspect. The detective quickly arrested one. *(The woods contained poison ivy and the guilty man had a terrible rash.)*

While driving, the couple's car ran out of gas. The man went for gas, instructed his wife to roll up all the windows, lock the doors, and let no one in. When he returned, his wife was dead and there was a stranger in the car. *(The wife had died during childbirth.)*

In a jail cell, a Ping-Pong ball falls into a 12 " long pipe stuck in the cement floor. The only things in the room are ball of string, a wooden ruler, a pocket mirror, a paper clip, and a small magnet. After some time, the Ping-Pong ball is recovered.
(One must "pee" into the pipe to get the ball to float.)

It was claimed that the woman died from fright during and intensely scary dream.
(Since she died in her sleep there is no way of knowing if she was dreaming.)

A crumpled piece of paper, a glass of water, a half-eaten apple, and a cookie are found at an empty house. The detective says that someone has been here within the last half-hour.
(The apple was still white.)

A man walked for 10 blocks through New York City without anyone seeing him. It was 2:00 in the afternoon and the streets were filled with people.
(He was walking in a sewer pipe.)

A convict, who cannot swim, escaped from a island prison. No other person or object was used in his escape. *(He walked or skated across the frozen water.)*

A box contains a vicious rat and a diamond. The diamond is safely removed.
(The box is turned upside-down.)

A car, which was parked on a hill, suddenly rolled down and crashed into a store. No one was in or near the car when it began to roll. *A stick and a piece of ice were holding the brake.*

The book with "How to Jog" on its spine had nothing to do with exercise.
(It was an encyclopedia with entries starting with "HOW" and ending with "JOG".)

A famous group of four seeks enlightenment.
(The Wizard of Oz. Dorothy, the Lion, the Scarecrow, and the Tin Man.)

A woman hops in a car and drives for hundreds of miles. When she stops and gets out, she finds herself in the same place she started. *(She was in a car race.)*

A bald male opens his eyes and finds himself naked in a small room full of people he doesn't recognize. Before he can say anything, a woman starts to hit him. He is so shocked he begins to cry. The woman smiles and walks away. *(A baby boy has just been born.)*

A woman walking on a sidewalk of a large city suddenly falls and dies. Her body is not moved for many days. (She dies in a severe earthquake.)

A group of men enter a house and quickly take all the possessions that the family owned. *(The men were the movers.)*

One man is responsible for the pain and tears of millions of children around the world.
(Dr. Salk, who invented the polio vaccine.)
In 1947, a man breaks something. He does not repair it.
(Chuck Yeager breaks the sound barrier.)

A young girl joins a group of social outcasts.
(Snow white and the Seven Dwarfs.)

A man is found dead in the snow, far from his home. There are no tracks around him.
(The man fell out of a ski lift.)

A rodent lives for over 60 years. Experts now believe that by using special techniques the rodent will still be around another 100 years. *(Mickey Mouse.)*

A man is attacked by a gang of five men, who shoot at him. He survives.
(A goalie on a hockey or soccer team.)

An elderly man goes for a walk. None of the people who are walking or running behind him can catch him. *(He is on a treadmill at a health club.)*

A man from Alaska puts on shorts and a tee shirt then goes outside. The wind is blowing and it is 20 degrees outside. The man remains calm and happy.

(He is on vacation. The temperature is 20 degrees Celsius.)

A train has been canceled. All, but five, people leave the train station.
(They speak a different language and didn't understand the announcement.)

A man is walking down a port city when he suddenly disappears. His body is later discovered washed up on shore. *(He fell into a sewer hole.)*

A man goes out for a drink every night. He does not get home until just before morning.
(Count Dracula goes out to drink blood.)

A masked man enters the crowded room and plunges a knife into a man's chest. The man dies. The masked man remains free. *(The masked man is a surgeon.)*

Two men enter a wealthy neighborhood in the early morning hours. They move from house to house taking everything they can. The police are never notified.
(The men are garbage collectors.)

A number of U.S. Navy ships embark on a mission. During the mission, one of the ships, containing over 100 men, sinks to the bottom of the ocean. The other ships never stop to search for or rescue the sunken ship.
(The ship is a submarine.)

A group of famous people is always seen together, even though some have never met each other.
(They are the men on Mt. Rushmore. Washington, Jefferson, Lincoln, Roosevelt)

A woman's body is found 100 feet below sea level. There are no injuries on her body and the cause of death is not drowning. *(She died of heat exhaustion in Death Valley.)*

A uniformed man responds to emergencies, helping people in dangerous situations. He does not get paid for any of his work. (It's Superman.)

Two men spend every day and night together. Going outside would kill them. Yet, they do go out for short walks and drives anyway. (The astronauts on the moon.)

A man captures an animal. Both he and the animal become well known.
(Curious George.)

A doctor creates a device that eases suffering. It works, yet thousands of people die from its use.
(The Guillotine)

A couple gets into a car. The car suddenly plunges down steep hill then flips. The car finally stops and the couple gets out smiling. *(It was a roller coaster car.)*

A man screams at the top of his lungs and wakes up most of the neighborhood. No one complains. *(Paul Revere yelling "The British are coming!")*

A man has no symptoms of any problem and feels no pain. The doctor says he needs surgery and Jason leaves bleeding and in terrible pain. *(His wisdom teeth are removed.)*

A young man travels to a distant land and frees a woman and an animal. A native who has a keen sense of smell chases them. *(Jack and the Beanstalk)*

A British subject takes a nasty fall and is never quite the same. *(Humpty Dumpty)*

A man travels to a distant land. The natives he meets do not speak English. They have committed no crime but he takes them to his country and puts them behind bars. *(Monkeys in a zoo.)*

A man turns on a machine. 33 1/2 hours later he turns it off and the people cheer. *(Charles Lindbergh crosses the Atlantic in a plane.)*

A woman witnesses a murder. There is a reward for information about the crime but she never reports any information even though she knows where the murderer is. The criminal is never caught. *(She is the murderer.)*

An American woman is accused of a crime. The court finds her guilty and she is sentenced to death. She has not hurt anyone in anyway. *(She was convicted of witchcraft.)*

A man straps himself to a machine and turns it on. A number of explosions occur before he is able to turn it off. He is pleased with how the machine worked. *(The machine is a car.)*

A shot is fired and six women take off running. The women are not caught and the man is not arrested. *(The women have just run a 100-meter race.)*

A woman gets paid for sitting all day, looking out her office window. *(A bus driver.)*

Forty-nine states try to stop a woman from getting the job. *(Miss America title/job.)*

In his native land, the well-known King never wore a crown and was not given any special privileges. *(Martin Luther King)*

The parents quickly flee the room as a large creature appears. The children are left in the room.
(Barney the dinosaur appears on the TV.)

Two women make money in real estate. Although they never break a law, one ends up going to jail. *(She lands on "Go to Jail" in Monopoly.)*

A woman is driven from her home to a government building.   She is fingerprinted, photographed, and given a series of test.   She drives home relieved.
(Drivers license building.)

A man at work watches a woman remove items from the shelves. She is told to keep her mouth shut and leaves without paying for them.   *(She is at a library.)*

A man is found not guilty. He is sent to prison with no word of possible parole.
(He was already serving a life sentence.)

A family lives in a building free of charge.   A large group of people decides how long they can live there. *(The President and his family.)*

A highly skilled woman goes to work on day and never returns. She is never found.
(Amelia Earhart.)

A woman carries around pictures of a number of dead people. She occasionally hands these out to others who thank her.   *(Money.)*

A golfer performs a feat that no other golfer has accomplished. It has not yet been repeated.
(Buzz Aldrin plays golf on the moon.)

The Captain enters the room.   Some stay to listen, others leave.
(Captain Kangaroo.)

A woman carves a statue weighing hundreds of pounds.   The buyer calls and says it has disappeared and would like to buy another one.   *(It's an ice sculpture.)*

A group of heavily armed men enter a bank and take a large sum of money.   Their slow vehicle is never followed.   *(Armored truck with security guards.)*

A doctor goes into surgery and passes out. The surgery is considered a success.
(The surgery is on the doctor who passes out from anesthesia.)

A group of young men dress up for a party. As the party proceeds, they end up destroying other people's property.   The police are never called.   *(The Boston Tea Party.)*

An elderly woman dies from something she has eaten. *(There was an old lady who swallowed a fly....)*

A man wants to leave his job to travel around the world with a famous group. The group tells him that he cannot join them. *(He wants to fight for his country during a war but is found unfit.)*

A person finally gets financial backing for a business venture. He hires employees, buys materials, and begins work. The venture does not accomplish its goal but the people are happy anyway.
(Christopher Columbus)

A man brings home the frozen food but does not put it in a refrigerator. The food is not eaten for many days. The family is not worried about spoilage and the food is still in good condition.
(The family lives in an igloo in Alaska.)

A man, who has never set foot in single state, is considered an United State citizen.
(He was born and lives in Washington, D.C.)

A famous person dies. There is no television coverage of the incident.
(The event happened before TV.)

A man responsible for the windows used in many large organizations, never washes his own.
(Bill Gates of Microsoft.)

A woman is being followed by two police cars that have their sirens and lights on. She drives as fast as she can, weaving through traffic. She never receives a citation. *(She is a police officer, leading other patrol cars to a scene of a crime.)*

A woman lights her cigarette and is fired for destroying her bosses work.
(She lit the cigarette in a dark room destroying the photographs.)

A world class runner falls at the end of his race. Before he can be rushed off to a hospital, a man appears and shoots him. He dies, as the killer walks away, not being stopped by anyone.
(The runner is a horse who has broken its leg.)

After having many drinks at a party, a guest drives home. His friends had told him that driving under his condition was illegal. He crashes and dies on his way home.
(He was driving under driving age.)

A man and women are having a conversation. Even though the man was wearing a seat belt, he is severely injured in the car wreck. The woman, who was not wearing a seat belt, is not inured.
(The man was talking to the women on a cellular phone.)

A man is found dead in a field. His wife is arrested when the mans sock is examined.
(The pilot's windsock is found to be heavily starched giving him a wind misreading.)

The stain on her coat saved her life. *(A seals fur had been stained. Fur merchants would not want her pelt.)*

The man grabs the electrical lines but is not hurt. *(The lines are hanging and his feet are not touching the ground.)*

A man, on a cruise, destroys his cabin with spray paint and a hammer. He is never required to repair it or pay for the damages. *(He was on the Titanic.)*

A man sits down to read a note from his dead brother. While reading the note, he dies. *(While having a drink from the dead brother's bottle, the man reads his brother's suicide note indicating that he had poisoned his drink to commit suicide.)*

After watching TV, the man shaves his beard off, cuts his hair, packs, and leaves town. *(He was watching America's Most Wanted when his picture appeared on the Television.)*

A man dies in a small room of a large building. Days later, another man, who was miles away of the death scene, is charged with murder. *(The man died in prison in the gas chamber. The other man had cut the telephone lines so the call ordering off the execution could not take place.)*

While vacationing, a couple is murdered. Even though the murderers are known, they are never sent to prison. *(They were visiting Pearl Harbor on December 7, 1941.)*

Because she did not have the bottle, the woman dies. *(The bottle contained a bee sting antidote.)*

A driver collides into another vehicle. All passengers walk away from the accident. Later, the man is charged with negligent homicide. *(The vehicle that was hit was carrying a liver for transplant. It was destroyed in the wreck.)*

A group of people leaves for Germany. They never arrive. *(They left on the Hindenburg.)*

A man, who had drowned, was found on the ocean shore. Later, at a motel room, a man was arrested for the murder. *(Pool water was found in the man's lungs.)*

A building goes up in flames. The building was completely secured yet the fire was started from inside. Later, a man is arrested for starting the fire. *(He used a lens to focus sunlight through a window.)*

Working in a garage, a man dies while working on a car. The owner of the car is accused of murder. *(The tires were filled with poisonous gas and the worker was changing the tires.)*

On a picnic, the girl accuses her boyfriend of seeing her sister. Although he denies it, she knows it is true. *(The blanket he brought had her sister's distinct perfume smell on it.)*

A woman suddenly disappears leaving everything she owns, even the clothes she was wearing.
(The Wicked Witch of the West, in The Wizard of OZ.)

He ate the candy and died. His wife was accused of murder. *(The man was a diabetic who had taken to much insulin and needed some candy. The wife had given him candy with artificial sweeteners.)*

Although they only found a can of black and a can of white paint in the apartment, they knew they had found the killers. *(They had used the paint on the roads, causing cars to go off the banks.)*

A rope broke, a bell tolled, a man died. *(A buoy that a blind man usually uses for guidance on his walks broke away during a storm. The man followed the sound over a cliff.)*

A man was found dead in a room with 53 Bicycles. *(They were Bicycle playing cards and he had an Ace up his sleeve.)*

She walked to the counter with a book. The man said, "That will be four dollars." She paid, then left with out taking the book. He didn't try to stop her.
(She paid a library fine.)

A plane is at an altitude of 1 mile. Huge mountains loom ahead. The pilot does not change speed, direction, or elevation. *(The plane is parked on the airport in DENVER.)*

This book was once read by only the very rich. *(The phone book.)*

The sheep always went to the road. *(It was winter and they wanted the salt off the road.)*

He returned to quickly and died. *(He was a scuba diver and surfaced too quickly.)*
She found a large sum of money but spent none of it for seven years.
(She had found a treasure chest was stuck on an island for seven years.)

The cut on his finger completely disappears after he places his hand in the water.
(The water was a river full of piranhas!)

A man jumped 150 feet and landed safely. *(It was a ski jump.)*

A man was trapped on an island in the middle of a large lake. He managed to escape.
(The lake froze and he walked off.)

He covers the solid metal ball. When he returns and lifts the cover, it is nowhere in sight.
(Either, 1, the cover is magnetic and picks up the ball or, 2, the ball is frozen mercury that melts while he is away.)

It costs him $10, yet he sells them it for $5 and becomes a millionaire.
(*He _was_ a billionaire.*)

The hikers guide falls off a cliff. (*The guide is a book.*)

There was something with a head and a tail in his sleeping bag. He could feel it.
(*A coin.*)

They did not allow him to enter the dance contest. (*It was limbo and he was a dwarf.*)

He fell out of a 20-story building and survived. (*He fell out on the 1ˢᵗ floor.*)

Only 12 people have ever done this. (*Walked on the moon.*)

The dog brought the stick back and died.   (*It was a stick of dynamite.*)

He dies of thirst in his own home.
(*His home is a yacht and he is stuck in the middle of the ocean.*)

The hatch was open but the bombs did not fall out of the plane. (*It was flying upside down.*)

It gets wetter as it dries. (*A towel.*)

You and I can see one but God never will. (*An equal.*)

He noticed he had a flat tire but drove a 100 miles anyway.
(*It was his spare that was flat.*)

It is so fragile that when you say it's name it breaks. (Silence.)

Make up your own! There are endless situations that can be made up. They do not have to be "Tricky". For instance:
A man gets in his car and goes to the store.
Players must discover that the man had forgotten birthday candles for his daughter's cake. Or, eggs for his omelet, or chips for the football game.
Whatever gets people asking good questions and ...
... THINKING!

About the Author

Kevin Brougher lives in Auburn, Washington with his wife, Karen, daughters, Rebekah and Lisa, a 4-½ foot Texas Bull snake, a guinea pig, and a cat. Kevin taught in the elementary school setting for 17 years but is now devoting his time to his interests of music composition, writing, curriculum development, inventing games and running a custom sportswear company. His other book, <u>State Debate</u>, also published by Missing Piece Press, is quickly becoming popular in home schools and classrooms across the nation.

Ordering Information

State Debate
BOOK & CARDS

50 information packed cards and 50 GREAT games! An all around winner. Lots of learning - lots of fun!

$16.95

State Debate
Card Pack

Extra cards for the State Debate Games. Call for teacher discounts!

$6.95

THINKLERS!

A wonderful resource of thinking activities. Position Puzzles, TWOsomes, Commonyms, and much more! 300+ pages.
$16.95

Dream by Kevin Brougher

Kevin's first produced inspiring instrumental album. 71 minutes.
$10

The Road Ahead

Original instrumental music composed, played and produced by Kevin Brougher 56 minutes.
$10

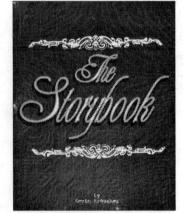

The Storybook by Kevin Brougher

$9.95

Sarah Kane loves to read. Her teacher knows that good reading can lead to good writing so he gives her a magical book to help develop her skills. But when she tries to get out of "having" to write a story, all kinds of problems happen. Follow Sarah as she gets herself out of trouble and becomes a writer in the process.

This "Kids-in-Mind" book has word activities, puzzles, questions, suggested craft ideas and framed blank pages for drawing built into the book! Watch for future "Kids-in-Mind" books! CALL for availability.
